WES

THE POWER OF PREMONITIONS

D0177235

ALSO BY LARRY DOSSEY

The Extraordinary Healing Power of Ordinary Things

Healing Beyond the Body: Medicine and the Infinite Reach of the Mind

Reinventing Medicine: Beyond Mind-Body to a New Era of Healing

Be Careful What You Pray For . . . You Just Might Get It

Prayer Is Good Medicine: How to Reap the Healing Benefits of Prayer

Healing Words: The Power of Prayer and the Practice of Medicine

Meaning & Medicine

Recovering the Soul: A Scientific and Spiritual Approach

Beyond Illness: Discovering the Experience of Health

Space, Time & Medicine

THE POWER OF PREMONITIONS

PREMONITIONS

HOW KNOWING THE FUTURE
CAN SHAPE OUR LIVES

LARRY DOSSEY MD

First published in the United States of America by:

Dutton, a member of the Penguin Group (USA) Inc. 375 Hudson Street, New York, New York 10014.

Published and distributed in the United Kingdom by:

Hay House UK Ltd, 292B Kensal Rd, London W10 5BE. Tel.: (44) 20 8962 1230; Fax: (44) 20 8962 1239. www.hayhouse.co.uk

Published and distributed in Australia by:

Hay House Australia Ltd, 18/36 Ralph St, Alexandria NSW 2015. Tel.: (61) 2 9669 4299; Fax: (61) 2 9669 4144. www.hayhouse.com.au

Published and distributed in the Republic of South Africa by:

Hay House SA (Pty), Ltd, PO Box 990, Witkoppen 2068. Tel./Fax: (27) 11 467 8904. www.hayhouse.co.za

Published and distributed in India by:

Hay House Publishers India, Muskaan Complex, Plot No.3, B-2, Vasant Kunj, New Delhi – 110 070. Tel.: (91) 11 4176 1620; Fax: (91) 11 4176 1630. www.hayhouse.co.in

Distributed in Canada by:

Raincoast, 9050 Shaughnessy St, Vancouver, BC V6P 6E5. Tel.: (1) 604 323 7100; Fax: (1) 604 323 2600

© Larry Dossey M.D., 2009

The moral rights of the authors have been asserted.

All rights reserved. No part of this book may be reproduced by any mechanical, photographic or electronic process, or in the form of a phonographic recording; nor may it be stored in a retrieval system, transmitted or otherwise be copied for public or private use, other than for 'fair use' as brief quotations embodied in articles and reviews, without prior written permission of the publisher.

The author of this book does not dispense medical advice or prescribe the use of any technique as a form of treatment for physical or medical problems without the advice of a physician, either directly or indirectly. The intent of the author is only to offer information of a general nature to help you in your quest for emotional and spiritual wellbeing. In the event you use any of the information in this book for yourself, which is your constitutional right, the authors and the publisher assume no responsibility for your actions.

Set in Fairfield with Futura

Internal design by Daniel Lagin

Jacket design by Kathleen Digrado

A catalogue record for this book is available from the British Library.

ISBN 978-1-8485-0166-9

Printed and bound in Great Britain by TJ International, Padstow, Cornwall.

While the author has made every effort to provide accurate telephone numbers and Internet addresses at the time of publication, neither the publisher nor the author assumes any responsibility for errors, or for changes that occur after publication. Further, the publisher does not have any control over and does not assume any responsibility for author or third-party Web sites or their content.

FSC
Mixed Sources
Product group from well-managed
forests and other controlled sources
Cert no. SGS-COC-2482
www.fsc.org
© 1996 Forest Stewardship Council

For Barbara

CONTENTS

FOREWORD

I live at 7,500 feet in the foothills of the Sangre de Cristo Mountains, a majestic tongue of the southern Rockies that extends into northern New Mexico. This is one of those blessed places where nature always seems to be in high-drama mode.

At this moment the world outside my window is transitioning from a harsh, snowy winter to a borderland season that is no longer winter, but not quite spring. The most obvious indicator that something is up is the birds. The finches, juncos, chickadees, nuthatches, doves, and flickers at the feeders are getting flirtatious. Yesterday, taking the cue, I emptied the birdhouses of last year's nesting materials in preparation for another round of nest building and offspring.

It's not just the birds that are getting frisky. Although the piñon and juniper trees are still hunkered down, the daffodils have made a foolhardy advance and are showing green shoots, which usually means they are about to get clobbered by a spring snow. Even the skies are livelier. The clouds are evolving toward showy cumulus formations, a dress rehearsal for their leading role in the violent thunderstorms of summer. Still, these rhythms of nature are protracted. It will be two full months before the earth tilts sufficiently toward the sun to banish frosty nights and permit me to plant my vegetable garden. In the meantime, I try to notice what's happening.

Notice. What a simple word for something so difficult! I've been trying to get the hang of it for most of my adult life, ever since a little book gobsmacked me in the 1970s and revealed to me that I was quite a poor noticer. That grenade, *How to Meditate*, was authored by psychologist Lawrence LeShan, who did landmark research in the connections between the psyche and cancer at a time when the field hardly existed. LeShan's shorthand definition of meditation was the art of doing one thing well—which, it turns out, is impossible without paying attention, without noticing. This is one of the most difficult tasks we can attempt, as anyone can discover in only a few minutes of trying to notice something intently, without the intrusion of extraneous thoughts and sensations.

The connections between noticing, meditation, and premonitions are profound. Meditation takes us outside the hubbub of flowing, rushing time into temporal stillness. During meditation, we sense our connectedness with all things in the past, present, and future. In this state, premonitions begin to seem not only possible, but likely. They begin to make sense.

Because both premonitions and meditation crash the barriers of time, meditation is a garden in which premonitions often flower. So as you read this book, I hope you will set aside time for stillness, whether you call it meditation, reverie, or solitude. All these activities are versions, literally, of "time out" and "out of time." Become a good noticer. Pay attention to the feelings, hunches, and intuitions that flood your life each day. If you do, you will see that premonitions are not rare, but a natural part of our lives.

A bumper sticker says, GRAVITY. IT'S NOT JUST A GOOD IDEA. IT'S THE LAW. So it is with premonitions. They are a fact. They are ubiquitous. They follow certain patterns we'll try to discern. Our task is to acknowledge and claim this stunning ability, this great gift, in the task of becoming fully human.

AUTHOR'S NOTE

Some of the premonitions and dream narratives that follow have been compressed, paraphrased, or edited for reasons of clarity and coherence.

To protect privacy, some names and identifying characteristics of individuals have been changed.

A word about the terminology I'll be using. Extrasensory perception, or ESP, involves three basic categories of phenomena: telepathy, clairvoyance, and precognition. Generally speaking, telepathy is mind-to-mind communication; clairvoyance is a direct non-sensory awareness of objective physical events, not necessarily involving another mind. The non-sensory, non-inferred foreknowledge of a future event is precognition or premonition.

The term *parapsychology* ("alongside psychology") was popularized in the 1930s by J. B. Rhine as a substitute term for what earlier researchers called *psychical research*. Parapsychology, also called *psi*, is an umbrella word that includes telepathy, clairvoyance, precognition, and psychokinesis, or PK. This latter term involves mentally affecting some physical object and is commonly called *mind over matter*.

In this book I'll use the terms *parapsychology*, *paranormal*, and *psi* interchangeably. I'll stick with these words because they have filtered into common usage. I'm not happy with *parapsychology* or *paranormal*, however, because they convey a false impression. If these events occur, as I believe they do, they are a part of nature and are not *para*, or apart. This means they should be considered an integral part of natural science, not as some ill-bred stepchild that embarrasses the rest of the family. As British biologist Rupert Sheldrake once observed, "Being a biologist, I wouldn't have much use for a field called *para*biology." As a physician, neither would I have much use for a field called *para*medicine. But alas, there is no ideal term to describe these challenging phenomena.

For generations, researchers have floundered in the search for the perfect term for psi phenomena. They still can't agree. It's rather like Louis Armstrong's celebrated response to a reporter who asked him to define jazz: "If you don't know, I can't explain it to you." Why are premonitions and other psi events so slippery where language is concerned? Perhaps it's because our language is geared to the see/touch/feel world. Psi, including premonitions, defy the senses. So it's not surprising that language limps in our attempts to grasp these events verbally.

I'll interchange *premonitions* with the terms *precognition, future knowing*, and *foreknowledge*. Premonitions are also commonly referred to by a host of colloquialisms such as *gut feelings, instinct, intuition, hunches, vibes*, or *sixth sense*. If you wish, pick your own term. Be inventive, like a friend of mine who prefers to call her premonitions *Factor X*.

INTRODUCTION

ometimes things grab hold and just won't let go. That's what it's been like with premonitions for me. I've been wrestling with them for a long time, unable to detach, rather like Jacob's struggle with the angel in the Old Testament. The main difference is that Jacob's brawl lasted only one night. My tussle with premonitions has persisted for more than three decades and shows no sign of ending. Frankly I didn't know what I was getting into when I began my encounter with them. The entire experience is not unlike entering a quiet cave, only to arouse a sleeping grizzly.

It all began innocently enough, with a dream that occurred during my first year in medical practice. In it, Justin, the four-year-old son of one of my physician colleagues, was lying on his back on a table in a sterile exam room. A white-coated technician tried to place some sort of medical apparatus on his head. Justin went berserk—yelling, fighting, and trying to remove the gadget in spite of the technician's persistent efforts. At the head of the table stood one of Justin's parents, trying to calm him and lend support. The technician repeatedly tried to accomplish her task but failed as Justin became increasingly upset. Exasperated, she threw up her hands and walked away.

I awoke in the gray morning light feeling shaken, as if this were the most vivid dream I'd ever experienced—profound, numinous, "realer than real." But in view of the dream's content, my reaction made no sense. I did not understand why I felt so deeply moved. I thought about waking my wife and telling her about it but decided against it. What sense would it make to her? We hardly knew Justin, having seen him only three or four times.

I dressed and went to the hospital to make early-morning rounds. As the busy day wore on, I forgot about the dream until the noon hour. Then, while lunching in the staff area with Justin's father, Justin's mother entered the room holding the boy in her arms. He was visibly upset, with wet, unkempt hair and tears streaming down his face. Justin's mom explained to her husband that they had just come from the electroencephalography (EEG) laboratory, where the EEG technician had tried to perform a brain-wave test on the youngster. The tech prided herself in her ability to obtain EEG tracings in children, which can be a demanding task, and her record was virtually flawless—until she met Justin. After relating to her husband how her son had rebelled and foiled the test, Justin's mom left with the disconsolate boy in her arms. Her husband accompanied them out of the dining area and went to his office.

My dream memory returned. I was stunned. I had dreamed the sequence of events in almost exact detail before they happened. I went to see Justin's father in his office and asked him to share with me the events leading up to the aborted EEG.

Justin, he related, had developed a fever the day before, which was followed by a brief seizure. Although he was certain the seizure was due to the fever and not to a serious condition such as epilepsy or a brain tumor, he nonetheless called a neurologist for a consultation. The specialist was reassuring; nothing needed to be done immediately. He would arrange an appointment for the following day for a brain-wave test, just to make sure nothing else was going on. It was a simple procedure and the EEG technician, he said, had a special way with kids.

Could anyone else have known about these events? I asked. I wanted to know if someone could have leaked information to me that I might have forgotten, that could have influenced my dream. Of course not, Justin's dad said; no one knew except the immediate family and the neurologist.

Then I told my colleague about my dream. He realized in an instant that if my report were true, his orderly, predictable world had been suddenly rearranged. If one could know the future before it happened, our understanding of physical reality was seriously threatened. He sensed my disturbance as well. Our conversation turned silent as we contemplated the implications of these strange happenings. I turned, left his office, and closed the door behind me. I did not bring up the event with him again.

Within a week I dreamed two more times about events that occurred the next day, and that I could not possibly have known about ahead of time. Why had a cluster of precognitive dreams erupted when I'd never experienced them before? It was as if the world had decided to reveal a new side of itself, for reasons I could not fathom.

In all three instances time seemed to be reversed, with effects appearing before their causes. Rationally I knew this could not happen. Time simply could not reverse itself and flow backward, carrying information into the present from a future that had not yet occurred. I wondered whether my mind could somehow have strayed from my body into the future, retrieving information about events that would later unfold. Both possibilities violated common sense and every ounce of my medical training. My consciousness was localized to my brain and to the present; *all* doctors knew that.

I did not experience another precognitive dream until around ten years later when I purchased my first computer. It was a clunky, cumbersome contraption that seemed to have a mind of its own. It had a distinctly stubborn personality, often refusing to carry out my commands. It came with an instruction manual that made little sense, and which was written by someone whose mother tongue obviously was not English. One day I found myself struggling with how to enter footnotes into the text I was working on. I followed the instructions scrupulously, step-by-step, for a couple of hours, trying all combinations. Nothing worked. I decided to abandon my efforts and try again the next day. That night I dreamed I was sitting before the computer writing as usual, when it came time to enter a footnote. I saw clearly how to do it, and where the instruction book had gone wrong. I awoke, went to the computer, and performed the keystrokes I'd seen in the dream. The procedure worked perfectly. I decided not to throw the machine out the window.

I haven't had a precognitive dream since. It was as if the universe, having delivered a message, hung up the phone. It became my job to make sense of it—which I try to do in this book.

My training in medicine has sensitized me to premonitions. Health and illness, clinics and hospitals, are prime stalking grounds for these phenomena. Yet we physicians have a tortured relationship with them. We are trained to honor evidence-based medicine, with its rigid algorithms and decision trees. This approach deliberately excludes hunches, intuition, premonitions, and other varieties of knowing that don't conform to reason and analysis.

I have spent my professional life in the field of internal medicine, from which I am now retired. Integral to my life as a physician has been a fascination with the role of consciousness and spirituality in health and illness.

Although I've published books exploring this issue in various ways, I've never focused explicitly on premonitions. But since my "Justin dream" clobbered me, I've been unable to suppress my curiosity about them. I've combed the neurological, psychiatric, and parapsychological literature in search of answers: how and why premonitions happen; what purpose they serve; what they imply for our understanding of consciousness, space, and time; and how to cultivate them.

Over the course of the last three decades, I've seen the landscape of this field change considerably. Solid breakthroughs have occurred in premonition research that were totally unanticipated. Ingenious computer-based experiments by consciousness researcher Dean Radin and others now show that perhaps everyone has an innate ability to sense the future. Scientists around the world replicated and, indeed, have confirmed the studies, so that we can now responsibly use *science* and *premonitions* in the same sentence.

As the new information has become available, my attitude toward premonitions has changed. I no longer believe my premonitions have dried up. I think they have merely taken other forms, becoming more subtle and less visible but always active. I believe that to be alive is to have premonitions. Premonitions are not something we can avoid. They are our birthright. They come factory-installed, part of our original equipment.

A premonition—from the Latin *prae*, "before," and *monere*, "warn"—is literally a forewarning. It is a glimpse of the future, a feeling or sense that something is about to happen. Premonitions are not explainable by inference from prior information or past experience. They come in many flavors. They may warn us of something unpleasant, such as imminent danger or a health crisis, or announce something agreeable, such as what the winning lottery numbers are or where to find a parking spot. Premonitions may be vague, or vivid and dramatic, as in a dream that contains complex characters and plotlines. They may occur while we are awake or asleep. We may be fully conscious of them, or they may be buried in our unconscious mind so deeply they prompt us to act without knowing why.

The sheer heterogeneity of premonitions is dizzying, confusing, maddening. Why should premonitory dreams warn us one night of a national disaster, and the next night reveal where we lost our glasses? Why do they range from the trivial to matters of life and death? Why do some premonitions arrive in vibrant detail, while others are an imageless hunch or a vague intuition? And why do they turn up not just in humans but in animals as well? Premonitions are fickle; sometimes they are valid, but often are misleading. Why aren't they consistent? Why won't they respond when bidden? These are some of the questions we'll try to unravel.

So as we begin, let's acknowledge that premonitions are utterly paradoxical; this will help us keep our balance as we explore this perplexing territory. A paradox is something that's considered to be senseless, logically unacceptable, or self-contradictory, but there are other views. My favorite comes from English essayist and novelist G. K. Chesterton, who said that a paradox is "truth standing on its head to attract attention." Maybe that's one reason why premonitions are so bizarre. If they weren't, we might not pay attention to them.

Our journey through *The Power of Premonitions* consists of five stages.

One—"The Cases"—describes actual instances of premonitions. I've selected examples that reveal the main characteristics of foreknowledge—how it often saves lives from impending disasters, and also how it often fails to do so because of its incomplete fragmentary nature. We'll see how premonitions often herald illness or death. The role of premonitions in premodern cultures will be examined, as well as people's use of premonitions to make money and acquire wealth.

Two—"Evidence"—examines the recent contributions of modern science to premonitions. We'll see how the various presentiment experiments indicate that perhaps everyone has an innate ability to see what will unfold in the near future. These little-known computer-based experiments reveal that premonitions are not fantasy or wishful thinking, but are a natural inborn ability that usually operates outside our conscious awareness.

Three—"Premonitions: Why, What, How?"—explores why premonitions exist and what purpose they serve, why they are not more accurate and widespread, and how to interpret them.

Four—"Why Should We Want to Cultivate Premonitions, and How Do We Do It?"—further unpacks the importance of premonitions, the penalties we often pay for ignoring them, the role of personality and temperament in premonitions, and some of the cautions and dangers of these experiences.

Five—"Premonitions and Our Worldview"—examines the impact of premonitions on how we see the world and our place in it. We explore not only our ability to see and change the future, but the past as well. We'll explore the influence of premonitions on perhaps the biggest questions of all—the nature of the mind, our origin, and our destiny.

In the Appendix, we'll review what some of the greatest minds in the history of science have had to say about the nature of consciousness. We'll see that these timeless views of the mind are cordial to the existence of foreknowledge.

The allure of future knowing is ancient and powerful. As author and remote-viewing researcher Stephan A. Schwartz says, "There is no siren whose call is quite so exquisite as the music of the future. For as long as writing has existed there are records showing we have sought to know its form. Last year alone, literally billions were spent by widows, lovers, spies, and presidents—all seeking, like an arrow through time, some way to answer: 'In the future, what will . . . ?'"

For most of human history, foreknowledge has not been regarded as hypothetical, but as a natural part of the human endowment. People saw evidence for this everywhere. Premodern cultures routinely used, and still use, premonitions pragmatically—knowing where danger lay; where to find game and shelter; when to plant and harvest; where to locate strayed animals; or which part of which plant, harvested in which season, prepared in which way, would cure a specific illness. In addition to the utilitarian side of precognition, there were more subtle benefits that were equally important.

The ability to know the future is a stepping-stone outside the here and now. The intensity of the trials of life—the daily dose of hunger, suffering, and death—was lessened for our predecessors because foreknowledge made it clear they were part of something outside the here and now, something transcendent. Our forebears could better endure the nastiness, horrors, and pain of the present because they were not time-bound.

They kept their links to the past alive through oral history, ritual, myth, and story, which often included honoring their ancestors. Their link to the future was fashioned through foreknowledge, which for them was an obvious, demonstrable fact.

Our forebears knew something we don't: the links between the past, present, and future are real. But how can we know this for ourselves? There are two main ways I'll pursue this in this book. One approach is to examine the actual precognitive experiences of ordinary people. Second, actual experiments demonstrate that we can know the future before it happens.

Systematic research in premonitions has a long and storied history, beginning most emphatically in 1882 with the founding of the Society for Psychical Research (SPR) in the United Kingdom. The SPR was later imitated in other countries, including the United States, where William James, widely regarded as the father of American psychology, helped found the American version in 1885. The founders of the SPR were among the most eminent, respected scholars of their day. Their dedication to the principles of science was profound. Sigmund Freud and Carl G. Jung were members of the organization. Past presidents have included several Nobelists.

Another major event in precognition research was the founding of the Duke Parapsychology Laboratory in 1935 by the legendary J. B. Rhine. Rhine is rightly considered the founder of modern parapsychology research, and he did more than anyone in the twentieth century to anchor it in rigorous science. Rhine and his colleagues brought a statistical and laboratory approach to studying extrasensory perception (ESP), which continues to this day. Rhine's initial laboratory has morphed into the Rhine Research Center, with headquarters in Durham, North Carolina.

In 1957, following an initiative by Rhine, the Parapsychological Association (PA) was formed with the intention of providing a nucleus for an international society. In 1969 the PA became formally affiliated with the American Association for the Advancement of Science. The archives of the PA are a rewarding entry point for anyone wishing to pursue the history of research in precognition.

Though my focus in this book is on the most recent research in precognition, I mean no disrespect to the early trailblazers. Those wanting a more comprehensive approach might consult the recent scholarly books *Irreducible Mind* by Edward F. Kelly and colleagues, and *Varieties of Anomalous Experience: Examining the Scientific Evidence,* edited by Etzel Cardeña, Stanley C. Krippner, and Steven Jay Lynn.

One of the most striking features of psi-related experiences (PREs) is their high prevalence in nearly every culture studied. A 1987 survey by the University of Chicago's National Opinion Research Center found that 67 percent of adult Americans say they have had PREs. In most other countries where similar surveys have been done, more than half the population reports PREs. This includes all of North America, the United Kingdom, and other countries in Europe, the Middle East, Brazil, Asia, and Australia.

The most common PRE involves telepathy, reported by one-third to half of the population. About one-fifth report clairvoyance. Psychokinesis is reported by only 5 to 10 percent of the population.

Where do premonitions fit in? Around 60 percent of PREs are *contemporaneous*, meaning that they link two concurrent events. Nearly all the remainder are *precognitive*, relating to the future. Precognitive ESP, or PREs, are what we call premonitions.

Most contemporaneous PREs are intuitive imageless impressions—a hunch or "just a feeling." By contrast, precognitive experiences or premonitions usually occur as realistic visual images, most commonly in dreams.

There is a dark side to premonitions. Because they provide foreknowledge, people throughout history have coveted this ability as a way of exercising influence over others. In their quest for power, people throughout history have won—and lost—kingdoms and fortunes by trusting premonitions. Adolf Hitler's premonitions of Aryan supremacy and a Third Reich that would reign supreme for a thousand years destroyed Germany, ravaged Europe, and led to 50 million deaths in World War II. The Allies' premonitions that the D-Day invasion at Normandy would be successful, in spite of horrid weather and ferocious German resistance, won the day.

Today it is difficult for us to appreciate the extent to which premonitions, visions, prescient dreams, prophecy, and divination have influenced civilizations. "The concept of divination is basic to not only shamanic but also Judeo-Christian traditions," say psi researchers Elisabeth Targ, Marilyn Schlitz, and Harvey J. Irwin in *Varieties of Anomalous Experience*. "As in other places, leaders in ancient Greece relied heavily on the prophetic efforts of sibyls at the Oracle of Delphi to make strategic decisions. In modern Asia, the time of escape for His Holiness, the 14th Dalai Lama, after the Chinese invasion was determined through directions from the Nechung oracle, who helped guide the spiritual and political leader of Tibet into safety in India."

The Nechung Oracle remains the official state oracle of the exiled government of Tibet. The Kuten, the medium of the oracle, occupies the rank of a deputy minister in the Tibetan government. His Holiness the Dalai Lama has dealings with him several times a year. The reason is pragmatic. As His Holiness says in his autobiography, "This may sound far-fetched to twentieth-century western readers. . . . But I do so for the simple reason that as I look back over the many occasions when I have asked questions of the oracle, on each one of them time has proved that his answer was correct." But he cautiously adds, "That is not to say that I rely solely on the oracle's advice."

At least the Tibetans are open about their reliance on future knowing. Our government tends toward secrecy in these matters. First Lady Nancy Reagan consulted an astrologer in managing President Ronald Reagan's schedule. The Carter administration successfully used remote viewers to locate a downed spy plane that satellites could not see. The CIA for decades employed remote viewers to gather intelligence in the highly classified Star Gate program.

Premonitory abilities can be extremely seductive. This is why many spiritual traditions have regarded them as detriments to one's spiritual development, and why some religions condemn them as satanic. This reaction is perhaps overwrought, at least in some instances. Fire can be used to cook our food or burn heretics, but no one suggests that we ban it because it can be used in nefarious ways. So it is with premonitions. Surely wisdom and discernment, not censorship or condemnation, is the better approach toward a gift that humankind has possessed for probably its entire history, and whose impact on us is, on the whole, benevolent.

I'm not asking you to take anything in this book on blind faith, but to open yourself up to the *possibility* of premonitions and the evidence supporting them. Listen to the stories people tell. Explore the research that demonstrates our capacity to sense the future. Ponder the implications of mind outside of time. Invite premonitions into your life and see what happens. If you do so humbly and reverently, your life will likely become more premonition-prone, and you may touch that exquisite infinite realm to which premonitions, now as always, are a door.

—Larry Dossey, M.D
Santa Fe, New Mexico

THE POWER OF PREMONITIONS

"I'm sure [my memory] only works one way," Alice remarked. "I can't remember things before they happen."

"It's a poor sort of memory that only works backwards," the Queen remarked.

> —Lewis Carroll, *Alice's Adventures in Wonderland* and *Through the Looking-Glass*

ONE

THE CASES

Premonition (noun): an intuition about the future; a feeling that something is about to happen, especially something unpleasant; a forewarning. From the Latin *praemonere*: *prae,* "before," + *monere,* "warn."

Amanda, a young mother living in Washington State, awoke one night at 2:30 A.M. from a nightmare. She dreamed that a large chandelier that hung above the baby's bed in the next room fell into the crib and crushed the infant. In the dream, as she and her husband stood amid the wreckage, she saw that a clock on the baby's dresser read 4:35 A.M. The weather in the dream was violent; rain hammered the window and the wind was blowing a gale. The dream was so terrifying she roused her husband and told him about it. He laughed, told her the dream was silly, and urged her to go back to sleep, which he promptly did. But the dream was so frightening that Amanda went to the baby's room and brought the child back to bed with her. She noted that the weather was calm, not stormy as in the dream.

Amanda felt foolish—until around two hours later, when she and her husband were awakened by a loud crash. They dashed into the nursery and found the crib demolished by the chandelier, which had fallen directly into it. Amanda noted that the clock on the dresser read 4:35 A.M. and that the weather had changed. Now there was a howling wind and rain. This time, her husband was not laughing.

Amanda's dream was a snapshot of the future—down to the specific event, the precise time it would happen, and a change in the weather.

This incident illustrates the literal meaning of "premonition"—a warning that precedes a future event, a happening that is usually unpleasant. It is on file in the archives of the Rhine Research Center in Durham, North Carolina, which houses the world's largest collection of premonitions.

Another typical "warning case" from the Rhine archives involved a man from Charlotte, North Carolina, who had experienced several precognitive dreams in years past. Not until a tragedy occurred did he put much stock in them. In one dream he met Rick, his cousin, on a Massachusetts street. When he reached out to shake his hand, Rick was struck from behind and fell to the ground. The man dismissed the dream as a terrible nightmare. Not long afterward, he was notified that Rick was viciously attacked and killed by a mentally deranged man while taking a walk during his lunch break. "It was the first time I recognized the phenomenon of precognition," he regretfully admitted. It took a catastrophe to convince him he could see the future.

This man deserves our sympathy. He, like most in our culture, has been conditioned to consider premonitions as illusions. Speaking openly and acting on them can cause embarrassment and social repercussions, particularly if they don't prove true. But even if we're open to them, says psychologist Sally Rhine Feather of the Rhine Research Center, "It is very hard, at times, to recognize the difference between an ordinary nightmare and a true, precognitive warning. No special markers distinguish one from the other. We learn the difference only when one or more precognitive experiences comes true in a dramatic enough way to make us consider the possibility."

Sometimes an intuition or gut feeling can be so strong that it prompts an intervention that goes against common sense. Physicist Russell Targ relates such an experience in his book *Limitless Mind.* One evening, while sitting at his desk paying bills, he began to worry obsessively about what would happen if he lost his credit card. This was strange; he'd never lost one before. The fear was so strong that he stopped what he was doing, went to the next room to get his credit card from his wallet, and compulsively wrote down its number in his personal phone book. The next day he went to a big street fair in Palo Alto, California, where he lived. He made a purchase with cash, and soon afterward paused to buy a beer to slake his thirst on this very hot day. He discovered he had no more cash, so he went to an ATM at a nearby bank. With cash in hand, he returned to the beer stand. Two days later, while buying groceries, he discovered with a shock that his credit card was missing from his wallet. He deduced that he'd left it at the ATM. Because of his gut feeling, he had the card number written down. He called the credit card company, cancelled the old card, and asked for a new one before any damage was done.

There are endless ways, it seems, in which we can be confused by premonitions. Sometimes they prove accurate, with the exception that one character has been substituted for another. This happened to Feather early in her career, when she was working at the Parapsychology Laboratory at Duke University. She awoke one morning following a vivid dream that her mother had died. To her knowledge, it was the only time in her life she'd had such a dream. Knowing more than most people about such things, she was understandably worried. Feather was working at the time with a lab colleague who was from another country. They learned later that the colleague's mother had died unexpectedly, far away in her homeland. "Why did my extrasensory perception substitute my mother for her mother?" Feather asks. "I have always supposed it was a sympathetic type of response for the sorrow that I knew she would feel."

Places can also be switched. While in a doctor's office, Feather once smelled smoke so strongly she asked the physician, "Is there something burning in here?" He assured her nothing was burning. When she arrived home soon afterward, she saw fire engines surrounding her house. Her child and a neighborhood playmate had been fooling around with matches.

Granted, the fragmentary nature of premonitions can impede people from intervening in a foreseen happening. But if they tried to intervene, could they? Sometimes the answer is yes, sometimes no.

In one case reported to the Rhine Research Center, Susan, a woman from New York, dreamed her four-year-old son was bitten by a dog, which she clearly visualized. The dream was so vivid she kept her child indoors for the next three days. On day four, however, he ran next door to the store. Before she could get to him, Susan heard her child screaming. He had rushed into the store and bumped into a dog with a sore tail. The dog attacked him, striking an eye. Seeing the blood, Susan was certain he was blinded, and she fainted. Fortunately the bite was just under the eye. "It was the same dog I dreamed of that bit him," she said.

There is good news. The Rhine analysis of 433 premonition cases shows that most of the attempts to intervene are *not* futile. "The important point we learned from this study was when ESP experiencers did actually try to intervene, they were successful about twice as often as not," Feather states. "A future foreseen is not a future written in stone. . . . [The] failed intervention attempts are greatly outnumbered by successful interventions."

One of the most compelling cases in the Rhine archives demonstrating successful intervention following a precognitive dream involved a streetcar conductor in Los Angeles, which operated a streetcar system until the 1960s.

In his dream, the conductor crossed an intersection just as the northbound no. 5 trolley passed him. As he waved at the no. 5 trolleyman, suddenly a big red truck made an illegal turn and cut in front of him without warning. There was a horrible crash. The truck overturned and people were thrown everywhere. Of the three occupants of the truck, two men were killed and a woman was screaming in pain. When the conductor walked over to the woman and looked down into her striking blue eyes, she shouted, "You could have avoided this!" The man awoke from his dream in a sweat. He went to work and the dream faded from his mind.

Eventually he found himself at the same intersection as in the dream. Then he saw the northbound no. 5 trolley and felt nauseated. When the trolleyman waved at him, his dream came flooding back into memory. Without delay he slammed on his brakes and cut off the power—just as a partially red panel truck drove directly into his path. Had he not taken immediate reflexive action, he would have hit it. Three people were in the truck—two men and a woman. As the truck passed, the woman leaned out of the window and gave him an A-OK sign, thanking him for stopping. She had piercing blue eyes, just as he'd dreamed.

The trolleyman was so upset by the sequence of events and the near accident that he had to be relieved from work.

Experiences such as these suggest that events that are foreseen are not immutable, but they can be modified by the decisions we make in the present. Let's look at one more case that affirms this possibility.

Dale E. Graff is a physicist, aerospace engineer, and a former manager of the highly classified project Star Gate, one of a number of civilian and government programs that investigated remote viewing phenomena over three decades, beginning in the 1970s during the Cold War.

One of Graff's interests is precognitive dreams; he has kept a dream journal since 1970. In one dream in which he saw an unfolding tragedy, he promptly intervened upon waking, possibly saving a life.

During the dream his attention was focused on a white station wagon in the driveway, which belonged to his wife, Barbara, which he almost never drove. He noticed a small cylindrical object on the backseat floor. One end of the object began to glow bright red. It exploded, enveloping the entire car in flames. Graff was so startled he awakened.

Having kept a dream journal for decades, Graff developed an intuitive feel for dreams that are likely to jibe with future events. "Due to its brevity and highly destructive imagery," he says, "I suspected that was either a significant, personal, symbolic dream or a precognitive warning dream." That morning he inspected the backseat, suspecting a leaking can of flammable material. He found nothing suspicious, so he checked the underside for gasoline leaks. Again nothing suspicious showed up. Just to make sure, he took the car in for a routine tune-up and safety check.

A few days later, the garage owner called to tell him the car was ready. "I have something interesting to show you," he said. He showed Graff a small cylindrical object and said, "Do you realize you were driving a time bomb? Look at the fuel pump. One end is charred and the insulation on the connecting wires is burned off. You had an electrical short that could have led to a gas tank explosion. It's good you brought it in when you did. On this model car, the fuel pump is inside the gas tank."

Graff stared at the damaged fuel pump, almost in disbelief. The long fuel pump resembled the cylinder he'd dreamed about. He had no idea it was mounted in the gas tank. In all the other cars he'd owned, the fuel pump was mounted forward in the engine area.

Graff considered that the fuel pump might simply have stopped working, or it might have triggered a catastrophic explosion, although there was no certainty this would have happened. But the dream provided him with what he most needed to know: his wife's life was in grave danger. This, and the dream's salient features, were all this dream expert needed to take action to possibly change the future.

Graff believes that precognitive information is not about fixed incidents, but is about possibilities. Some futures are so highly probable they are essentially certain. They will happen. Other less probable futures, while likely, can nevertheless be avoided or prevented by taking appropriate action if sufficient information is present in the precognition. These probabilistic futures, he believes, suggest that "something quantum physical" is operating in premonitions. Perhaps a quantum-like barrier between now and the future may exist, he suggests, that can be tunneled through if we can muster the required focus and mental intention. Future events are always casting their shadows across our paths in the present, Graff says. But to notice them, we first have to be open to their possibility, otherwise they will flicker in and out of our experience without being recognized.

Few of us, however, are dream experts like Graff. How can we amateurs separate valid premonitions from invalid ones? One way is to follow a simple, old-fashioned method he has employed since 1970: write down all that dream stuff. Feather concurs. "Keeping a diary of our dreams," she says, "can help us recognize the difference between an ordinary nightmare and a true precognitive warning we need to act on."

WARNINGS OF ILLNESS

Forewarnings of illness are one of the most common varieties of premonitions. One celebrity example, featured on *60 Minutes* in March 2008, helped raise public concerns about the safety of the nation's hospitals.

In November 2007, the twelve-day-old twins of actor Dennis Quaid and his wife, Kimberly, were admitted to Cedars-Sinai Medical Center in Los Angeles with possible staph infections, for which routine IV antibiotics were given. On their second day of hospitalization, the Quaids were told the babies were doing fine, so the tired parents went home for a few hours' rest. They left instructions to be called if any problems arose. At nine P.M. that evening, Kimberly had a mother's premonition that something was wrong. "I just had this horrible feeling come over me, and I felt like the babies were passing. I just had this feeling of dread," she said. She even made a note at the time, scribbling "9:00 P.M. Something happened to babies." Quaid called the hospital and was put through to the nurse who was in the room with the infants. He asked how the babies were doing, and was told they were fine.

In fact, they weren't fine. Around the time of Quaid's call, the nurses had discovered that both twins were in grave danger. Instead of being given ten units of heparin to flush out their IVs and prevent them from clotting, they were given ten thousand units of the adult version of the drug, not once but twice. The infants began to bleed from bandages placed over blood draw sites.

It turned out that two pharmacy technicians had mistakenly delivered one hundred vials of adult-strength heparin to the pediatric unit. It wasn't until the next morning, however, that the Quaids learned what had happened. Their pediatrician informed them that an identical mistake had earlier killed three infants in Indiana. It was touch and go for a while; but after spending eleven days in intensive care, both twins made a full recovery.

Time-specific premonitions are not uncommon—as Sherman L. Cohn, professor of law at Georgetown University Law Center in Washington, D.C., discovered. In 1958, while living in Alexandria, Virginia, he and his wife visited his parents in Erie, Pennsylvania, where he grew up. As they departed, Cohn's father was standing on the front steps waving. Cohn said to his wife, "Look back at Dad. This is the last time we will see him alive." Six weeks later, when his father was taken to the hospital with a "chest cold," Cohn turned to his wife and said, "He will not make it." She asked how he knew, and he said he just did. The next morning, while in synagogue, Cohn knew at a certain moment that his father had died. He looked at his watch; it was ten forty-five. When he returned home, his wife told him he had gotten a call from his sister, informing him that his dad had died at ten forty-five.

Premonitions of illness are often stunningly accurate in pictorial detail.

One morning, while at my office at the Dallas Diagnostic Association, a patient of mine knocked on my door unannounced. I had cared for her for years. She was a highly intelligent, middle-aged attorney who was quite successful in her profession. This morning, however, she was distraught and near tears. Without wasting time on formalities, she got to the point.

"I need your help," she said. "Last night I had a dream in which I saw three little white spots on my left ovary. I'm terrified they are cancerous."

That was all there was to it—no symptoms, just a disturbing dream. I took her report seriously. But when her exam proved normal, she was not consoled.

"The dream was one of the most vivid I've ever had," she said. "I can't dismiss it. I know something is wrong."

"Let's do a sonogram and get a picture of your ovaries," I suggested.

She eagerly agreed, so I escorted her down the hall to the radiology department and introduced her to a no-nonsense colleague whose technical skills were superb. When the radiologist asked her what the problem was, she described her dream without hesitation—three little white spots on her left ovary. He was not exactly enchanted by this clinical tidbit, and he gave me his best you've-got-to-be-kidding glance. It was obvious that this was the first procedure he'd ever performed because of a dream. Nevertheless, I left them alone and walked back to my office to see other patients.

Within an hour the radiologist was in my office. The fact that he chose to personally deliver the sonogram report suggested he'd found something interesting. Moreover, he was nervous and pale, as if he'd seen a ghost.

"What on earth is wrong?" I asked. "What did you find?"

"Three little white spots," he stammered. "On her left ovary."

"Just like she saw in her dream?" I asked, rubbing it in.

"Yeah," he conceded. "Just like in her dream."

"Cancer?"

"No. They're ovarian cysts, completely benign."

My patient was deeply relieved to discover that her ovarian lesions were not cancerous. She was delighted to learn that, although she'd experienced an accurate image, her self-diagnosis was wrong.

Supernormal Physical Senses?

In the days that followed, I discussed this case with some of my physician colleagues. Some argued that this woman's dream was not a premonition, but an example of highly developed body awareness. I am not persuaded by this idea, because there is no known mechanism by which one can know the precise anatomic detail of organs deep within the body, especially when they are not causing symptoms. One of my colleagues suggested that the woman did have symptoms but was not consciously aware of them, and that the body translated this subtle awareness into a dream. But the very definition of *symptom* involves awareness by the patient; an "unaware symptom" is an oxymoron, a contradiction in terms. And even if her symptoms were so subtle they did not register in her conscious awareness, symptoms involve sensations such as pain, nausea, or weakness, not visually precise configurations such as she described.

Invoking the physical senses to explain complex phenomena such as this woman's dream is an old argument. In the nineteenth century, one of the fallback arguments of skeptics toward clairvoyance, or distant knowing, was "hyperacuity of the senses," even when the event in question involved situations in which the senses are not known to operate. Even when great distances were involved, skeptics breezily attributed subjects' knowledge to superbly developed vision, hearing, and smell. To be sure, supernormal functioning of the human senses is real; some individuals do have amazingly keen vision, olfaction, and so on. But to attribute extraordinary knowing to hyperacute senses when utterly remote distances or the future are involved—situations in which the senses can't sense—is to engage in paranormal explanations without realizing it.

Such dreams are not rare. They frequently are repetitive, as if they are clamoring for attention. In one example, a woman dreamed repeatedly for a year that a nurse was holding a lighted candle to her left lower leg. She could not figure out the meaning of this recurrent dream until a year later when she developed osteomyelitis, a painful bone infection requiring surgery, at the site the nurse was illuminating.

In another example, a heavy smoker dreamed repetitively that he was in the army in combat. Seeking cover from machine-gun fire, he took refuge in the hollow trunk of a large tree. The bullets penetrated the tree, however, and methodically cut the man in half from the left side of his lower chest to the right. A medical checkup revealed a small tumor on the left lower lobe of his lung, which had not metastasized and was surgically resected.

In another case, a medical student dreamed she was sinking into a cavity in the earth and was suffocating. Two months later she was diagnosed with tuberculosis, which can be associated with cavities in the lungs and shortness of breath.

These three diseases—osteomyelitis, lung cancer, and tuberculosis—notoriously cause symptoms, which may have provoked a symbolic dream, as my skeptical colleague suggested. But we should be cautious in giving everything over to the body and its physical mechanisms, in view of instances in which health-relevant warnings apparently cannot operate via the physical senses, as in the above event of the falling chandelier.

Survival Value

From the standpoint of evolutionary biology, the ability to bypass the physical senses is just the sort of ability that an intelligent, survival-oriented organism might sooner or later develop. Any organism possessing such an ability could scan the event horizon, assess impending dangers, and take appropriate measures. Such an organism would have a distinct advantage in the high-stakes game of survival of the fittest. This skill might become internalized as part of one's genetic endowment, and would be passed on to succeeding generations.

My patient's premonition was not completely accurate. She suspected that the ovarian abnormalities meant cancer, when in fact they were benign cysts. Her waking mind exaggerated the danger. This is quite common; dreams of impending dangers are often misinterpreted. When this happens, dreams function like a diagnostic test whose sensitivity is too high, causing it to generate "false positives." From a survival perspective, false positives are much better than false negatives, which occur when a dream or a test is too insensitive. If we want to survive, an occasional false alarm is better than no warnings at all.

Yet there are unhealthy extremes. In some people this early warning system may be pathologically sensitive—in paranoid individuals, for instance, who see danger lurking everywhere, all the time, or in hypochondriacal individuals, who continually sense the presence of disease.

A challenge facing any creature with such a warning system would be how to distinguish the false alarms from the accurate ones. People I've known who are good at interpreting their premonitions say that valid dreams have qualities that set them apart from bogus ones. They say, as we'll see, that dreams that turn out to be true have a numinous or noetic quality that causes them to seem hyper-real.

My patient had never previously cried wolf because of a dream about her health, and she never did so afterward. Her dream life seemed well-calibrated, telling her when to pay attention to dream messages and when to disregard them.

When to Take Seriously?

Dismissing dire nocturnal premonitions as "just" dreams is risky.

Psychologist Carl G. Jung described how one of his patients disregarded a dream premonition that literally indicated the method of his death. The man was involved in a number of shady affairs. He developed an "almost morbid passion" for high-risk mountain climbing, which Jung interpreted as a sort of compensation for his other activities. In Jung's words, "He was trying to 'get above himself.'" In one dream the man saw himself stepping off the summit of a high mountain into the air. "When he told me his dream," Jung says, "I instantly saw the risk he was running, and I tried my best to emphasize the warning and convince him of the need to restrain himself. I even told him that the dream meant his death in a mountain accident. It was in vain. Six months later he 'stepped off into the air.'"

It's easy to criticize Jung's patient in retrospect, but in practice it is not always easy to know how to respond to a health-related dream. The language of dreams is notoriously symbolic, and symbols require interpretation. How can we know whether to interpret the symbols in dream premonitions literally, or to consider them metaphorically?

Jungian psychologist Jerome S. Bernstein suggests that when a dream premonition is extraordinarily vivid and deals with the body, physical health, and life or death, we would be wise to seriously regard this as a literal message and take action, for we may not have a second chance.

TELESOMATIC EVENTS:
THE IMPORTANCE OF FEELING

A premonition often involves a sense that a loved one is going to be harmed, as in Amanda's precognitive dream that a chandelier was about to fall and crush her sleeping infant. Her experience is emblematic of many precognitive experiences. One simply cannot explore them without being impressed by the significance of empathy, concern, compassion, and love in their origin.

There is another class of nonlocal experiences called telesomatic events, in which emotions also play a central role. Neurologist Berthold E. Schwarz coined the term *telesomatic* from words meaning "distant body." The term is appropriate, because the involved individuals behave as if they share a single body, even though separated by great distances and, in some cases, by time.

A classic telesomatic example, reported by the nineteenth-century English social critic John Ruskin, involved Arthur Severn, the well-known landscape painter. Severn awoke early one morning and went to the nearby lake for a sail. His wife, Joan, who remained in bed, was suddenly awakened by the feeling of a severe, painful blow to the mouth, of no apparent cause. Shortly thereafter Severn returned, holding a cloth to his bleeding mouth. He reported that the wind had freshened abruptly and caused the tiller to hit him in the mouth, almost knocking him from the boat at the estimated time his wife felt the blow.

Mathematician-statistician Douglas Stokes reported a similar instance in 2002. When he was teaching a course on parapsychology at the University of

Michigan, one of his students reported that his father was knocked off a bench one day by an "invisible blow to the jaw." Five minutes later his dad received a call from a local gymnasium where his wife was exercising, informing him that she had broken her jaw on a piece of fitness equipment.

An example that captures the feeling-and-need side of remote knowing is again from the Severn clan, who seemed to be good "receivers" of such things.

One day while Joan Severn was sitting quietly with her mother and aunt, the mother suddenly screamed, collapsed back onto the sofa, covered her ears with both hands, and exclaimed, "Oh, there's water rushing fast into my ears, and I'm sure either my brother, or son James, must be drowning, or both of them!" Then Joan looked out the window and saw people hurrying toward the nearby shore. Shortly thereafter her uncle came to the house, looking pale and distressed, and reported that James had indeed drowned.

The late psychiatrist Ian Stevenson, of the University of Virginia, has investigated scores of comparable instances in which distant individuals experience similar physical symptoms. Most involve parents and children, spouses, siblings, twins, lovers, and very close friends. Again, the common thread seems to be the emotional closeness and empathy experienced by the separated persons.

In another example, a mother was writing a letter to her daughter, who had recently gone away to college. For no obvious reason her right hand began to burn so severely she had to put down her pen. She received a phone call less than an hour later informing her that her daughter's right hand had been severely burned by acid in a laboratory accident, at the same time that she, the mother, had felt the burning pain.

In a case reported by researcher Louisa E. Rhine, a woman suddenly doubled over, clutching her chest in severe pain, saying, "Something has happened to Nell; she has been hurt." Two hours later the sheriff arrived to inform her that Nell, her daughter, had been involved in an auto accident, and that a piece of the steering wheel had penetrated her chest.

Actual physical changes sometimes accompany a premonition that something is wrong. In 1892, British Maj. Gen. T. Blaksley described a case involving a soldier in the Twelfth Regiment who was a close friend of his. One morning, while walking to the firing range, his friend said, on the basis of a premonition, "My twin brother died this morning on his ship on the west coast of Africa, at eight o'clock, and I know that the effect on me will be a serious illness." General Blaksley tried to console him by assuring him that he had been dreaming, to no avail. "No," his friend insisted, "it is certain; through our lives there has always been such strong sympathy between us that nothing has ever happened to one without the other knowing about it." His premonition proved true; he came down with an attack of jaundice. News eventually arrived that his twin brother had died at the time he had stated.

Hospitals, clinics, and medical offices are among the most common settings for these events. Psychologist Paul Pearsall relates, "The wife of one of my patients was speaking with me in my office while her husband was undergoing a heart test called an angiogram. As we talked, she suddenly doubled over, grabbed her chest as if in severe pain, and cried, 'My God. He's had a heart attack. Joe just had a heart attack.' I called for a stretcher and, as we wheeled her to the cardiac unit, her husband was wheeled past her as the nurses brought him out of the exam room. Husband and wife looked at each other and, before they could speak, one of the nurses sensed the wife's fear. She said, 'He's okay. He had a little trouble in there and his heart stopped for just a few seconds. We got it going again and he's going to be fine.'"

These examples of remote knowing are contemporaneous, not precognitive. I mention them to illustrate the importance of emotional closeness and empathy in psi events in general, including premonitions.

A remarkable example of how telesomatic events can be interwoven with premonitions is that of Larry Kincheloe, an obstetrician-gynecologist in Oklahoma City. I received a remarkable letter from him, in which he described how premonitions and bodily sensations can combine to influence patient care.

After completing his training in obstetrics and gynecology, Kincheloe joined a very traditional medical group and practiced for about four years without any unusual events. Then one Saturday afternoon he received a call from the hospital that a patient of his was in early labor. He gave routine orders; and since this was her first baby, he assumed that delivery would be hours away. While sweeping leaves, he experienced an overwhelming feeling that he had to go to the hospital. He immediately called labor and delivery and was told by the nurse that everything was going fine; his patient was only five centimeters dilated, and delivery was not expected for several more hours.

Even with this reassurance, the feeling got stronger and Kincheloe began to feel an aching pain in the center of his chest. He described it as similar to the feeling one has at sixteen years old after losing his first love—an achingly sad, melancholy sense. The more he tried to ignore the sensation the stronger it grew, until he felt he was drowning. Desperate, he jumped into his car and sped away, feeling better only as he neared the hospital. When he walked onto the labor unit, he felt overwhelming relief.

The nurse was just walking out of his patient's room. When she asked why he was there, Kincheloe honestly admitted that he did not know, only that he felt he was needed and that his place was with his patient. She gave him a strange look and told him that she had just checked the woman and that she was only seven centimeters dilated. At that moment a cry came from the labor room. Anyone who has ever worked in labor and delivery knows that there is a certain tone in a woman's voice when the baby's head is on the perineum, nearing delivery. He rushed to the room just in time to deliver a healthy infant. Afterward, when the nurse asked how he had known to come to the hospital after being told that delivery was hours away, he had no answer.

After that day, Kincheloe started paying attention to his feelings. He's learned to trust them. Having experienced these intuitive sensations hundreds of times, he routinely acts on them. Usually by the time he gets a call from labor and delivery, he is already getting dressed or is in his car on the way to the hospital. He often answers the phone by saying, "I know. I am on my way," knowing that it is labor and delivery calling him to come in. This is now such a common occurrence among the labor and delivery staff that they tell the new nurses, "If you want Dr. Kincheloe, just think it and he will show up."

Recently he had the old feeling, called in, and talked to a new nurse who was taking care of a patient of his who was in active labor. She reported that the patient was resting comfortably with an epidural and that she had a reassuring fetal heart rate pattern. He again asked her if she was sure that nothing was happening that required his attention. Exasperated, she said, "I told you I just checked her and everything is fine." In the background Kincheloe heard another nurse say, "Ask him if he is having chest pains." Confused, the new nurse asked him. He replied yes. He heard the new nurse relay his response to the older nurse, who said, "Since he's having chest pains you had better go check the patient again."

"Just a minute," the new nurse said to Kincheloe, and she put down the phone and went to check the patient. She hurriedly related that the baby was nearing delivery and that he needed to come immediately.

Dr. Kincheloe's experiences show how physical sensations can alert us to something important about to happen—an early-warning premonition system. Physical symptoms are like psychic cell phones uniting distant individuals. The cell-phone metaphor is appropriate, because our reliance on electronic gadgets to communicate may be one reason our psychic connections have withered. But they have not totally atrophied. Individuals like Dr. Kincheloe, who are able physically to sense when someone else is in need, are proof that such linkages still exist.

I envision a day when our medical schools honor our distant connections and teach young physicians and nurses how to cultivate them. Then the healing professions will be transformed and humanized, for it will be obvious that healing is not dependent solely on drugs, mechanical devices, and scalpels.

PREMONITIONS OF INFANT DEATH: SIDS

We pay a price for excluding premonitions from our concepts of healing. This is nowhere more obvious than in sudden infant death syndrome, or SIDS.

Sudden infant death syndrome is the sudden and unexplained death of an apparently healthy baby. It is the leading cause of death in infants between the ages of one month and one year in the United States.

Infants are most susceptible to SIDS between two and four months of age. SIDS is not contagious or hereditary, and it affects families of all social, economic, and ethnic groups. Although the basic cause of SIDS remains unknown, certain practices can make sleep safer, such as allowing babies to sleep on their backs on firm surfaces. Since these practices were popularized in the early 1990s in the Back to Sleep Campaign and continue to be promoted by SIDS organizations, SIDS deaths have been reduced by more than 50 percent.

Premonitions are a recurring feature in the experiences of SIDS parents. Don, a physician in a large metropolitan area, sensed during the first trimester of his wife's pregnancy that the happiness his son's birth would bring would be short-lived. A few months before the birth, he occasionally found himself contemplating a nearby cemetery, where his son would be buried. When Don first held him in his arms, he felt for no obvious reason that the newborn was not supposed to be with them. After the baby came home, Don was awakened from sleep with thoughts of SIDS. He even heard a voice very similar to his own say repeatedly, "Take a good look. This is the last time you will see him."

Don's apprehensions increased when his wife planned a flight with the baby to visit her parents, who lived in another state. Although they disagreed about whether the baby should go, Don didn't make his fears clear to his wife. As he was driving them to the airport, negative feelings came flooding in. At the airport, walking to security, he heard a clear warning that he'd never see his son again. He knew his baby would die during the trip. While walking back to the parking lot, the voice told him to go back and get his son. Finally the voice softened and stopped, as Don ignored it and kept walking. Early the next morning his wife called, hysterically relating that their son had died. He later would find that his aunt had similar apprehensions about the baby.

Looking back, Don said, "The process has been a shock to me since I knew beforehand this [death] was going to happen. The only thing I didn't know was when and where. . . . I have no idea of its meaning. The only thing I can say is that perhaps if I would have listened to 'my heart' many mishaps could have been prevented. . . . I think people have the ability to perceive things and give it a purposeful meaning which can be used for any future event."

Don was one of many SIDS parents who participated in the largest study ever done examining premonitions of SIDS, and the effect of the premonitions on grieving and healing, conducted by the Southwest SIDS Research Institute of Lake Jackson, Texas, near Houston. Of 174 SIDS parents, 21.8 percent (or roughly 38 parents) sensed that something was going to happen to their infants, while only 2.6 percent (or roughly 15) of 568 control parents whose infants did not develop SIDS sensed their child might die. For the majority of the SIDS parents, the premonition took the form of a vague, uneasy feeling without any obvious cause. More than half of the SIDS parents described a vivid dream or, like Don, an auditory or visual hallucination while awake.

Most of the SIDS parents believed their premonitions had a negative effect on their grieving process. Even though the interviews took place an average of four years following the death of their infant, they continued to experience fear, anger, and guilt. "If only they had listened" was a lingering thought and a recrimination of the physicians and nurses they'd relied on. They remembered, with bitterness, that they'd not been taken seriously when they had disclosed their concerns to their pediatricians. A third of the SIDS parents actually visited their physician following their premonition. Although they requested further medical intervention and tests, *non-routine medical follow-up was not recommended for any of the SIDS infants studied.* When the parent expressed concern about the future death of the apparently healthy baby, and the exam was normal, responses from pediatricians ranged from outrage ("How could you say such a thing?") to denial ("Your baby's perfectly fine! Relax and enjoy him!").

The parents frequently blamed themselves for not pushing back hard enough ("I knew something was going to happen, and I had the responsibility to do something to prevent it."). Their feelings of guilt had continued, and they were relieved to discuss their feelings. They did not renounce their premonitions and, as a group, were left with a strong belief in trusting their instincts.

Many of the SIDS parents experienced dreams, visions, or feelings of being in contact with their infants following death. They felt uniformly positive about these experiences, and were left with a sense that their baby was being cared for and was in a better place.

In a lecture I once gave on the nature of consciousness, I discussed our ability to acquire information outside the present. As an example, I described the premonitions of parents whose children died of SIDS. During the discussion that followed, one woman was furious. "How terrible to have a premonition that doesn't prevent the horrible fate of losing your child!" she said. I could see heads nodding in agreement throughout the audience. "No wonder those parents felt angry and bitter," she continued. "Their premonitions left them feeling that their fate was controlled by devils, not God. Those poor SIDS parents are actually in greater pain from having experienced premonitions!"

Would the SIDS parents have been better off without a premonition of their baby's death? Only the parents themselves can answer that question. I doubt they would all answer the same. Some would probably have preferred a premonition of danger, because it might have given their infant a better chance to survive. Others might choose not knowing, in hopes of diminishing the anger, remorse, and pain that followed.

Surely the attitudes of the SIDS parents toward premonitions depended heavily on whether or not they acted successfully on the forewarnings. This is true not just for SIDS parents, but for any parent. For Amanda, for example, whose dream of a falling chandelier prevented it from crushing her sleeping infant, she and her husband were immeasurably grateful for her precognitive dream. But Amanda honored her premonition and acted on it immediately, while Don, the SIDS parent, to his regret, did not, even after repeated warnings. Their feeling toward their premonition could not possibly be the same.

Of the SIDS parents who did try to act on their premonitions, all were thwarted by pediatricians. In the case of the falling chandelier, Amanda did not have to go through a third party. Although her husband dismissed her dream as silly, she initiated action on her own that saved her baby's life. But the decisions of the SIDS parents were not that simple; even when they tried, they were unable to overcome the barrier of their skeptical pediatricians. Their experiences reveal the complexity of premonitions. When an entire team of individuals is involved—parents, physicians, and nurses—the belief systems of several individuals must be aligned for effective action to be taken.

And why did only a minority of the SIDS parents experience a premonition? Were the other infants unworthy of a warning? Do the premonitions gods play favorites? Do they tease and taunt humans, giving them just enough information to make them miserable when they fail?

It would be improper for me to speak for any of those SIDS parents. I can say, however, that for my part I'm glad that premonitions exist, in spite of their often infuriatingly imprecise nature. I'd always choose poor vision over total blindness. After all, there might be ways I could improve my vision—glasses, surgery, and so on. My vision might improve on its own, or I might compensate for my visual deficits by bringing other physical senses into play, as people with sensory defects commonly do. But I would never reject what sight I do have in favor of none at all. Just so, I prefer to hang on to my underdeveloped premonition sense.

There are premonition prodigies in whom the ability for future knowing seems highly developed, just as there are a few among us who can run a four-minute mile or high-jump eight feet. Most of us, however, can only look on those rarities with envy. Those exceptions, however, whether in athletics or foreknowledge, show us what is possible. In the history of our species, there were surely rare individuals who were on the leading edge of the ability to walk upright and vocalize clearly. Those abilities, in time, spread to the rest of the population. Perhaps in time, clear, precise premonitions will too. Meanwhile, I believe we should be grateful for what meager abilities we may have. And we should comfort one another when our reach exceeds our grasp.

THE ABERFAN DISASTER

If all premonitions were as accurate as Amanda's there would be little debate about them, because their value would be obvious with disasters averted and lives saved. Yet premonitions can be graphically precise, but because key pieces of information are missing it is difficult or impossible to put them to practical use. The missing information is usually date, time, and place, as we'll now see.

Coal mining and death have always kept close company. In 1906, the Courrières mine disaster, Europe's worst mining accident, killed 1,099 miners, including many children. In China, 1,549 miners died in a 1942 mine explosion—the world's deadliest mine disaster. America's worst mining tragedy took place in a coal mine in Monongah, West Virginia, in December 1907, when an underground explosion killed 362 men and boys, created 250 widows, and left more than 1,000 children without support. The 2006 Sago Mine disaster in Sago, West Virginia, and the 2007 collapse of the Crandall Canyon Mine in Crandall Canyon, Utah, reminded Americans that coal mining remains dangerous, even in modern times.

Coal miners are not the only victims of mining accidents, which the villagers of Aberfan, Wales, discovered on Friday, October 21, 1966. At nine fifteen A.M., a mountain of coal waste that had long loomed above the town broke loose. Destabilized by recent rains, a river of black coal sludge, water, and boulders flowed into Aberfan with the vengeance of a mass murderer, crushing or suffocating 144 people, including 116 children. First to be killed were the occupants of a cottage high up the slope. Next in its path were the children and teachers at Pantglas Junior School, who had just returned to their classrooms after singing "All Things Bright and Beautiful" at their assembly. Before the black monster came to rest, it engulfed twenty more houses. Then there was total silence. As George Williams, who was trapped in the debris, recalled, "In that silence you couldn't hear a bird or a child."

Mine employees stationed up on the slope, who were responsible for monitoring the mountain's stability, had seen the avalanche start but could not sound the alarm because their phone had been stolen. The landslide happened so quickly that nobody down below saw anything. Everyone heard the noise, however. "It was a tremendous rumbling sound and all the school went dead," recalled eight-year-old Gaynor Minett. "You could hear a pin drop. Everyone just froze in their seats. I just managed to get up and I reached the end of my desk when the sound got louder and nearer, until I could see the black out of the window. I can't remember any more but I woke up to find that a horrible nightmare had just begun in front of my eyes."

As word of the horrific event spread, people all over Wales dropped what they were doing, threw a shovel in the car, and drove to Aberfan to help. They discovered that about half the students at the school had died, along with five of their teachers. After eleven A.M., nobody was rescued alive. It was almost a week before all the bodies were recovered.

There had been many previous mining disasters in Britain in which the death toll was far greater, but this time it was different. Now it was innocent children who were killed.

On October 26, following resolutions by both houses of Parliament, a tribunal was convened to investigate. It sat for seventy-six days and was the longest inquiry of its kind in British history up to that time. One hundred and thirty-six witnesses appeared before the tribunal and nearly three million words of testimony were recorded.

Blame and legal liability for the disaster was assigned to the National Coal Board (NCB). Excuses were made. The chairman of the NCB attributed the catastrophe to "natural unknown springs" beneath the waste deposits, but all the villagers knew this was incorrect. The investigation showed that the NCB had been dumping coal waste on top of springs that it was well aware of, as they were shown on maps of the neighborhood and in which village schoolboys played.

The tribunal's report was unsparing. Colliery engineers, it found, had concentrated on conditions underground. In a stinging rebuke, the report described them as "like moles being asked about the habits of birds." Nine NCB employees were singled out, but no one would face criminal charges.

In words that would be applied to the American government's response to Hurricane Katrina thirty-nine years later, the final report stated, "[T]he Aberfan Disaster is a terrifying tale of bungling ineptitude by many men charged with tasks for which they were totally unfitted, of failure to heed clear warnings, and of total lack of direction from above. Not villains but decent men, led astray by foolishness or by ignorance or by both in combination, are responsible for what happened at Aberfan."

Aberfan remains a defining moment in Welsh history and has become part of England's collective memory. The event shook the entire nation. Like Americans who remember where they were and what they were doing when President John F. Kennedy was assassinated, or when they first heard of the September 11 tragedies, most British people born before 1960 recall the 1966 Aberfan disaster in the same way. People across Britain felt a special sympathy for the victims, because during World War II many of them had been evacuated to safety in South Wales to escape the bombing of London and other large English cities. During that time, many evacuees developed a fondness for the people of the region. Fifty thousand letters of condolence that poured into Aberfan still survive. David Kerr, speaking on the floor of Parliament shortly after the tragedy, summed it up, saying, "This tragedy has reminded people a long way from Wales that we are still one nation."

Today visitors to the cemetery where the victims are buried can stroll the dignified memorial garden, where flowering plants with pink and blue blossoms remind them of the girls and boys whose lives were snuffed out that October morning. The villagers welcome respectful mourners, but casual tourists are discouraged. After thirty years, Aberfan remains a place of tears.

Within weeks of the Aberfan disaster, reports of premonitions began to surface from all over Wales and England. Fourteen months after the tragedy, many of them were published in *The Journal of the Society for Psychical Research*, in a paper authored by Dr. John Barker, a psychiatrist near Aberfan, entitled "Premonitions of the Aberfan Disaster." He had persuaded a local newspaper to run an article to solicit any premonitions people might have had about the calamity. Barker received seventy-six letters. Although many letters were vague, he selected thirty-five that seemed possibly valid. In twenty-four of those, the respondents had related the information to someone else before the avalanche occurred. In the promising cases, Barker obtained the names and addresses of family members and friends who might substantiate or discount the report, and he interviewed them as well as the initial letter writers.

In many of the reports, dreams were involved. In one case, the dreamer saw the word *Aberfan* spelled out in huge brilliant letters. In another dream, a telephone operator from Brighton talked helplessly to a child who walked toward her, stalked by a billowing cloud of black dust or smoke.

Most who responded to Barker's request did not live near Aberfan, had never heard of it, and had no connection with it. But ten-year-old Eryl Mai Jones, the only known Aberfan student to have had a premonition of the disaster, had told her mother before the devastation, "Mummy, I'm not afraid to die." Her mother responded, "Why do you talk of dying, and you so young; do you want a lollipop?" "No," she said, "but I shall be with Peter and June." The day before the devastation she said, "Mummy, let me tell you about my dream last night." "Darling, I've no time to listen," her mother said. "Tell me again later." "No, Mummy, you must listen," she persisted. "I dreamt I went to school and there was no school there. Something black had come down all over it!" The child was killed the next day and was buried in a communal grave with two friends who also lost their lives—Peter on one side, June on the other. The story was put together by a local clergyman and was verified and signed by both the little girl's parents as correct.

Mary Hennessy wrote to Barker about a dream she had the night before the disaster. She dreamed of Aberfan and of children in two rooms. Soon they moved to a larger room, broke into smaller groups, and appeared to be praying. Hennessy wrote, "At the end of the room there were long pieces of wood or wooden bars. The children were trying somehow to get over the top or through the bars. I tried to warn someone by calling out, but before I could do so one little child just slipped out of sight. I myself was . . . watching from the corridor. The next thing in my dream was hundreds of people all running to the same place. The looks on people's faces were terrible. Some were crying and others holding handkerchiefs to their faces. It frightened me so much that it woke me up."

Hennessy was so horrified on waking that she called her son and daughter-in-law. She was worried that the dream might indicate approaching harm to her two young grandchildren. "I know I dreamed about schoolchildren," she explained to the parents, "but just take special care of them, please?"

Carolyn Miller also reported a vision she had on the evening of October 20, the day before the disaster. She saw "an old schoolhouse nestling in a valley, then a Welsh miner, then an avalanche of coal hurtling down the mountainside. At the bottom of this mountain of hurtling coal was a little boy . . . looking absolutely terrified to death. Then for a while I 'saw' rescue operations taking place. I had an impression that the little boy was left behind and saved. He looked so grief-stricken. I could never forget him, and also with him was one of the rescue workers wearing an unusual peaked cap."

If the premonitions Barker reported had been known ahead of time, could an analysis of them have prevented the 144 Aberfan deaths? Some thought the answer might be yes, and that the risk of ignoring such warnings would have been inexcusable. Thus, the following year Barker established the British Premonition Bureau, whose mission was to prevent disasters by collecting and screening premonitions that involved warnings. A year later a kindred organization, the Central Premonition Registry, was established by Robert and Nancy Nelson in New York City for the same purpose. Neither venture was successful because of several factors, including negative public relations, underfunding, and a great deal of inaccurate information.

A systematic effort to predict future events through premonitions has recently been reborn at The Arlington Institute (TAI) in Arlington, Virginia. TAI specializes in thinking about global futures and trying to influence rapid positive change. John L. Petersen, president and founder, is considered by many to be one of the best-informed futurists in the world. Petersen's institute works with what they consider to be "precognizant dreamers" who have had experience with governmental intelligence services. The institute's premise is that "the human collective unconscious somehow anticipates large impending perturbations," and that this knowledge may be useful in averting disasters.

Premonition alert systems seem so simple: just gather the intuitions of a select group of premonition-prone individuals and identify any patterns they may portend. But for the individuals involved, things may not be this straightforward. Missing information—date, time, or place, as in the Aber-fan catastrophe—can sometimes lead to profound mental distress.

I once had a patient whose foreknowledge seemed to come to him natu-rally and unbidden. His mother possessed this ability, as did his mother's mother. The man worked at a local police station as a radio dispatcher. One morning while at work he developed an unsettling sense that a toddler was walking toward a swimming pool and was about to fall in the water. His imagery was extraordinarily vivid and was accompanied by a certainty he had learned to trust over the years. But there was a problem: he could not identify the address of the imperiled child. He was in an ideal situation as a dispatcher to intervene by alerting a patrol car, but he could not do it. Within an hour a police unit called in, saying that they had just discovered that a small child had drowned at a certain apartment complex.

The man was devastated. He blamed himself for the child's death. If he had been more aware, the child would still be alive. He cursed his "gift" and wanted to be rid of it. Overwhelmed by guilt and shame, he quit his job.

I referred him to a psychologist who honored the ability of consciousness to operate beyond the senses. He was the perfect therapist for the patient. Over many months of counseling, the man made peace with his gift and reclaimed it. He gave up his expectation that it operate perfectly. He devel-oped a sense of gratitude for his ability he had not felt before, and he began to regard it as a blessing, a grace. He found that the sensitivity and reliability of his premonitions increased, though not to the level of perfection he'd de-manded earlier.

PREMONITIONS AND IMMORTALITY: DUNNE'S EXPERIMENT WITH TIME

When premonitions happen, most people aren't as shaken up by them as the former police dispatcher was. Most individuals simply note the premonition as an odd experience and the event recedes into memory or is forgotten alto-gether. Occasional individuals, however, find that they cannot dismiss pre-monitions that easily, particularly if they recur. A rare individual will put them under the microscope and attempt to understand the significance of premonitions for his or her life, and for human existence in general.

A Gallup Poll in 2005 found that three in four people in America believe in the paranormal. There is also evidence that precognitive dreams are among the most common psychic events to appear in the life of the average person, and that dreams of future events make up more than half of the ESP experiences people report. But in the early 1900s the high prevalence of these experiences was unknown. So when John William Dunne began dreaming about things that showed up in the newspapers the following day, he was worried. He thought he might be a "freak" and that he was "a great deal madder than [he] could bring [himself] to believe." Dunne need not have worried; he was not the freakish type.

Dunne was born in 1875 into the Anglo-Irish aristocracy in County Kildare. His father was Gen. Sir John Hart Dunne KCB, who served in the Crimean War of 1854 and in north China in 1860. Dunne followed in the family tradition, serving in the Second Boer War in 1900. He was furloughed with typhoid but returned for further duty in 1902.

Dunne was a friend of famous literary figures such as H. G. Wells and J. B. Priestley. He was an outstanding aeronautical engineer during the early days of aviation and held so many patents he was able to retire at a relatively young age and live comfortably off the income they afforded him. In 1904 he invented the Dunne plane, a daringly designed tailless craft with swept-back wings. The aircraft builder Burgess bought it, and the Burgess-Dunne biplane was adopted by Canada as that country's first airplane for military aviation. Dunne was also an accomplished fly fisherman, and his 1924 book *Sunshine and the Dry Fly* is a classic. He wrote two books for children as well, *The Jumping Lions of Borneo* and *An Experiment with St. George*. Dunne was active politically; he proposed the creation of the League of North-West Europe, a NATO-like organization he believed would provide political stability in Europe against communism and fascism.

As an accomplished scientist, Dunne was not someone who was attracted to crystal balls, Ouija boards, or séances. So what was he to think when he had a series of disconcerting dreams about catastrophes that later came true?

One occurred in 1902 while Dunne was a soldier in the field in southern Africa during the Boer War. The dream, a nightmare, involved the eruption of a volcano on an unidentified island. He saw fumaroles, jets of steam, spewing upward from around the mountain. "Good Lord, the whole thing is going to *blow up!*" he told himself in the dream. Dunne was seized with a desire to save the island's four thousand unsuspecting inhabitants. He realized the only way this could be done was with ships. But he could not get the incredulous French authorities on a neighboring island to budge. He found this infuriating, and said to all who would listen that "Four thousand people will be killed unless—." Without realizing it, Dunne had apparently dreamed of the infamous eruption of Mount Pelée on the northern tip of Martinique in the Caribbean, which would turn out to be the worst volcanic disaster of the twentieth century.

Mail was delivered infrequently to Britain's soldiers in the field in 1902, but when a copy of the *Daily Telegraph* (London) eventually arrived, Dunne opened the center sheet and read, VOLCANO DISASTER IN MARTINIQUE, TOWN SWEPT AWAY, AN AVALANCHE OF FLAME, PROBABLE LOSS OF OVER 40,000 LIVES, BRITISH STEAMER BURNT:

> One of the most terrible disasters in the annals of the world has befallen the once prosperous town of St Pierre, the commercial capital of the French island of Martinique in the West Indies. At eight o'clock on Thursday morning the volcano Mont Pelée which had been quiescent for a century, etc. etc.

Dunne, always a stickler for detail, was stunned by the accuracy of his dream, with the exception of the number of deaths involved. In the dream it was four thousand; in reality it turned out to be forty thousand. "I was off by a nought [zero]," he said. This observation is telling, because it shows that Dunne did not shade the facts, but faithfully reported them as they happened, like the good mathematician and engineer he was. He continued to do so in the years that followed as he struggled to make sense of what was happening.

And so it went, year after year, as Dunne dreamed, recorded, and analyzed his nocturnal premonitions. By the time he published *An Experiment with Time* in 1927, he had concluded what many consider the first systematic experiment of precognition.

Dunne's premise is that time does not proceed the way we normally experience it during our ordinary waking existence, as unrolling from the past, to the present, and into the future. A truer sense of time, he felt, comes during dreams, in which these temporal distinctions are transcended, and time's three divisions seem to be present simultaneously. If one can know the future, the barriers between the present and the future cannot be absolute. These barricades must be porous, capable of being bridged. Dunne concluded from his "experiment with time" that time is best viewed as an "eternal now."

Dunne cultivated the ability to recall his dreams by immediately recording them upon waking. He suggested that people place themselves in environments where their consciousness could escape the waking experience of time as a linear, sequential flow. I suspect, based on my own experiences, that his admiration of fly fishing was in part due to the reverie and enchantment that come from standing in clear, flowing water, entering into an otherworldly sense of connectedness with nature, and becoming lost in time during the process.

Although Dunne was intrigued by his ability to glimpse the future, he did not believe that the value of premonitions was limited to this life. For him, the mother lode of premonitions was the eternal now that made premonitions possible. He reasoned that if we are able to experience an eternal now in dreams, we must possess some quality or faculty that is itself eternal. Premonitions therefore led Dunne to the belief in immortality. He expanded his views of immortality in his 1946 book *Nothing Dies*.

Throughout human history, countless native cultures have held beliefs about time and immortality similar to Dunne's. The view that waking consciousness restricts and limits one's apprehension of reality, and that a truer view can be gained in dreams and altered states of awareness, is practically universal, as shown by scholar of world religions Mircea Eliade in his landmark book *The Myth of the Eternal Return*, first published in English in 1954.

Dunne's influence has been immense. His views of time anticipated the concepts of many subsequent scholars and scientists, such as physicists David Bohm and Julian Barbour. Echoes of his ideas on premonitions, time, and consciousness can be found in the works of some of the most famous literary figures of the twentieth century, including T. S. Eliot, C. S. Lewis, Jorge Luis Borges, Vladimir Nabokov, J. R. R. Tolkien, J. B. Priestley, and Robert A. Heinlein.

Dunne believed he had shed light on the most important premonition there is: the foreknowledge of what happens when we die. For me, his contributions are profound. His insights into the question of the survival beyond bodily death and the possibility of immortality have been vastly undervalued. Dunne was born during the heyday of spiritualism, when contact with the dead during séances was all the rage. As a mathematician and engineer, he favored a completely different approach to resolving questions surrounding survival. His method involved revisioning time by empirically validating premonitions, thereby transcending religion and belief. In the end, he believed, all shall be revealed. First, however, life must be entered fully. "We must live," he said, "before we can attain to either intelligence or control at all. We must sleep if we are not to find ourselves, at death, helplessly strange to the new conditions. And we must die before we can hope to advance to a broader understanding."

AVOIDING TRAINS AND PLANES

Skeptics often dismiss a premonition as an anecdote, as "just a story." Researchers have countered skepticism by applying statistical analyses to large collections of similar events. These analyses can reveal whether or not premonitions are correlated with the event in question, or whether the premonition is a chance happening, just "one of those things."

William Cox, a North Carolina researcher and businessman, discovered a pattern by surveying the passenger loads on American trains involved in accidents between 1950 and 1955. Cox compared the number of passengers present on the accident run with the passenger load on the same run of each of the preceding seven days, as well as the preceding fourteen, twenty-one, and twenty-eight days. He discovered that in every case fewer people rode the trains that crashed or were wrecked than rode similar trains that did not crash. The odds against a chance explanation for this finding were greater than one hundred to one. As a single example, the Georgian, operated by the Chicago & Eastern Illinois Railroad, carried only nine passengers the day of its accident, June 15, 1952, compared to a typical load of sixty-two passengers that it had carried five days earlier.

It's not that people wake up on the morning, envision a train wreck, and decide not to board. They are more likely to experience a sense of physical unease, depression, or distress that has no discernible source or reason. A typical expression is, "I feel like something bad is going to happen." Sometimes the motivation to avoid travel is lodged so deeply in the unconscious that it does not even rise to this level, in which case people may cancel their travel plans without a clue about why.

Further evidence for the role of the unconscious in premonitions comes from the event that changed America: September 11, 2001.

Premonitions of September 11

One the largest collections of ESP cases in the world is maintained by the Rhine Research Center in Durham, North Carolina. Since the 1920s people have sent descriptions of their experiences to the center because they know they will be taken seriously. Dr. Sally Rhine Feather, an experimental and clinical psychologist and daughter of legendary J. B. and Louisa Rhine, the founders of modern psi research, continues to collect and analyze anecdotal experiences.

Although reports trickle in at a steady rate, they flooded in following September 11, 2001. In fact, the events of 9/11 generated the largest outpouring of disaster premonitions ever received at the RRC related to a public national catastrophe.

In one case, "Becky," a North Carolina mother and housewife, contacted psychologist Feather for help in dealing with a disturbing series of events. In July she had paid for airline tickets for a trip to Disney World in Florida for her son Matthew, her brother Steve, Steve's son, and herself. Both families were giddy with excitement. The departure date was September 11. But as the date grew near, Becky, who had no fear of flying and loved to travel, became increasingly anxious, agitated, and disturbed about the trip. Becky felt a smothering sensation, as if the trip were pressing down on her physically. Her husband, John, an assistant district attorney, was quite irritated by her irrational attitude and how it was upsetting everyone involved with the trip. Becky's son Matthew was devastated when she finally suggested they delay the excursion.

On September 4, one week before United Airlines pilot Michael Horrocks's 767 was hijacked and flown into the South Tower of the World Trade Center, Becky awoke at three A.M. from a bizarre dream. She felt as if she were spinning into blackness, and a man's voice was repeating the same number: "2830, 2830, 2830." The voice was also repeating a name she could not make out. "It sounded like Rooks or Horooks," she said. Becky turned on the light, found a pen, and wrote down the name and number, as the voice con-tinued in her head. She considered waking up her husband. She'd had many premonitions in the past that foresaw the death of relatives and friends, in-cluding her father, mother, and cousin, but John, a rational lawyer, remained unconvinced by them.

Becky was emphatic that some important event lay ahead that she should take seriously. In spite of the family protests, she cancelled the September 11 airline reservations for Disneyland. When United Airlines Flight 175 crashed into the South Tower of the World Trade Center, killing pilot Mi-chael Horrocks and his fifty-six passengers, things began to make sense for Becky. She immediately connected his name with the name she heard in her dream. She knew too why she'd needed to cancel her Disneyland flights: America's airports were shut down and no commercial flights were allowed following the terrorist attacks. She could not have flown even if she had wanted to.

John had suspected that his wife's concerns were the product of an over-active imagination. When things began to fall into place, he did a one-eighty. His skepticsm evaporated like a snowball on a hot stove.

But what about "2830," the number that was repeated in the dream? On May 15, 2002, nine months and four days following the fateful day, a paper was published about the attacks, "Effects of the Terrorist Attacks of Sep-tember 11, 2001, on Federal Emergency Management in the United States," by professors Claire B. Rubin and Irmak Renda-Tanali, of the Institute for Crisis, Disaster and Risk Management of George Washington University. They reported that "approximately 2,830 deaths have been confirmed" in the World Trade Center disaster.

Becky and John went to psychologist Sally Rhine Feather for counseling following these events. Their marriage had been strained because Becky felt muzzled, unable to discuss the psychic impressions she'd had all her life with her rational, analytical husband. Her premonitions of September 11 were a turning point in their marriage. "Like Saint Paul on the road to Damascus, John had been knocked off his horse by the Light," Feather said. And like Saint Paul, he was "converted" by the experience. As this happened, Becky found her freedom. She ceased hiding her premonitions and apologizing for them, and her husband stopped behaving disapprovingly when she spoke about them.

Shortly after America's day of terror, Feather received another call from a well-educated woman named Marie (not her real name) living in North Carolina. Two weeks before 9/11, Marie and her husband were vacationing in Washington, D.C. The usual places had been on their itinerary, including the Pentagon, but because the traffic was heavy and the weather sultry they skipped this particular site.

As they were exiting the city, Marie closed her eyes in the passenger seat of the auto to relax. Her husband, who was driving, remarked, "When we come around the bend up ahead, you should get a good view of the Pentagon because our road goes right by it."

When Marie opened her eyes and looked to her right, the Pentagon had huge billows of thick, black smoke pouring out of it. There were no obvious flames, just towers of smoke rising into the sky, as if a bomb had gone off. Marie yelled, slammed her hands on the dashboard, and continued screaming. She was so emotionally upset she hyperventilated and lost her breath. She felt overwhelmed and felt as if she were falling, which had prompted her to try breaking her fall by reaching out to the dashboard.

Marie's outburst quickly subsided and they drove on, but she continued to feel as if they were in grave danger. She felt that the Pentagon was on fire. Her husband assured her it wasn't; he could see the massive building too. Then Marie's vision of the burning Pentagon suddenly disappeared.

Marie, a down-to-earth woman with a business degree, was confused and distraught by her experience. Although she had had premonitions all her life, this one was different—more real, vivid, and frightening.

Two weeks later, at 9:45 A.M. on September 11, 2001, her premonition came true, as American Airlines Flight 77 slammed into the Pentagon, killing 184 people and setting off fires that created clouds of thick, black smoke.

Marie's premonition deserves notice for several reasons. She was fully conscious at the time, and the premonition was visually accurate, geographically specific, and involved a witness, her husband. The missing elements were the date and time.

Marie's premonition was not unique. As Jungian analyst Jerome S. Bernstein reports in his book *Living in the Borderland,* anecdotal reports and news stories revealed that scores and probably hundreds of individuals all over the country had premonitory dreams and waking fantasies prior to the events of 9/11. Dozens of people reported premonitions that saved their lives.

These took the form of inexplicable dread or sudden illness that kept them away from their jobs that day, or intuitions that prompted them to simply turn around and go home before the planes crashed into the WTC or the Pentagon.

Skeptics have criticized these accounts as "just stories." They are stories, but that does not mean we should ignore them. The way we respond to stories is hugely subjective. An old saying in medicine makes the point: "If you don't like a patient's story, you call it an anecdote. If you like it, you call it a case history."

Many of the premonitions of people employed at the World Trade Centers came to light when *The New York Times* published "Portraits of Grief" on July 14, 2002, personal remembrances about the nearly three thousand individuals who lost their lives on September 11.

One portrait was of thirty-six-year-old Lawrence Francis Boisseau, the fire safety director at OCS Security in the World Trade Center. In early September he had a dream that the WTC was crashing down on him. Maria Teresa, his wife, had a dream a few days later about debris, followed the next night by a nightmare in which people were bringing a great deal of food. On September 9, 2001, sobered by their dreams, they talked about death while driving to a christening. Lawrence said to Maria Teresa, "You know, if the time comes, if you need somebody to take care of you, I don't mind." She replied puckishly, "In my case, if I die first, you are not getting remarried." He responded, "Oh, that's not fair. How come? I'm allowing you to remarry if you need to." "No," his wife said, "I don't want to share this feeling. I don't want any woman to share this relationship with you, just me. The feeling that I have, I just want to lock inside my heart."

Lawrence Boisseau was killed on September 11 while helping knock out the windows of a child-care center on the ground floor of the WTC. The grandparents of several of the children he helped rescue attended his memorial service.

Boisseau's example shows the poignant "what-if" side of premonitions: what if they had been taken seriously? His dream was camera-like in its visual accuracy: the WTC was literally falling down on him. Moreover, his dream was affirmed by his wife's precognitive dream of debris. Why did he not act on his premonition? Psychoanalyst Bernstein believes that Boisseau's dream was not dramatic enough to dissuade him from going to work, or to vacate the building as quickly as possible once the attack occurred. The Boisseaus, he suggests, like most people in Western cultures, were biased in favor of rational, analytical thinking. This would have made it difficult for them to consider their premonitions as literally prophetic, rather than "just dreams."

But wait. It's easy to criticize people for ignoring premonitions, and that's not my intent. In defense of the Boisseaus, they did not dream the date of the WTC crash. Even if he had wanted to take his dream seriously, which day should he have picked to stay away? And once the WTC tragedy had begun to unfold, how could he have deserted the daycare children whose lives were in danger? Premonitions are not like digital photographs; they don't come with the date emblazoned at the bottom of the image.

A friend of mine who has lived in Manhattan for many years, and who endured the horrors of 9/11, does not find premonitions like the Boisseaus' compelling. "God knows how many neurotic New Yorkers have inexplicable dreads that keep them away from work on any given Monday," she says. "This is not good evidence because it's retrospective, and you have to examine a random sampling over time to see how many people stayed home from work on any given day of their lives because of impulses or whatever. Sometimes folks just take the day off! And existential angst is not a premonition."

How, then, can one know whether or not to take a premonition seriously?

A clue, Bernstein suggests, is the psychic energy that is connected with it. Does it pack an emotional punch, or is it a ho-hum experience that fails to leave much of an impression? For Bernstein, the term that captures the psychological juice of a dream is *numinous*—from the Latin *numen*, meaning "divine power."

Numinous was coined in 1917 by Rudolf Otto, a German theologian and scholar of comparative religion. Otto defined the numinous as a nonrational nonsensory experience or feeling whose primary and immediate object is outside the self.

Numinous events typically fill us with a sense that we are in contact with something more significant and greater than the individual self or ego. Numinous dreams typically feel like revelations, as if the gods whispered to us while we slept. On waking, they can seem "realer than real," deeply profound, utterly moving. We may tell ourselves that the experience is "only" a dream, but the psychological wallop numinous events deliver can motivate us to take them seriously and share them with others, as the Boisseaus did with each other.

Liza Leeds, a movie producer and jewelry designer living in New York City, experienced a numinous dream premonition the night of September 6, 2001, and related it to her friend, investigative journalist Randall Fitzgerald. In her dream she is sitting in her car in Manhattan, which is unnaturally quiet. A policeman taps on her window and tells her to move her car. She sees that something is terribly wrong—it's completely dark and debris is everywhere. Cars are flattened; the area looks like a war zone. Out of the debris four firemen walk toward her car. They tell her that a building has exploded.

Liza woke up, deeply upset. Feeling she had dreamed a truly "big dream," she immediately wrote it down. She was certain at the time that it was a precognitive dream.

Shortly after the tragedies on 9/11, stories began to surface from people who had changed their travel plans at the last moment because of a vague, gnawing feeling that something was not quite right. In one widely circulated account, a woman suffered crippling stomach pains while standing in line to board one of the planes that would soon fly into the Twin Towers. She went to the lavatory and recovered spontaneously, but missed her flight and lived to tell the story. Such stories are not convincing for unconscious premonitions, however. Many passengers miss flights because of full bladders, traveler's diarrhea, fear of flying, and so on. Far more intriguing are the vacancy rates of the doomed planes.

American Airlines Flight 77, a Boeing 757 that crashed into the Pentagon, could have carried up to 289 people, yet only 64 seats were occupied, a 78 percent vacancy rate. American Airlines Flight 11, a Boeing 767 that crashed into the North Tower of the World Trade Center, could have carried 351 passengers, but was 74 percent unoccupied with only 92 on board. United Airlines Flight 175, a Boeing 767 that flew into the World Trade Center's South Tower, also could have carried 351 people, but only 65 passengers flew that day, an 81 percent vacancy rate. United Airlines Flight 93, the Boeing 757 that crashed in Pennsylvania, was 84 percent unoccupied, with only 45 of 289 seats filled. All in all, the four planes were only 21 percent full.

Was William Cox's train-avoidance effect operating? It's impossible to tell. To know if premonitions of 9/11 caused the high vacancy rates on the doomed planes, one would have to compare vacancy rates throughout the year against the rates on September 11. This was the approach Cox used with train wrecks, and is the reason his research is so compelling. It has proved impossible for researchers to make comparisons, however, because the airlines are unwilling to provide vacancy information. Perhaps they cannot provide it. When British biologist and psi researcher Rupert Sheldrake tried to obtain this information to determine if there were more cancellations and no-shows for the crashed planes on September 11 than would be expected by chance, he was directed to a high-ranking executive at American Airlines. "He was friendly and open-minded, but unfortunately could not help," Sheldrake says. "He told me that all the data for the 11 September flights had been impounded by the FBI, who were investigating in minute detail every booking, cancellation and no-show."

All we can say is that the low passenger occupancy rates suggest, but do not prove, that premonitions may have saved passengers' lives on the mostly vacant planes that crashed that tragic day.

In general, there are weaknesses in most of the premonitions of 9/11. Most of the accounts are retrospective, recounted after the event happened. There is always the chance that people will embroider their accounts, perhaps without knowing they are doing so. Memory plays tricks on everyone, making false memories a fact of life.

Another issue confounding premonitions of 9/11 is inference. One of the defining features of premonitions is that the event that is foreseen cannot be inferred from prior happenings. But there was a highly significant prior event that created an atmosphere of fear and dread that many New Yorkers continually lived with—the bombing of Tower One (the North Tower) of the World Trade Center in 1993, killing six people and injuring more than a thousand. This attack no doubt prompted thousands of residents to infer that another attack would occur, inferences that were misconstrued as premonitions. As of this writing, Google lists more than a quarter million Web sites devoted to "premonitions of 9/11." How many of these are inferences from the 1993 bombing?

But it would be reckless, I believe, to dismiss all intimations of 9/11 because they *might* be false. For instance, consider the waking premonitions and dreams that a Lower Manhattan dweller posted on YouTube. In one dream he saw two pterodactyls flying over the WTC area. He reasoned that ptero meant "terror," and that he should stop flying in airplanes for a while. He also had dreams of men in biohazard suits walking in Lower Manhattan. He had visions of "ghosts" walking the streets, which he later connected with the ash-covered throng that fled the falling towers on 9/11. His revelations are highly suggestive of symbolic prophecy.

Consider too the painting *Gaia* by highly acclaimed visionary artist Alex Grey. Painted in 1989, it shows two planes flying over the Word Trade Center buildings in a polluted, ravaged landscape. Was this a warning of 9/11? Similarly, cover art for the CD *Party Music* by the alternative hip-hop group The Coup, based in Oakland, California, shows the Twin Towers of the World Trade Center detonating. The image is an eerily precise premonition of the horrific tragedy. The art was created in June 2001, but after 9/11 the release of the CD was delayed to allow new cover art to be developed.

Do artists and musicians intuitively tap into the future more readily than others? Could their prophetic talents be put to practical use?

The Pentagon evidently thinks so. In October 2001, about two dozen writers and directors were commissioned to brainstorm with Pentagon advisers and officials in an anonymous building in Los Angeles. The Pentagon wanted to know what could happen next, following the September 11 attacks. A BBC investigation found that "Hollywood had researched scenarios such as hijacks, bombs in New York, manhunts for Muslim extremists, and even the use of planes as guided missiles aimed at Washington," well before September 11, and that "some former CIA agents and intelligence officers shared Hollywood's premonition of terrorism but their warnings were ignored." The Pentagon's film liaison officer officially maintained, however, that any connection between Hollywood movies and real-life terrorism is "just coincidence."

In any case, Hollywood's visions suffer from the shortcomings of premonitions we've already seen—the absence of a specific time and place of future terrorism. Was something more than coincidence involved in their film scenarios? It is impossible to know for sure.

What we do know, however, is that several scientific studies suggest a relationship between creativity or artistic ability and psi performance.

In one study involving music, drama, and dance students at the elite Juilliard School in New York City, participants achieved one of the highest scores ever recorded in a so-called ganzfeld experiment, a particular type of ESP study.

No one has subjected the outpouring of premonitions of 9/11 to the kind of analysis that would satisfy the requirements of good science. But that does not mean we should ignore them. Anecdotes don't always lie.

How might those who experienced premonitions of 9/11 been taken more seriously? One way would be to keep a diary or dream journal, in which the premonition or dream is recorded and dated right away. This helps prevent the problems of retrospection and false memory. Another precaution is to have the description notarized, and store it in a safety deposit box. Notarization documents the date, time, and content of the premonition, and is evidence that the premonition was not fabricated at some later time. For individuals who for personal reasons wish to preserve a record of their premonition experience, notarization and safe storage may well be worth the expense. Another backup strategy is to tell at least one other person about the premonition, so they can serve as a witness if the premonition is ever questioned.

I acknowledge how sensitive the issue of premonitions remains for many New Yorkers, Washingtonians, and Pennsylvanians who lived through the terrible events. One Manhattan resident told me, "September 11 was a tragedy on an unparalleled scale, and since no premonition prevented it, I'm not too thrilled with them. What good does it do me if some lady sees this disaster and nothing comes of it? It was my city. I feel personally upset at these premonitions because they did no good!"

I'm sympathetic. If I had been in Manhattan on 9/11, I might feel the same way. On the other hand, is it proper to "kill the messengers" for their premonitions because they failed to prevent tragedy? Presumably most messengers were ordinary folks who were minding their own business; they weren't *trying* to dream up disaster scenarios. If they'd come forward, would anyone have listened? We often are deaf to conventionally gathered intelligence, let alone that reported by visionaries, particularly those without a specific time and date of reference. Insiders in the intelligence community have suggested that information of an impending terrorist attack was ignored by our government. If intelligence gathered by professionals was ignored, what's the likelihood anyone would have taken seriously the premonitions of nervous citizens?

The criticisms against premonitions—that they are so vague and imprecise they're worthless—are not unique. In fact, those objections are the very reasons the U.S. government gave for failing to act on warnings of the 9/11 attacks. In her testimony in 2004 before the 9/11 Commission, then National Security Advisor Condoleezza Rice said, "More often, it [the intelligence] was frustratingly vague. Let me read you some of the actual chatter that we picked up that spring and summer: 'Unbelievable news coming in weeks,' 'Big event . . . there will be a very, very, very, very big uproar,' 'There will be attacks in the near future.' Troubling, yes. But they don't tell us when; they don't tell us where; they don't tell us who; and they don't tell us how." And in response to intelligence suggesting Osama bin Laden and other top Al-Qaeda members were planning another attack on the United States, Homeland Security Secretary Tom Ridge said in 2004, "We lack precise knowledge about time, place, and method of attack. But along with the CIA, FBI, and other agencies, we are actively working to gain that knowledge." So the real reason authorities reject premonitions is *not* that they are vague—so, too, is much of conventional intelligence—but because of the assumption that they cannot be valid in principle. It's the old "everyone knows" reaction: "Everyone knows" we can't know things before they happen. But some premonitions of 9/11 were much more detailed than the intelligence from conventional origins.

Would anyone have listened? Would anyone have cared? These questions have been asked before. Swiss psychologist Carl G. Jung, who was keenly interested in premonitions, said at mid-twentieth century that although inner experiences of this sort were very meaningful to his patients, "In most cases they were things which people do not talk about for fear of exposing themselves to thoughtless ridicule. I was amazed to see how many people have had experiences of this kind and how carefully the secret was guarded." But guarding the secret can be lethal.

On May 3, 1812, John Williams, an Englishman, dreamed he was in the lobby of the House of Commons and saw a small man enter dressed in a blue coat and white waistcoat. He observed another man entering, dressed in a snuff-colored coat with metal buttons. He fired a pistol at the smaller man, and a large bloodstain spread on the left breast of the white waistcoat before he fell to the ground. Several men nearby apprehended him. The dreamer asked the identity of the victim and was informed that it was Spencer Perceval, the prime minister.

Williams told his wife the dream upon waking. She told him to disregard it. He went back to sleep, but had the dream again and told his wife a second time. She said it was just a dream and that he should simply ignore it. Williams experienced the dream a third time that night. He became agitated and consulted with several friends about whether he should alert someone in authority. They strongly advised him against it, lest he be ridiculed as a fanatic. Eight days later, on May 11, 1812, in the lobby of the House of Commons, John Bellingham, a deranged merchant seeking government compensation for his business debts, shot Perceval in the heart. Perceval uttered the words "I am murdered," and died almost instantly. Bellingham surrendered immediately and was convicted and hanged a week later. Williams's dream proved eerily prophetic. The details of the assassination were identical to those of his dream, including the colors of the clothing, the buttons on the assassin's jacket, and the location of the bloodstain on Perceval's white waistcoat. Spencer Perceval is the only British prime minister to have been assassinated.

No one wanted to hear John Williams's premonition in 1812. Things haven't changed all that much. In our culture, as in nineteenth-century England, a stigma often attaches to those who come forward with visions. We are more likely to trust electronically gathered intelligence than information that surfaces via premonitions, even when the electronic kind is less accurate. I suggest that both sources can be valuable. Premonition prodigies such as John Williams still exist. If we chose to do so, we could tap them for their expertise as an adjunct to intelligence of the conventional kind.

Many of our bodily functions, such as our heartbeat, are involuntary and operate outside our conscious awareness. Let's look at a well-documented example suggesting that premonitions do so as well.

THE EXPLODING CHURCH

On Wednesday evening, March 1, 1950, an extraordinary event unfolded in the quiet prairie town of Beatrice, Nebraska, that stunned the locals, riveted the nation, and raised fundamental questions about the nature of consciousness.

Beatrice—"bee-AT-ris," as the residents call it—is a peaceful, friendly, no-nonsense kind of town of around twelve thousand folks. It is located near the geographic center of the continental United States. The town is the county seat of Gage County, a fertile piece of American heartland in southeast Nebraska in America's Great Plains.

The area is rich in history. Wild Bill Hickok, the legendary army scout, lawman, and gunfighter, was tried for murder in Beatrice (and acquitted on a plea of self-defense). Clara Bewick Colby, Nebraska's leading suffragette, was from Beatrice. In 1883 she founded *The Woman's Tribune* in Beatrice, which became the leading women's suffrage publication in the nation.

Beatrice was founded in 1857 by a group of hardy pioneers who called themselves the Nebraska Association. They traveled up the Missouri River from St. Louis on the steamboat *Hannibal*, disembarked, explored the surrounding area, and found a hospitable township site where the Big Blue River is joined by Indian Creek. The community got its name from Julia Beatrice Kinney, the eldest daughter of Judge J. F. Kinney, the Nebraska Association's first president. The county itself was named in honor of Rev. William D. Gage, a Methodist minister who was chaplain of the first territorial assembly in 1856. Between 1855 and 1882, the southern half of Gage County served as the Otoe-Missouri Indian Reservation.

Beatrice was still in winter's grip on an eventful Wednesday evening in March 1950. It was so cold that Pastor Walter Klempel went early to the West Side Baptist Church on West Court Street to light the furnace before the fifteen choir members arrived for practice. His task completed, he went home, planning to return to the church with his family when the choir members began to arrive. He knew they'd show up at 7:15 P.M. for practice at 7:20. They probably would not be late. Over the years a tradition of punctuality had arisen, because no one liked to sit around waiting for stragglers.

At 7:25 P.M. the church blew up. Its walls exploded outward and the heavy wooden roof crashed straight down. The cause, fire experts said later, was natural gas leaking from a broken pipe, ignited by the flame in the furnace.

Windows in nearby homes were shattered and a radio station was knocked off the air. The blast was heard throughout the town, and citizens wondered in dread who had been injured or killed. It was certain to be someone they knew—a friend, a neighbor, a relative—because Beatrice was a small, intimate community where people knew and cared about one another. But when the townspeople scurried to the demolished church, they realized that something astonishing had happened: No one was hurt when the church exploded, because nobody had been there.

A complete no-show at choir practice had never happened before, and rational explanations didn't add up. There was no bad weather, except for the cold, that might have prevented choir members from going to church that night, and it was unlikely that those hardy Nebraskans would have been intimidated by cold weather. There were no competing events in town that might have lured them away. When a reporter from *Life* magazine showed up a few days later, citizens told him they believed fifteen lives had been saved by "an act of God."

It wasn't just the townspeople who marveled. The incident captured the attention of Warren Weaver, one of the twentieth century's foremost experts on probability theory. In his book *Lady Luck: The Theory of Probability,* Weaver used the Beatrice event as an example of a highly improbable happening. He calculated that the chances of all fifteen choir members being late on this particular night was a staggering one million to one. The Beatrice incident also fascinated South African biologist and author Lyall Watson, who wrote about it years later. He placed the odds even higher, at one in a billion.

When the event was reported in *Life*, one of America's most popular magazines at the time, the country became aware that something extraordinary had taken place in tiny Beatrice. But, as always, memories gradually dimmed and the incident receded into the past. In the decades that followed, some critics who heard about the event dismissed it as a tall tale, an urban legend. But recently Snopes.com, the well-known Web site dedicated to investigating urban legends, probed the historical record and declared the story true. The sleuths at Snopes, like earlier investigators, were impressed by the sheer improbability that no one was harmed. Their report states, "It is impossible to calculate precise odds for all these events occurring at once. But past performance indicated that each person would be late for practice one time in four—producing a one-in-a-million chance that the entire choir would be late that night."

The citizens of Beatrice may have seen the hand of God in the event, but Weaver and other probability experts didn't. For them, it was a chance happening, which by definition is meaningless, "just one of those things." Highly unlikely events are bound to occur sooner or later, the experts explained. For example, even though the odds against dealing a perfect hand in bridge is seventy-nine billion to one, some bridge player somewhere in the United States accomplishes this feat roughly every three or four years. Or, to invoke a perennial argument of the statistically obsessed: put a bunch of typewriters in a room full of monkeys, and, given enough time, some monkey will eventually peck out a perfect version of *Hamlet* by merely playing around with the toy.

Yet the Beatrice event seemed different from a perfect hand at bridge. For one thing, the stakes were not the same. The exploding church was a life-and-death situation in which fifteen people could have been blown to smithereens, but weren't. Moreover, card dealers don't have a choice in which order the cards fall, but the Beatrice choir members did have a choice on whether to go to the church on time that night. This suggests that the incident was not a mindless, meaningless happening, but was somehow connected with the conscious—or unconscious—decisions made by the fifteen tardy choir members.

When the reporters who invaded Beatrice began asking questions, they discovered that none of the choir members had any conscious premonition that a potentially lethal event was about to happen. They gave a variety of reasons why they didn't show up on time, all of them mundane. One was delayed while his daughter changed into a clean dress. Two women's cars wouldn't start. Several others were teenagers absorbed in homework and listening to the radio. Others overslept, were taking care of their kids or stopping in to see their parents or writing letters. Another felt "just plain lazy" that night.

Were the probability experts correct in declaring the scenario a chance happening? They were relying on a venerable principle in science called Ockham's razor, which says that the simplest explanation is always the preferred one. But Einstein postulated in "Einstein's razor" that theories should be made "as simple as possible, but not simpler."

I suggest that the Beatrice church explosion illustrates the subtlety of premonitions—how they often manifest so faintly in our unconscious mind that we respond to them without realizing it. Conscious premonitions may make better headlines, but it is in the delicate, faint traces of awareness that future knowing most commonly presents itself.

THE *FARMER'S ALMANAC*

Because the averted Beatrice disaster involved fifteen individuals, it is more difficult to dismiss as merely a happy coincidence. But when single individuals are involved, we can be left scratching our heads about whether premonitions were operating or not. Take the following example from the *Farmer's Almanac*.

As the manuscript for the 1816 edition of the *Farmer's Almanac* was going to press, someone realized there was no weather prediction for July 13. The founding editor had gone home ill. A copy boy was told to put in anything he wanted, so he inserted "rain, hail, and snow." When parts of New England got all three on that summer day, the editor took full credit and declared, "I told you so." Thereafter, the *Farmer's Almanac* took on an oracular glow for millions of Americans. According to climatologists, the weird weather in this "year without a summer" was caused by the 1815 eruption of Mount Tambora in Indonesia. The cooling dust cloud from the volcano set off the "Little Ice Age," which resulted in unseasonably cold weather the following summer in New England, where ponds and lakes never thawed, there were twenty-inch snowdrifts in June, and an August freeze killed the corn crop.

How did the copy boy get it right? Was this an uncanny premonition, or just a crazy collision of chance happenings? Maybe it was a lucky, or even an educated, guess, but I'd like to know more about the boy himself. Was this a one-time occurrence, or did he often make accurate predictions? Was he known to have "second sight"? Did other members of his family have "the gift"? These questions have never been answered. In any case, Americans aren't deterred; the annual distribution of the *Almanac* is still at more than three million copies.

Our exploration of premonitions does not depend on ambiguous experiences such as the copy boy's, however. Premonitions have often been put to the test in real-life settings, sometimes by daring explorers.

ACROSS SPACE *AND* TIME: TWO EXPLORERS TEST THE LIMITS OF PREMONITIONS

History casts both light and shadows, illuminating some great figures and eclipsing others—often, it seems, capriciously. An example of the latter is the Australian Sir George Hubert Wilkins. Although he is largely forgotten now, he was a superhero to anyone who had access to the media in the 1920s to 1940s. Wilkins was a larger-than-life individual who became a celebrated newsreel cameraman, reporter, pilot, spy, war hero, scientist, explorer, geographer, and adventurer. He was the first person to fly across the polar ice cap from Barrow, Alaska, to Spitsbergen, Norway, in 1928, a feat that many consider the greatest of all Arctic flights. Wilkins also circled the globe in a zeppelin, took the first submarine under Arctic ice, was the first to fly in the Antarctic, and was a pioneer in planetary weather forecasting and the study of global warming.

Wilkins's exploits as a movie cameraman in the killing fields of the Western Front in World War I are almost incredible. He repeatedly cheated death, in spite of several wounds and uncountable near misses. His biographer, Simon Nasht, has recently brought this remarkable man's story back to life, after being forgotten for generations. He describes in *The Last Explorer* how Wilkins calmly wandered the blood-soaked fields of Flanders as bullets bounced off his tunic and shells fell unexploded at his feet. Wilkins believed that luck alone could not explain his survival in this deadly environment. He had premonitions of danger that he believed came from "Providence," showing him the way and guiding him to safety.

Wilkins grew up in rural South Australia among Aboriginal people. He often noticed that they appeared capable "of knowing of some event which was taking place miles beyond their range of sight and hearing." Wilkins remained fascinated with the nonsensory, nonrational operations of consciousness for the rest of his life.

In 1937, when six Soviet fliers crashed in the Arctic in Alaska, the Soviet government commissioned Sir Hubert to lead an aerial search for them. Seeing an opportunity to put telepathy to a test, he and Harold Sherman, a New York psychic and writer, decided to collaborate on a six-month experiment. Three nights a week, between eleven thirty and midnight New York time, Wilkins, the "sender," would attempt to project his thought impressions from whatever location he was in, to Sherman, the "receiver," who wrote down what came through while sitting in the darkened study of his Riverside Drive apartment. Each night, Sherman would seal his written impressions and send them to Dr. Gardner Murphy, a psychologist at Columbia University, who would serve as an independent judge of whatever correlations might turn up. When Murphy eventually compared Wilkins's log to Sherman's written impressions, he found too many matches to be handily dismissed as chance. When they later reviewed the results, Wilkins and Sherman estimated a match rate of 60 percent.

Some of the correspondences were almost identical. On December 7, while at Point Barrow, Alaska, Wilkins heard a fire alarm ring. He went to the window and saw a Native house blazing in the night. Sherman, 3,400 miles away in New York City, recorded that same night, "Don't know why, but I seem to see a crackling fire shining out in the darkness—get a definite fire impression as though a house burning—you can see it from your location on the ice." This and many similar examples convinced the explorer and the psychic that mental impressions could be transferred between two people at a distance.

On the surface, it seemed that Wilkins and Sherman were involved in a simple telepathy experiment, but the situation was more complicated than that. Wilkins's duties were so urgent and dangerous in the Arctic that he rarely took the time to purposefully "send" mental messages to Sherman in New York. It became clear that Sherman was receiving information before Wilkins sent it, and often before it even happened. Sherman was clearly invoking precognition, picking up on events that would *later* happen.

Sherman realized the significance of this: he and Wilkins seemed to be communicating across space *and* time. The greater the danger, the more acute Sherman's premonitions were felt. He accurately predicted the only two accidents that befell Wilkins in the Arctic. He wrote, "[M]ore than telepathy is involved. . . . At times your mind will pick up impressions of past and future events. . . . I sensed and accurately recorded, the only two accidents which were to befall Wilkins' plane in the Far North, at least ten days in advance of the actual happenings."

Wilkins was seldom given to hyperbole, and was often described as demonstrating "aggressive modesty" in his claims. Yet he could not hold back his enthusiasm for the significance of his experiments with Sherman. He considered the results "a rousing, staggering indication of the powers of the mind." Sherman was equally emphatic. "There is a growing abundance of evidence now that precognition is a fact," he said. "Man's mind can go backward and forward in Time, with equal facility, when so moved to function."

The world was at war in 1942, so the Wilkins-Sherman book went largely unrecognized, but it has recently been republished and has become a cult classic. Surely there has never been a book like it, filled with the real heroic and hazardous Arctic rescue attempt (the Soviet fliers were never found), and layered with experimental findings of "thought transfer" through space and time.

The Wilkins-Sherman experiments would be essentially replicated in 1971 by another explorer, astronaut Edgar Mitchell, the sixth man to walk on the moon. Mitchell was the lunar module pilot for the Apollo 14 mission. Prior to the mission, he and two research physicists on the Apollo program, Drs. Boyle and Maxie, who were also interested in this field, devised a "thought transfer" experiment. Wilkins, Sherman, and others had shown that information could be transferred mentally over thousands of miles, but no one had tested this phenomenon on an interplanetary scale. The Apollo 14 mission offered the opportunity to do just that.

Mitchell's experiment involved four transmission sessions during rest periods programmed into the flight. Using random number tables—printed columns and rows of random numbers that were used prior to computers—Mitchell generated four tables of twenty-five random numbers using just the numbers one to five. Then he randomly assigned a symbol from Zener cards to each number. Zener cards are used in standard tests of ESP, and include stars, crosses, waves, squares, and circles. For each transmission session, which took about six minutes, Mitchell would check the particular table of numbers and think about the corresponding symbol for fifteen seconds. He did this before going to sleep at night.

Like Wilkins thirty-four years earlier, Mitchell was so busy he could find time for only four transmission sessions. Despite the best-laid plans, Mitchell's transmissions did not correspond to the receiving sessions for the four individuals on Earth. That didn't seem to make any difference. The receivers, it turned out, wrote down their impressions before Mitchell's sending sessions even began, converting the experiment into a successful test of precognition or future knowing.

NASA, sensitive as ever to public relations, ignored history's first space-based thought-transfer experiment, except to say that it was a personal test without official sanction. Back on Earth, however, Mitchell found that the experiment generated excitement among "quite a few engineers" and legendary rocket genius Wernher von Braun. Mitchell described how many of these scientists came to his office, closed the door, and asked him to tell them about the experiment, which he did.

Von Braun wanted to carry the experiments further. He suggested that Mitchell do a survey of NASA installations to see if there was an appropriate place where this kind of work could be done in a deeper way. However, both Mitchell and von Braun left NASA before any further experiments could be accomplished. When Mitchell established the Institute of Noetic Sciences after leaving NASA, the two men remained friends, with von Braun speaking at a fund-raising dinner.

The two sets of experiments—one by Sir Hubert Wilkins from the Arctic across 3,400 miles, and the other by astronaut Edgar Mitchell some 200,000 miles from Earth, are near replicas. Both demonstrated that distant receivers can acquire information precognitively, before it is sent.

MAKING MONEY

Premonition literally means "forewarning," usually of events that are unpleasant or disastrous, as in the examples of Aberfan, 9/11, and the Beatrice church explosion. But future knowing can also be employed for agreeable purposes, including financial gain and success in business.

I've suggested that the ability to see the future gave our ancestors an evolutionary advantage, because it made it more likely they'd survive dangers that lay ahead.

The meaning of survival, however, changes from era to era. Today, one of the most hostile environments in our culture is the hypercompetitive upper echelon of corporate management. Survival for CEOs, for instance, is not usually a literal matter of life and death as it was for our ancestors, but CEOs struggle to survive nonetheless. Might they be employing premonitions, as our ancestors probably did in their struggles to survive?

Many people think so, although the favored term for this ability is not premonitions, precognition, or future knowing, but *intuition*. There is a growth industry purporting to teach people how to unleash their intuitive powers in the business world. Nearly a quarter million Web sites are devoted to "business intuition."

But what, exactly, does *intuition* mean? Most people would agree that it's a kind of instinctive knowing, without the support of actual evidence. When an intuition involves a prediction or a sense of what will happen in the future, the intuition becomes indistinguishable from a premonition, a feeling or belief that something is going to happen.

Businessmen may prefer to call their instincts about the future intuition, but this doesn't change their premonitory nature. All businessmen invoke premonitions routinely. Examples include a sense of which direction business cycles are headed, the future strength of the stock market, what actions "the fed" will take, and what the level of consumer confidence will be over the next year. Decisions about acquisitions, sell-offs, and investments in capital equipment are often made on hunches and gut feelings, not logical inferences or rational predictions. Even though businessmen sometimes refer to their decisions as educated guesses, genuine premonitions are not "educated"; they are not based on logical reasoning and cannot be inferred from past events. Investors often speak of "rolling the dice" in making a decision, implying that they're relying on something other than logic. Many famous titans among the nation's CEOs are famous for being right more often than wrong in making these kinds of decisions.

In a classic study at the University of Texas at El Paso in the 1980s, management professor Weston H. Agor tested the intuition of two thousand managers and found that the top-level leaders scored higher on intuition than those ranking lower in the corporate hierarchy. Top executives typically digested all the relevant information first, but when the data was incomplete or confusing they shifted to intuitive approaches in making a decision. Interestingly, they were hesitant to disclose to their colleagues that they relied on intuition, preferring instead to be thought of as cool intellectuals guided solely by reason.

In the mid-1970s, parapsychology researcher E. Douglas Dean and professor of engineering John Mihalasky of New Jersey Institute of Technology (formerly the Newark Institute of Technology) performed a series of experiments that shed light on this area. They spent ten years studying 385 chief executive officers of U.S. corporations. The CEOs were asked to guess at a hundred-digit number that did not yet exist at the time the guesses were made. Then the number was produced by a computer using random generating techniques. The results were then correlated with the financial reports issued by the executives' corporations. Dean and Mihalasky found that 80 percent of executives whose companies' profits had more than doubled in the past five years had above-average precognitive powers. "It was so definitive," writes remote-viewing researcher Stephan A. Schwartz in his review of these experiments, "that Dean was able to examine financial reports and predict *in advance* how a given CEO would do in his experiment."

There is no way the CEOs could have used logic or inference in predicting a string of numbers before the computer had even generated them. They were using premonitions, not educated guesses.

Since the Dean-Mihalasky number-guessing findings were published more than thirty years ago, the test has been administered to people of all ages and in various walks of life. Results indicate that precognitive ability does not correlate with intelligence. In fact, Dean and Mihalasky found that engineering students with higher grade-point averages did slightly worse than those making lower grades.

An interesting outcome of Dean and Mihalasky's work with CEOs was the high percentage of them—around 80 percent—who acknowledged a private belief in ESP. When questioned, they admitted their belief was not based on either a familiarity with the scientific literature or an acquaintance with psychics, but because they'd seen it work in their own lives.

Many experts whose careers are based on prediction are uncomfortable with the image that they're employing premonitions or precognition. Examples include the originators of the Delphi method, a forecasting technique developed at the RAND Corporation at the beginning of the Cold War to predict the impact of technology on warfare. The creators of the method are said to be unhappy with the name, which is derived from the Oracle of Delphi of ancient Greece. Their concern is that the name implies "something oracular, something smacking a little of the occult." In the Delphi process, carefully selected experts answer questionnaires in two or more rounds. After each round a facilitator summarizes the anonymous opinions and the reasons given for the judgments. Then the participants are encouraged to revise their predictions. It's said that, as the process proceeds, the range of answers narrows toward a "correct" position.

If it makes experts less squeamish to substitute *intuition* for *premonitions*, so be it. Everyone isn't fooled, however. As one organization devoted to developing premonitory ability flatly states, the developers of the Delphi method at RAND "used what ESP researchers would call precognition."

The same pattern is found in stockbrokers as in CEOs. In 2007, researchers Christian Harteis and Hans Gruber, of the Institute of Education at the University of Regensburg in Germany, found that "in most cases intuitive predictions of stock market development are better than rationally justified ones. . . . Stock market investment decisions rely on forecasts of market development. . . . As complete information is not available, entirely rational decisions cannot be made, and it becomes necessary to rely on intuition."

Some business consultants have passed through the eye of the needle and acknowledge that business executives really do employ precognition routinely. Carol Kinsey Goman, Ph.D., the author of nine books on creativity in business, actually advises business executives to write down their dreams, feelings, and hunches—a time-honored way of cultivating premonitions.

The financial crisis of 2008 may illustrate the value of premonitions in the "survival of the fittest" in the highly competitive credit and investment world. Those CEOs who were gifted with future knowing would have been more likely to steer clear of risky subprime mortgage investments and survive the crisis, while those who were less gifted with intuition were less likely to do so. The meltdown may also illustrate how greed can neutralize or sabotage premonitions, even when they are present.

What happens when premonitions, acknowledged as such, are put to the test in a business context?

In 1982 the *St. Louis Business Journal* pitted nineteen prominent stockbrokers against a St. Louis psychic, Beverly Jaegers. Jaegers was a reluctant psychic—originally a skeptic and debunker of psi phenomena—until her own experiences changed her mind. In the experiment, each participant was asked to select five stocks whose value they believed would increase over the next six months. Although Jaegers had no training in corporate analysis, she outperformed eighteen of the nineteen financial experts. The Dow Jones Industrial Average fell 8 percent over the six-month period, but the stocks picked by Jaegers increased in value by 17.2 percent. Only one stockbroker did better—barely—at 17.4 percent.

Jaegers had attracted national attention in the 1970s when Pete Dixon, a commodities broker, decided to put her psychic skills to the test. He came to her with a sealed envelope containing a prediction that coffee prices would increase, and asked her to elaborate on its contents. In reporting the incident in a retrospective of Jaegers's career, journalist Stefene Russell says, "[She] saw heavy rain and people carrying baskets with a few shriveled red berries in the bottom of each." Dixon was excited. He promised to buy Jaegers a new house if what she said proved true. "He bought voluminous shares in coffee, just in time to watch the price shoot up after a freeze in Brazil decimated the crop. He made millions and made good on his promise, giving Jaegers a check . . . which she used to buy a new house."

If all premonitions were as straightforward as suggested in the Jaegers case, all psychics would be wealthy and on the boards of large corporations, commanding huge salaries. The fact that they are not attests to the imprecise, capricious, and often invalid nature of premonitions.

Historian Brian Inglis saw a pattern in the attempts of psychics to make money. "Divination," he wrote, "whether spontaneous or induced, was rarely to make anybody's fortune; either something would happen to prevent a bet from being laid, or the information could turn out to have been subtly misleading."

Inglis cites the experience of Dr. Christopher Knape, a court apothecary in Berlin. In 1768, while an apprentice, Knape dreamed the winning numbers of the state lottery and won a modest sum. He dreamed them again eight years later but was distracted by a noise before he could write them all down. When he did so, he could only recall with certainty the first two, and relied on his fuzzy recollection for the others. They nonetheless proved correct, but he was cautious and bought only a few tickets, thereby winning only twenty dollars instead of hitting the jackpot. The next year he dreamed a set of numbers he felt certain were correct, and decided to bet everything on it, only to discover that all the tickets for those numbers had already been sold. Although his premonition proved correct, he won nothing.

In his superb book *Healing Dreams*, author and filmmaker Marc Ian Barasch relates the experience of Thelma, a *sangoma* (traditional shamanic healer or herbalist) he met in a shantytown on the outskirts of Johannesburg, South Africa. She told Barasch how she once prayed for money to expand her house so she could take in more students. That night she dreamed that her grandfather was telling her she indeed needed a better house, and in the dream he gave her a six-digit number. On waking, she realized it could be a number for the Pick Six lottery. She had only sixty rand, however, and thought the ticket would cost more, so she did not buy it. "Then the next day," she said, "I saw the winning number was exactly the one in my dream. I cried for a week—it paid out a million rand!"

Yet Knape's and Thelma's experiences do not tell the whole story. Some individuals act decisively on dream information and sometimes report considerable, even repeated, success in making money by lottery and other means. An example is Jennie, a fifty-year-old housewife in upstate New York who wrote me about her premonitory dreams. Jennie's roof was in serious need of repairs, but she could not afford to have it fixed. She was quite religious and was cautious about greed, so she prayed to win the lottery—not the jackpot, but just enough to repair her roof. That night she dreamed a string of numbers, wrote them down, and entered them in a particular category of the state lottery. She won just the amount she needed for her roof repairs. Three years later she again found herself needing money to make ends meet. As before, she prayed for just the amount she required. The correct numbers again came to her in a dream, and the lottery paid her the amount she needed.

Jennie's experiences suggest that dream premonitions are need-based, and that they are more likely to occur if one sets a specific intention or a request that needs to be met.

When one particular experiment was made public in the 1980s, it was featured on the front page of *The Wall Street Journal* and became a NOVA film, *A Case of ESP.*

The experiment was designed to see if it was possible for a team of individuals to make money in the marketplace by using psychic functioning. The group consisted of Stanford Research Institute physicist and psi researcher Russell Targ, as well as a remote viewer who had successfully participated in prior experiments, an enthusiastic investor, a businessman, and an adventurous stockbroker. They called themselves Delphi Associates. The goal was for the psychic to forecast silver commodity prices a week into the future. It is well-known in psi research that reading numbers or letters psychically is a very difficult task. So the team did not ask the psychic to actually read the symbols on the big board at the New York Mercantile Exchange a week ahead of time, but instead used a technique called *associative remote viewing.* They devised a set of symbols that corresponded to the possible states of the silver market. They wanted to know if a commodity called "December silver" would be "up a little" (less than a quarter or unchanged), "up a lot" (more than a quarter), "down a little," or "down a lot." They asked the businessman to choose four strongly differing symbols, one for each of the four possible states of the silver market. The symbols were chosen from common items such as a lightbulb, a flower, a book, a rock, a stuffed animal, and so on. Only the businessman knew the four symbols he'd chosen, and to which state of the silver market they corresponded.

At this point Targ called the remote viewer over the telephone and asked him to describe his impressions of the object they would show him the following week when the actual state of the silver market was known. The broker then went into action, buying or selling silver future contracts based solely on what the viewer saw—a book, teddy bear, flower, whatever. Thus the psychic didn't actually read numbers, but named a symbol that was associated with what the silver market would do a week into the future, thus the term *associative remote viewing.* At the end of the week, when silver finally closed, the team liquidated its position and showed the remote viewer the object that corresponded with how the market had actually behaved. Providing feedback to the remote viewer in terms of success and failure rates, many researchers believe, is an important factor in generating future success in the precognitive process. All nine forecasts made this way in the fall of 1982 were correct, earning the team more than $100,000, which they divided with the investor.

The following year they were not as successful. The investor, seeing a good thing, wanted to carry out two trials a week. They tried, but the result was a rushed protocol and a compromise of the critically important matter of viewer feedback. The goal of the experiment changed as well. Targ's initial purpose was to raise money to fund his scientific work in psi experimentation. The goal of the investor in the second year was to make a killing. To further complicate things, one of the participants developed personal animosity toward Targ, and one team member wanted to change the agreed-on split in his favor. Hard feelings poisoned the group's smooth workings, and this time the calls were wrong every time. The reason for the change, Targ believes, is that the group lost its "spiritual focus." Part of the goal of the first series was scientific progress. In the second series, they were definitely out to break the bank. As Targ put it, "Serious greed had entered into our planning."

Could the initial success be recovered by improving the protocol with a different team that worked together harmoniously? In a subsequent formal precognitive experiment, again using associate remote viewing, psychics successfully predicted changes in the silver commodity market (up or down) in eleven of twelve individual calls. No one made money, however, because they had removed the investment factor from the study.

Purity of purpose seemed to be operating in a similar precognitive experiment involving prediction of silver futures. In this study, physicist Hal E. Puthoff, Targ's colleague at Stanford Research Institute, set out to raise exactly $26,000 for a new Waldorf School. He quickly did so and promptly withdrew from the market.

In another investment experiment, remote viewing researcher Stephan A. Schwartz and his colleague Rand De Mattei used associative remote viewing to make money to finance their research program by predicting the Standard & Poor 500 index. The result was a tripling of their investment.

Psi researcher James Spottiswoode set out to win the California State Lottery's Fantasy 5 jackpot in 1995, using precognitive remote viewers. This required guessing five numbers, which could be between one and thirty-nine. The odds against doing this successfully were 575,757 to 1. Spottiswoode recruited seventeen remote viewers to participate. He looked for consensus among them, using a technique too complex to describe here. After the remote viewers reported their visions to him, Spottiswoode discovered he had not allowed himself enough time to print the numbers on all the tickets and get them back to the shop where he'd purchased them. As a result, "He watched helplessly as [they] won the California lottery, but to no effect other than the satisfaction of doing it."

These experiments suggest that the underlying purpose of one's precognitive efforts may be a key in whether or not they are successful in business and investing. Greed seems to doom success; charitable, impersonal goals appear to favor it.

As I write, the U.S. Congress has fashioned a rescue plan for Wall Street and the nation's credit institutions, after many of them fell into bankruptcy. The most frequently cited cause for this financial disaster is greed. "CEOs got greedy," said President Barack Obama. His rival in the presidential election, Senator John McCain, also roasted Wall Street for its "unbridled greed." Some analysts attributed greed also to millions of homebuyers, who purchased overpriced property with loans they could not afford. The poster child for runaway greed is perhaps Bernard Madoff, the onetime NASDAQ chairman whose long-running Ponzi scheme appears to have bilked investors of fifty billion dollars. The whole mess sounds like a rerun of Targ's second silver futures experiment on a national scale, in which the craving for profit got the upper hand and doomed the experiment.

Contrast Wall Street's avarice with the approach of Warren Buffett, the world's second richest man, who continues to make his fortune in investment and turns it into philanthropy. Buffett is considered by many to be the most intuitive of current investor gurus. In 2006 he made American history by making the largest-ever charitable donation by an individual—$37 billion to the Bill and Melinda Gates Foundation. Buffett supports a variety of causes—at-risk and disadvantaged youth, cancer research, education, family and parenting issues, health, homelessness, organ donation, and poverty.

Or consider actor Paul Newman, who died in September 2008. Since founding his highly successful Newman's Own food company, which he established in 1982 to manufacture his special salad dressings, Newman donated more than $200 million to various causes—AIDS and cancer research, summer camps for children, drug abuse prevention, homelessness, hurricane relief, and more.

In contrast, Wall Street supports a single cause: profit—the more the better.

Experiments employing precognition to make money suggest that there may be an internal calculus whereby profits are linked to a "spiritual focus," as Targ suggests. No one ever accused Wall Street of being spiritually focused. Is this one reason for its current calamity?

We usually consider a premonition to be an experience of a single individual. In some situations, however, premonitions seem to emerge spontaneously in large groups of people. This is the theme of the book *The Wisdom of Crowds* by James Surowiecki, who writes the popular business column The Financial Page for *The New Yorker*. These collective premonitions can have enormous financial consequences.

On January 28, 1986, America was stunned by the explosion of the Space

Shuttle *Challenger*. Eight minutes after it blew up, the story appeared on the Dow Jones News Wire. "The stock market did not pause to mourn," Surowiecki observes. Within minutes, investors began to dump stocks of the four main companies involved in the *Challenger* launch: Rockwell International, which built the shuttle and its main engines; Martin Marietta, which manufactured *Challenger*'s external fuel tank; Lockheed, which provided ground support; and Morton-Thiokol, which constructed the solid-fuel booster rocket. A mere twenty-one minutes after *Challenger* blew up, Lockheed's stock was down 5 percent, Martin Marietta's had decreased 3 percent, and Rockwell's had fallen 6 percent. Morton-Thiokol took the biggest hit. So many investors were trying to dump their stock in the company that a trading halt was declared immediately. By day's end, the stock was down almost 12 percent, while that of the other three companies had begun to struggle back, to around a 3 percent loss.

How did thousands of stockholders across the nation single out Morton-Thiokol for punishment? It would be weeks before the country would learn that the flawed O-rings made by Morton-Thiokol had led to the disaster. Somehow "the crowd" knew ahead of time. But how did they have this premonition? Group foreknowledge and collective premonitions?

Surowiecki, a down-to-earth business columnist, is aware of how spooky and mystical this sounds. "But it just happens to be the way the world works," he says. Surowiecki's assertion that accurate premonitions can arise from large groups of nonexperts challenges the cherished concept of the expert CEO who is smarter than the company's employees and its thousands of investors and stockholders. In view of the current wreckage on Wall Street, perhaps it's time we listened less to CEOs and more to the premonitions of "the crowd."

Thus far, we've observed the "personality" of premonitions. We've explored how they crop up in the daily lives of ordinary individuals, with side trips into the worlds of exploration and business. We've seen that premonitions can be highly specific, but often are not; that they may manifest dramatically in our conscious awareness, but may also nudge us unconsciously to act; that they may occur in individuals or in groups; and that, although they usually warn us of threatening events, they can also be put to use in practical, agreeable ways.

Cases, stories, and anecdotes are important, but they don't tell the whole story of premonitions. It's time now to venture into the world of science to see how researchers have enlarged the picture of future knowing. Many scientists believe that the emerging evidence elevates premonitions to the level of established fact. Let's examine the reasons why.

TWO

EVIDENCE

"If it happens, it is possible."

—An unnamed law of the universe

AHEAD OF OURSELVES:
THE PRESENTIMENT EXPERIMENTS

Compelling laboratory evidence that we have an innate ability to sense the future has been growing quietly for nearly two decades. It has been gathered primarily by psi researcher Dean Radin, laboratory director at the Institute of Noetic Sciences in Petaluma, California. Radin has found that our central nervous system automatically responds to events that have not yet happened and of which we are unaware in the present. His findings are perhaps the most serious challenge ever mounted to the assumption that our consciousness can only access the past and present. Radin calls this faculty presentiment, which he defines as a vague, noncognitive sense that something good or bad will occur. It is difficult to overestimate the value of this line of experimentation, and as Stanley Krippner, the prominent psi researcher, states, theses studies "suggest that presentiment actually does reflect foreknowledge of future events. In my opinion, this is currently the most important experiment in psi research."

Part of the impetus for Radin's investigations came from the experience of a friend of his who was fond of firearms. After cleaning his pistol and replacing the bullets, he would always leave the last (sixth) chamber empty. However, after one particular cleaning he had a strong sense of foreboding when he was about to place the final bullet in its chamber. Yielding to this vague dread, he left the bullet aside. Several weeks later, in a drunken argument at his cabin, his father-in-law grabbed the gun and attempted to shoot him. Radin's friend would have died had that bullet been in its chamber. To this day, he keeps the bullet "with his name on it" in a safety deposit box.

In his presentiment experiments, which began at the University of Nevada in 1993, Radin took advantage of the well-known "orienting response," which is displayed by an organism in a fight-or-flight situation. When humans face a crisis or an unknown, fearful situation, there is a characteristic response of the autonomic nervous system: the pupils dilate, the brain waves alter, there is an increase in sweat gland activity, an increase in the heart rate, and blanching of the extremities as blood vessels constrict. These physiological changes make biological sense, because when we are in danger these modifications sharpen our perceptions, increase our physical strength, reduce the danger of external hemorrhage, and in general make it more likely that we'll survive whatever threat we face.

Subjects in Radin's experiment sat in front of a computer screen. On the subject's left hand, Radin and his team measured three responses of physiological arousal: heart rate, the amount of blood in a fingertip, and electrodermal activity or skin conductance, which is an indicator of sweating. In their right hands the subjects held a computer mouse. When they pressed the mouse, the computer randomly selected an image from a pool of 120 high-quality digitized photographs that were of two types, calm and emotional. The calm photos were pleasant images of natural scenes, landscapes, and cheerful people. Emotional photos were disturbing, shocking, or arousing, such as erotic, sexual pictures and grisly autopsies. After the mouse was pressed, subjects faced a blank computer screen for five seconds. Then the computer randomly selected an image and showed it on the screen for three seconds. Then the screen went blank for five seconds, and this was followed by a five-second rest period. Then another trial would begin. Twenty-four subjects participated, viewing a total of nine hundred pictures.

During the five seconds after the subjects pressed the mouse and the screen was blank, their electrodermal activity began to rise in anticipation of the subsequent photo: nothing surprising there. The stunning finding, however, was that the electrodermal activity increased *more* if the future picture was going to be emotional. In other words, the participants "pre-acted" to their own future emotional states *before* the emotional pictures were seen, and before the computer had selected them. Radin and colleagues, as mentioned, called this a presentiment effect, to indicate a prior sentiment or feeling.

By the late 1990s, Radin had concluded four separate presentiment experiments. Overall, the odds favoring a true presentiment effect in these studies was 125,000 to 1. The studies are a profound challenge to common sense, because they demonstrate, under double-blind conditions, that when the average person is *about* to see an emotional picture, he or she will respond before that picture appears.

Radin also hypothesized that the greater the emotionality of a picture, the larger or more robust the presentiment effect would prove to be. He tested this possibility and found it to be correct: the more the emotionality, the greater the presentiment effect, with odds against chance of 125 to 1.

The electrodermal activity or galvanic skin response that Radin measured is, of course, only one aspect of the body's fight-or-flight mechanism. Would other aspects of this emergency reaction pattern also reflect presentiment? To test this, Radin measured the diameter of the pupil, which dilates when the body is gearing up for fight or flight. He found the same pattern. As with electrodermal activity, pupillary dilation significantly increased several seconds prior to being shown images of sex, violence, or mayhem, when compared to peaceful, serene pictures. This suggests that the body's entire autonomic system may be capable of apprehending future events.

Do our eyes signal presentiment in other ways? On his blog "Entangled Minds," Radin invites questions and comments about his presentiment experiments. One individual wrote in 2007, "I strongly suspect that my daughter has some kind of presentiment-like effect with blinking and having her picture taken. The number of photographs of her with her eyes closed seems much higher than an estimate of how often she blinks. This is for photographs taken with a [digital camera] with a silent shutter and no flash." Radin replied that his pupillary dilation experiment did indeed show significantly more blinking, on average, across many subjects, just before seeing emotional versus calm pictures. "Perhaps if your daughter is shy of having her picture taken," he responded playfully, "she is sensing exactly the right time to ruin the shot."

On a blustery day in February 2008, Radin and I were scheduled to lecture at a conference in San Francisco on the primacy of consciousness. As is often the case at scientific meetings, the most interesting events occur not at the podium but during informal chats in hallways and at mealtimes. During a hallway moment, I asked Radin how he got the ideas for his landmark experiments. "I dream them up," he said. I thought he was using the term loosely, and smiled. He saw my amusement and continued, "Seriously, they occur to me in dreams. That tells me I'm on the right track and that it's OK to go ahead."

A crucial criterion for good science is whether other researchers can validate one's findings. To date, nineteen presentiment studies have been done by various researchers in different laboratories, ten of which have yielded statistically significant results.

Among those replicating Radin's findings is Dick Bierman, a professor of psychology at the University of Amsterdam and the University of Utrecht. Bierman employed essentially the same protocol as Radin, using photos of calm scenes as well as sex, violence, and mayhem.

Experiments in 2004 at the HeartMath Research Center in Boulder Creek, California, extended Radin's and Bierman's findings. Led by researcher Rollin McCraty, the HeartMath team showed emotionally arousing or calming pictures to twenty-six subjects who were experienced meditators or skilled in emotional management techniques popularized by the Institute of Heart-Math.

Unlike the subjects studied by both Radin and Bierman, the HeartMath subjects did not demonstrate a presentiment effect in skin conductance (galvanic skin response). The researchers suggested this was due to the fact that their subjects had been trained through meditation and other techniques to *not* react to stressful stimuli.

The HeartMath subjects, however, showed a significant presentiment effect in the behavior of the heart. Around five seconds prior to viewing the image, the subjects' heart rates began to change before being shown stressful images, but not prior to being shown calming images. Somehow the heart "knew" what lay ahead in the future, even though the subjects were consciously clueless about what lay ahead. Moreover, the HeartMath researchers found significant gender differences. Women demonstrated a greater presentiment response to future emotional stimuli than did men.

The HeartMath researchers also produced evidence that the heart may register future events before the brain does so, and that the change in heart rate originates within the heart, not in the brain. This goes against the conventional notion that the brain is in charge of how the heart responds to emotional stimuli, by sending signals to it via the autonomic nervous system. The HeartMath researchers maintain, rather, that "recent work in neurocardiology [suggests that] the heart is a sensory organ and an information encoding and processing center with an extensive intrinsic nervous system, enabling it to learn, remember, and make functional decisions independent of the cranial brain."

It's not necessary to decide which organ, the heart or the brain, senses the future first. Instead, the HeartMath researchers suggest that we should emphasize whole-body knowing. "The body's perceptual apparatus is continuously scanning the future. [T]he heart is directly involved in the processing of information about a future emotional stimulus seconds before the body actually experiences the stimulus. . . . What is truly surprising about this result is the fact that the heart appears to play a direct role in the perception of future events; at the very least it implies that the brain does not act alone in this regard."

These experimenters believe their findings fit with human experience. Nearly all cultures, they say, both ancient and modern, have regarded the heart as a conduit to a source of information and wisdom lying beyond the reach of the physical senses—whether called intuition, future knowing, or premonitions. Poets have long spoken of the heart as an emotional gateway. But the HeartMath findings appear to elevate this sentimental view from metaphor to empirical fact.

Some of the most dramatic evidence for presentiment has been found in experiments in which the stimulus was thoroughly obnoxious. Subjects can habituate or get used to offensive images, but the human body does not habituate to electric shocks, as all torturers know. When Hungarian physicist Zoltán Vassy used electric shocks as the stimulus to be precognized, the presentiment effect was "amazingly strong," as Radin observed, with significant odds against chance.

One of the most offensive stress-producing experiences in modern life, particularly for urban dwellers, is noise. In recent years, noise has become a major health issue in the developed world. In August 2007 the World Health Organization (WHO) released shocking statistics estimating the number of Europeans killed or disabled by noise exposure. Summarizing this information, *New Scientist* magazine reported, "[C]hronic and excessive traffic noise is implicated in the deaths of 3 percent of people in Europe with ischemic heart disease. Given that 7 million people around the globe die each year from heart disease, that would put the annual death toll from exposure to noise at 210,000 deaths." This compares with an estimated four million people who die worldwide annually from smoking-related illnesses. WHO plans to issue guidelines on noise exposure levels that can be used by local and national governments in justifying tough anti-noise rules. This is a major development, rather like the landmark U.S. Surgeon General's Report on Smoking and Health in 1964. WHO's estimates, like the surgeon general's report, will likely transform noise in the public's eye from the category of a mere nuisance or annoyance to that of a lethal factor in health.

If noise can be lethal, might our bodies be geared to anticipate and avoid it? Can future noise be detected as a presentiment?

In 2003 physicists Edwin C. May and James Spottiswoode measured the electrodermal response in more than one hundred subjects who were about to hear a random loud noise periodically through headphones. This simulates real-life exposure to offensive noises, which usually involves loud sounds we can't predict. The presentiment effect was quite strong: the nervous system reacted three to five seconds in advance of the disagreeable stimulus, with odds against a chance explanation of 1,250 to 1.

Physicist Vassy in Budapest replicated this study in fifty subjects, again with statistically significant findings.

Holger Klintman, of the Department of Psychology at Sweden's Lund University, began a series of experiments in the early 1980s that adds evidence to the presentiment effect. In his studies, a person was shown a patch of color—red, green, blue, or yellow—followed by the name of the color (that is, the word *green, red, blue,* or *yellow*). He asked the person to speak aloud the name of the patch of color shown to them as quickly as possible, and then speak aloud the name that followed as fast as they could. Klintman found that if the initial color patch matched the succeeding name, they could say the subsequent name quickly and accurately. But if the initial color patch mismatched the subsequent color name, the task became surprisingly difficult and frustrating and they spoke the subsequent color name more slowly.

Then Klintman decided to analyze the time it took for people to speak aloud the name of the color patch, the first stimulus. He was astonished to find that the initial reaction time was faster if the color patch matched the name that was to follow, and slower when they were mismatched. But how could the person have known whether the two were *later* going to be matched? Klintman believes this effect represents what he called time-reversed interference, in which a later event somehow traveled backward in time, causing cognitive interference when the future stimulus was mismatched, and slowing down the first reaction time. He devised a further double-blind experiment to test his hypothesis that involved twenty-eight subjects. It produced odds against chance of 67 to 1. He ran a total of five successful experiments, each with a somewhat different design, resulting in overall odds against chance of 500,000 to 1.

In summarizing these various experiments, Radin states, "[These] physiological presentiment experiments . . . suggest that under certain circumstances we can consciously or unconsciously respond to events in our future, events that we have no normal way of knowing."

Kary Mullis, a Nobel Prize–winning chemist, became fascinated with Radin's findings and decided to give the experiment a try in Radin's lab. The results shook him up. When he appeared as a guest on National Public Radio's *Science Friday* program in May 1999, he said, "I could see about three seconds into the future. . . . It's spooky. . . . [Radin has] done that over and over again with people. That, with me, is on the edge of physics itself, with time. There's something funny about time that we don't understand because you shouldn't be able to do that." Psychologist Dick Bierman, who also replicated Radin's work, says, "We're satisfied that people can sense the future before it happens. We'd now like to move on and see what kind of person is particularly good at it."

Just as Mullis had visited Radin's lab as a presentiment subject, Rupert Sheldrake, the Cambridge-trained biologist, author, and psi researcher, volunteered as a subject in one of Bierman's presentiment experiments at the University of Amsterdam in February 2001. As Sheldrake reports in his book *The Sense of Being Stared At,* he showed a strong emotional arousal before the erotic images appeared, even though he was unconscious of it. The dramatic rise in his electrodermal activity began five seconds before the erotic pictures were chosen by the computer, and before they appeared on the screen. No such arousal occurred before the calm images appeared, or even before the violent ones. Although he had read about the presentiment experiments before participating in them, he was nonetheless surprised like Mullis, who had found the experience "spooky."

Sheldrake emphasized the precision of the experiment. Since the randomization was automatic and took place inside the computer, there was no way he could have detected by any normal means what kind of picture would come up next, nor could he have picked up any clues from Bierman. Bierman himself did not know which images would appear, and in any case he was not in the room when Sheldrake did the tests. "I was alone," Sheldrake said, "with the computer, the images, and my emotions."

Meanwhile Chester Wildey, a student pursuing a master's degree in electrical engineering at the University of Texas at Arlington, heard the Mullis interview on NPR and was fascinated. He convinced his thesis committee to permit him to explore presentiment and the electrodermal skin response, using a monitoring circuit that he designed. Although electrical engineering usually steers clear of such things, Wildey convinced his committee that if a Nobel chemist (Mullis) was interested in this phenomenon, they should let him have a go at it. They did. Like Radin and the other scientists, Wildey found evidence for a presentiment effect.

He then wondered whether the effect went beyond humans. Did it extend down the evolutionary scale to animals, and if so, what kind? Intrigued by the suggestion of Cambridge mathematician Roger Penrose and University of Arizona anesthesiologist Stuart Hameroff that consciousness should occur in animals with brains the size of those found in worms, Wildey added a new twist: he would test presentiment in earthworms. But what stimulus would be appropriate? Visual or auditory stimuli wouldn't work with earthworms; they don't have the necessary sensory apparatus to detect them. Wildey hit upon the perfect stimulus: vibration, to which earthworms are extremely sensitive. Wildey conducted 231 controlled trials in his earthworms, finding odds against chance of 17 to 1. The presentiment window was narrower in his earthworms, however—only one second prior to the stimulus, compared to around three seconds in humans.

Wildey's bold study is important because it extends presentiment beyond humans into different biological domains. If a capacity exists in a variety of living creatures, this strongly suggests that the presentiment experiments involving humans are not a fluke.

It is interesting that the two future stimuli that most aroused Radin's and Bierman's subjects were photos that were sexual or violent in nature. This makes biological sense. If an organism were aware that sexual opportunity or activity lay ahead, he or she could prepare to procreate; or if violence or danger were about to happen, he or she could prepare for or avoid it. This

foreknowledge would be an advantage in meeting our evolutionary impera-
tive, which is to stay alive and reproduce.

Noteworthy also is the fact that the presentiment is unconscious; the
foreknowledge operated on its own, without the subjects' awareness.

Premonitions are often like this. An individual may slow down before
rounding a curve for some reason that is not apparent, only to find a few seconds later that the road ahead is blocked by an accident. An employee may
have decided not to go to work in the World Trade Center on September 11,
2001, because of nothing more than a vague hunch, which was in fact reported by many individuals following the terrorist attacks. As psychologist
and psi researcher James C. Carpenter says, extrasensory apprehensions are
usually "unconscious, and we can only glimpse their effects by suspending
cognitive work and consulting the vague material at the edges of experience."

The presentiment findings are supported by experiments that take place
not in the confines of a computer lab, but in the outside world in real life.
Among these are studies in remote perception conducted for more than two
decades at the Princeton Engineering Anomalies Research (PEAR) Laboratory at Princeton University.

The goal of these experiments is to see whether information can be ex-
changed mentally between two distant people—a sender or agent, and a receiver or percipient. According to the PEAR protocol, the percipient attempts
to record the information that an agent attempts to convey mentally from a
far-off target site. The specific target site is selected randomly beforehand
from a large pool of possible sites. The agent travels to the target and typically
spends ten to fifteen minutes there. Beginning at an assigned time, he looks
around and records his impressions of the scene in prose, according to a
thirty-item checklist on which the subsequent judging is based. The agent
also takes photographs of the target for future reference. The distant percipient records his or her impression, and this is eventually compared to the
agent's description of the target site. Scoring is done using the checklist, to
which yes or no answers can be given. For example, is the scene indoors or
outdoors? Are trees present? Water, mountains, valleys? Automobiles, planes,
boats, trains? Is the scene noisy or quiet, confined or expansive, hectic or
tranquil? What about architectural details—columns, towers, arches, monu-
ments? Animals, insects, birds, fish?—on and on, for the full thirty elements.

The percipient or receiver is unaware of the specific time the agent will be "sending" from the target site. The percipient is free to record his or her impressions at any time, whenever they seem to come through.

Hundreds of remote viewing trials have been conducted at PEAR with considerable success, showing odds against chance of 100 billion to 1. Spatial separation is not an important factor. The same degree of success is seen whether the agent and percipient are in the same city, or when they are separated by six thousand or more miles. Neither does time seem to matter, for in most of the trials the receiver "gets" the information from the sender precognitively—up to several days *before* it is sent, and *before* the image has been randomly selected from the target pool.

Critics of the presentiment experiments sometimes dismiss them as trivial, because they reveal precognition intervals of only a few seconds (although *any* precognitive interval should be astonishing). PEAR Lab's remote perception studies, however, demonstrate precognitive intervals up to approximately 150 hours, which is nearly a week. For this reason the PEAR team refers to these experiments as PRP, or precognitive remote perception.

In one PRP experiment, the agent visits the huge radio telescope at Kitt Peak in Pima, Arizona. The full description of the percipient is: "Rather strange yet persistent image of [agent] inside a large bowl—a hemispheric indentation in the ground of some smooth man-made material like concrete or cement. No color. Possibly covered with a glass dome. Unusual sense of inside/outside simultaneity. That's all. It's a large bowl. (If it was full of soup [the agent] would be the size of a large dumpling!)"

In this instance the agent and percipient were 2,200 miles apart. The percipient recorded this observation forty-five minutes before the agent visited the target site. According to the statistical analysis, there were only three chances in a hundred that the percipient could have arrived at this description by chance, by sheer guessing.

In another experiment, the target site visited by the agent was a modern bridge over the Danube River in Bratislava, Slovakia. The actual target site was one end of the bridge where there are two huge columns topped by a circular, disc-like structure that is a panoramic restaurant. The beautiful sleek bridge is suspended over the Danube by cables from the top of the columns. In the agent's photograph of the scene there is a river ferry. Under the bridge, where it meets the land, is a small building with a fence in front. People are strolling along the riverfront walkway.

The percipient recorded in part: "I have the feeling that [the agent] is somewhere near water. I seem to have the sensation of a very large expanse of water. There might be boats. Several vertical lines, sort of like poles. They're narrow, not heavy. Maybe lamp posts or flagpoles. Some kind of circular shape. Almost like a merry-go-round or a gazebo. A large round thing. It's round on its side, like a disc. Maybe with poles. Could possibly come to a point on top. Seeing vertical lines again. Seems to be a strong impression, these vertical lines. No idea what they could be. . . . A definite sensation of being outside rather than in. Water again. . . . To one side of where [the agent] is I get the feeling there's a kind of small building. Could be a shed. . . . Predominant colors seem to be blue and green. . . . Water again. Some very quick impression of a fence, a low fence. . . . Steps. Don't know where they're leading to. . . . The steps sort of lead up to like a path or walkway. Like a boardwalk. And there's a fence along it. There's people walking along it, and there's vertical lines along that walkway."

In this experiment, the distance separating the agent and percipient was 5,600 miles. The precognitive interval was 23.5 hours. According to PEAR's analytical method, the odds against guessing as an explanation for this description, which is nearly photographic in its accuracy, were a thousand to one.

More than three hundred remote perception studies have been done at PEAR; the majority are precognitive, in which the percipient registers the information before it is sent.

The information received is not always photographic in detail; interesting surprises occur. For example, the agent's target in one experiment was the components of the Saturn moon rocket at the NASA Space Center in Houston, Texas. The percipient, in Princeton, New Jersey, described an indoor scene with the agent playing with several puppies. This was considered a complete miss when formally analyzed. Later that evening, however, the agent, prior to learning anything about the perception, visited a friend's home where he frolicked at length with a litter of newborn pups, and was so moved by the experience he purchased one of them.

In a similar instance the agent was traveling to the selected target, a gambling casino in Nevada. On the way he stopped at a service station where, for amusement, he tried riding a collapsible bicycle. The percipient, in Chicago, included nothing in the description that was relevant to a casino, but accurately described the agent's clumsy attempt to ride the bike.

Although judged to be misses, these two instances suggest that the consciousness of the agent and percipient has "a mind of its own," and sends or receives information that may lie outside the strict protocols laid down by the experimenters.

These studies have been replicated in several institutions by many different investigators, among them Stanford Research Institute (SRI) in Menlo Park, California, and Science Applications International Corporation (SAIC) in La Jolla, California. The odds against chance in the SRI data are a billion billion to one. These results have been published in prestigious scientific journals such as *Nature, Proceedings of the IEEE,* and the *Journal of Scientific Exploration.*

Following his evaluation of the SAIC tests, Ray Hyman, a University of Oregon psychologist, who is a well-known skeptic of the field of parapsychology, conceded, "I cannot provide suitable candidates for what flaws, if any, might be present." Still, the recalcitrant Hyman was unwilling to acknowledge that distant mental communication is real.

Precognition tests aren't limited to remote perception, however; they come in many varieties, such as card-guessing experiments in which individuals try to predict which card will turn up next. In 1989, psi researchers Charles Honorton and Diane C. Ferrari analyzed the published studies in foreknowledge that had been done since 1935. They studied 309 precognition experiments that had been carried out by 62 researchers. These involved more than 50,000 subjects and more than 2 million individual trials. As physicist Russell Targ states, "Thirty percent of these studies were statistically significant in showing that people can describe future events, where only five percent would be expected by chance. This gave overall significance of greater than 10^{20} to 1, which is akin to throwing 70 pennies in the air and having every one come down heads. This body of data offers very strong evidence for confirming the existence of knowledge of the future that cannot be ascribed to somebody's lucky day."

ONLINE EVIDENCE

Further evidence for premonitions is an online experiment of Radin's that has been running since August 2000 called Got Psi?

The Got Psi? Web site has several tests for psi ability, all of which are sensationally popular. As of August 2006, more than twenty million trials had been recorded from participants from nearly all the world's countries. In only one year, these Internet-based psi tests collected more data than all of the ESP tests conducted over sixty years in the famous parapsychology research project led by the legendary J. B. Rhine and his colleagues. The simplicity of the test designs, the fact that people can take the tests at their leisure and track their repeat performances over time, and the fact that the Web is accessible to hundreds of millions of people worldwide have ushered in a new era in psi research.

In the online Card Test, the participant is asked to test his or her premonition by guessing which one of five cards has a picture on the other side. With mere guessing, a subject has a one-in-five chance of selecting the correct card. Runs consist of five, ten, or twenty-five trials.

A more complex card-guessing experiment is the Sequential Card Test, in which one guesses which of five cards the computer will select. If that card is the target, the trial ends. If not, the participant-selected card turns white, as if it has been turned over, and the participant selects one of the remaining cards until he or she eventually finds the target card.

One can also participate in the Remote Viewing experiment, in which one attempts to describe a complex image that will *later* appear.

In another test of precognition, the Location Test asks participants to guess where, within a given area on the computer screen, a target will appear after clicking on the square where one thinks it is going to pop up.

When analyzed, these tests give a statistical assessment of one's ability to peek into the future and anticipate what's coming up.

Over months and years, the level of success in the millions of trials from individuals all over the world varies somewhat, but generally stays within certain statistical boundaries. But sometimes the unexpected happens.

Beginning in July and ending in early September 2001, the success rate seen in the online card test rose dramatically and then fell to an unprecedented low just before September 11 and stayed there for more than two weeks. Then, almost immediately following September 11, the success rate rose steeply, returning to the levels seen all along. Although it is conceivable these deviations could have happened by chance alone, the probability is quite low, says Radin, and nowhere else in the entire six-year database of the Card Test is any similar excursion found.

Why did the psi ability of participants worldwide go haywire prior to September 11? Why did it return to normal immediately following that tragic day? Radin and physicist Richard Shoup, of the Boundary Institute, which cosponsors the online tests, suggest that the subjects unconsciously sensed the impending tragedy, and that this subliminal awareness interfered with their psi performance online.

The huge downward blip in psi performance a couple of weeks prior to September 11 creates intense interest in nearly everyone who encounters it, because it suggests an obvious question: could deviations in online psi tests be used to predict disasters?

We have to be cautious. As in the premonitions of the Aberfan disaster, knowing *that* a tragedy is about to happen is far different from knowing when and where it will occur. But that does not mean that the information is useless. Knowing that a catastrophe is impending might stimulate heightened awareness or security measures, thereby helping authorities thwart, say, a terrorist attack. We ought to be grateful for *any* warning that might be potentially helpful, whether it comes from high-placed intelligence sources, CIA spooks, or online subjects dabbling in psi tests.

Online tests herald a new epoch in precognition research. Millions of trials by thousands of individuals worldwide can be accomplished in relatively short time periods. This is simply not possible when subjects are tested conventionally as individual subjects, one by one, in a research lab. The huge database that results from online experiments yields astronomical odds against chance, which means they favor the veracity of premonitions. When the data is dissected, novel patterns can be found, such as the nosedive in accuracy of premonitions just prior to major disasters. These patterns substantiate what we've already seen—the largely unconscious nature of our ability to know the future.

FACING UP TO THE EVIDENCE

Though it did not involve premonitions per se, an interesting chapter in the history of research in distant mental phenomena is worth a brief detour, because it demonstrates the openness and courage that's required for an honest appraisal of the evidence underlying this field. Upton Sinclair, the Pulitzer Prize–winning social activist whose book *The Jungle* led to legislation that reformed America's meatpacking industry, and also whose 1927 novel *Oil!* inspired the 2007 Academy Award–winning movie *There Will Be Blood*, had a telepathic wife, Mary Craig Sinclair. In test after test, she showed she could mentally acquire accurate information remotely, without any sensory input. Against the stern advice of his friends, who were certain he would ruin his good reputation, Sinclair wrote the book *Mental Radio*, endorsing these phenomena. "Loyalty to the nature of the universe makes it necessary for me to say so," he said. "It is foolish to be convinced without evidence, but it is equally foolish to refuse to be convinced by real evidence."

Sinclair was famous, and he had famous friends. Among them was Albert Einstein, who wrote the preface for the German translation of *Mental Radio*. On May 23, 1930, Einstein responded with a statement that I have often thought should be tattooed on the brains of those fearful critics who refuse to acknowledge the evidence for remote, nonsensory knowing, no matter how good it may be. Einstein wrote, "I have read the book of Upton Sinclair with great interest and am convinced that the same deserves the most earnest consideration, not only of the laity, but also of the psychologists by profession. The results of the telepathic experiments carefully and plainly set forth in this book stand surely far beyond those which a nature investigator holds to be thinkable. On the other hand, it is out of the question in the case of so conscientious an observer and writer as Upton Sinclair that he is carrying on a conscious deception of the reading world; his good faith and dependability are not to be doubted. So if somehow the facts here set forth rest not upon telepathy, but upon some unconscious hypnotic influence from person to person, this also would be of high psychological interest. In no case should the psychologically interested circles pass over this book heedlessly."

Did Einstein have a mental lapse that made him open to the possibility of telepathy? Apparently not. Sixteen years later, in 1946, he wrote a similar message to Jan Ehrenwald, a psychiatrist and psi researcher with whom he had a brief correspondence. Einstein wrote, "I read your book (*Telepathy and Medical Psychology*) with great interest. It is certainly a good presentation of the problem, and I do not doubt that it will find a broad circle of readers. I can judge as a layman only and cannot state that I arrived at an affirmative or negative conclusion. In any case, it appears to me that from the physicist's point of view, we have no right to rule out a priori the possibility of telepathy. For that the foundations of our science are too uncertain and incomplete."

Einstein went on to say that he was unimpressed by and suspicious of card experiments, but found greater significance in the Sinclair experiments, in which Sinclair would make a drawing that was then received telepathically and duplicated by his wife. He continues, "In any case, your book was very stimulating to me and has somewhat 'softened up' my attitude which from the onset was distinctly negative towards the whole problem. One should not go through this world with blinders. . . . You may show this letter . . . to other people."

In hundreds of experiments, replicated in various labs by different researchers, we see evidence that the future is somehow shaking hands with the present, and cause and effect are trading places. However, confronting this evidence is not easy for many. One of Sinclair's friends said that he could not believe that his wife had gained distant information from telepathy, for this would require him to abandon "the fundamental notions" on which his "whole life has been based."

PREMONITIONS IN ANIMALS

Because premonitions seem clearly to exist in humans, it is likely that a precognitive sense exists as an evolutionary precursor in animals as well. Animals might have an even greater precognitive sense than we do, just as their senses of hearing, smell, and vision are often keener than ours.

In July 2007, a furor erupted over the existence of precognition in animals. The uproar involved a cat named Oscar, who overnight became the most famous feline on Earth after his story was published in the prestigious *New England Journal of Medicine*, widely considered the most influential medical journal in the world. Within two months more than two million Web sites featured Oscar. Paparazzi descended on him, and he was featured in newspapers and magazines worldwide. Oscar's meteoric rise to fame was the sort of thing publicity hounds dream about.

The excitement concerned whether or not Oscar had genuine premonitions that nursing-home patients were going to die, or whether he was merely behaving like, well, a nice kitty.

Oscar had been adopted as a gray-and-white brindled kitten two years earlier from an animal shelter by staff members of Steere House Nursing and Rehabilitation Center in Providence, Rhode Island. Steere House, founded in 1874, is a highly rated institution that prides itself on providing "old-fashioned hand-holding," innovative care and expertise, and attention to uplifting the spirit of its residents to "foster a sense of happiness, peace, security and well-being." The directors of Steere House are aware of the contributions pets make to the welfare of nursing-home residents, and the institution has long been pet friendly.

In 1991 the staff adopted Henry, a forlorn, mangled, and starving cat they found hiding under a car in their parking lot. Henry blossomed. For years he patrolled the halls at Steere, enjoying every moment of attention from the staff and patients. Henry died a few months before Oscar was adopted.

Oscar carried on in Henry's tradition. He grew up on the third-floor dementia unit at Steere, where elderly patients with end-stage Alzheimer's disease, Parkinson's disease, stroke, and other brain conditions are cared for. By this time Steere had become something of a menagerie, with five other cats; Cadbury, a floppy-eared bunny; Tilly, one of many parakeets; and Maxine the guard dog.

About eighteen months before the *New England Journal of Medicine* article made Oscar famous, the staff began noticing something unusual. Around two hours before a patient died, and never more than four, Oscar would enter the room, hop onto the bed, sniff the air, lick his paws, curl up next to the dying patient, and begin a deep-throated purring. He had not failed to spot a single death among the twenty-five that occurred following his arrival as a kitten in July 2005. In only one death was he absent—because the relatives of the patient asked him to be taken from the room. On this occasion Oscar objected strenuously, caterwauling and scratching the door so aggressively he had to be removed from the floor.

Some people who read about Oscar's death vigils considered them morbid, as if he were a feline angel of death. Home and Hospice Care of Rhode Island saw it differently. They presented him with an award—an Oscar of sorts—for his compassion in attending patients in their final hours of life, many of whom would have died alone had he not been there. The plaque was engraved: "Oscar—Steere House: for his compassionate quality end-of-life care."

As news of Oscar's ability spread around the world, a debate erupted. How does he do it? Can the cat see the future? Does he have premonitions of death? Not a single medical authority who was interviewed about Oscar's talents thought the cat was precognitive, although a few of them conceded that his skill was a mystery and that they simply did not know how he did it. Almost all the experts were eager to put a conventional spin on Oscar's talent and distance themselves from a premonition-based explanation.

Many nonscientists saw it differently, such as Laurie Cabot, who is known as "the official witch" of Salem, Massachusetts, where the infamous witch trials were held in the seventeenth century. She considers Oscar a "familiar," a term witches used for their cat companions in the old days. The term implies that Oscar has psychic powers and can communicate with the patients he serves. Cabot, whose ancestors came over on the *Mayflower* as Pilgrims, thinks Oscar is picking up on brainwave signals from the patients who are about to die. "This little cat Oscar," she says, "knows all the patients in the unit and he is trying to help them, just like the cats that I've always kept will curl up on my chest and try to heal me if I feel upset or am ill. In this case, though, Oscar is not trying to heal, he is clearly trying to help these people walk over into the other world." Cabot is describing the role of the psychopomp in Greek mythology, literally a "soul conductor" to the afterlife.

Physicians of course are nervous about endorsing the existence of the afterlife or future knowing, thus the stampede to analyze Oscar in everyday terms. "[Oscar] seems to understand when patients are about to die. . . . [The] cat might be picking up on specific odors surrounding death," said geriatrician David M. Dosa, author of the original *New England Journal of Medicine* article, and who is affiliated with the Warren Alpert Medical School of Brown University in Providence. Dr. Joan Teno, a professor of community health at the same medical school, who cares for Steere House patients and sees Oscar regularly, stated, "I don't think this is a psychic cat. I think there's probably a biochemical explanation." Dr. Teno offered another possibility. "I think he is following the patterning behavior of the staff," she says. "This is an excellent nursing home. If a dying person is alone, the staff will actually go in so the patient is not alone. They will hold a vigil." She was suggesting that Oscar, who has seen this routine many times, is a copycat. But Dr. Teno was ambivalent and conceded, "As a scientist, I want to offer a biological explanation for this. But I can't." Veterinarian Margie Scherk, of Vancouver, British Columbia, president of the American Association of Feline Practitioners, opted for the odor hypothesis. "I suspect he is smelling some chemical released just before dying," she said. "Cats can smell a lot of things we can't. And cats can definitely detect illness." Jill Goldman, Ph.D., a certified applied animal behaviorist in Laguna Beach, California, chimed in, saying, "Cats have a superb sense of smell. There has been ample opportunity for him to make an association between 'that' smell [and death]." Daniel Q. Estep, Ph.D., a certified applied animal behaviorist in Littleton, Colorado, offered a different possibility. "One of the things that happens with people who are dying," he said, "is that they are not moving around much. Maybe the cat is picking up on the fact that the person on the bed is very quiet. It may not be smells or sounds, but just the lack of movement." Dr. Nicholas H. Dodman, a leading animal behaviorist and professor at Cummings School of Veterinary Medicine at Tufts University, went further. "It may just come down to empathy," he said. Dr. Thomas Graves, a feline expert from the University of Illinois, in an interview with the BBC, was one of the few experts who dared to broach the "p" word, premonition. "Cats often can sense when their owners are sick or when another animal is sick," he said. "They can sense when the weather will change; they're famous for being sensitive to premonitions of earthquakes."

Following a televised Oscar story on *CBS News*, hypotheses got even more creative as viewers posted their views on the program's Web site. "Has anyone considered the possibility [that] the cat is carrying a disease and is CAUSING the patient's death instead of PREDICTING it?" wrote one individual. Others suggested "cat allergies" as an explanation for the connection between Oscar's presence and the demise of the patient. At a blog, one person wrote, "I have always suspected cats suck out your soul while you sleep." Television talk show host Glenn Beck, while interviewing Dr. Dosa, offered fraud on the part of the staff as an explanation. He suggested that "somebody is making [Oscar] right," which Dosa emphatically rejected.

How do the families who are involved with Oscar see it? Dosa reported in his *New England Journal of Medicine* article that when a grandson of a dying person asked why the cat was there, his mother explained, fighting back tears, "He is here to help Grandma get to heaven." However, unless Oscar starts talking we may never know if he's using the highly refined physical senses cats are known to possess, or premonitions, or both. So far, the cat's got his tongue.

Cases abound that suggest the existence of a human-animal bond that operates across space-time, a connection that is difficult to break, even when people try. For example, consider what happened when a man wanted to get rid of his dog and released him in a dense part of the city of Durham, North Carolina, five miles from his residence. When he returned home the dog was waiting for him, frisky and happy to be reunited with his master. The man's conscience was pricked, and he decided not to abandon his pet after all.

More extreme examples exist, such as Minosch, a German cat, who reportedly traveled fifteen hundred miles in sixty-one days to return home after being separated from its vacationing family. And there's Bobbie, a pedigreed Collie with a quarter strain of Scotch sheepdog in him, who got lost in Indiana on a family trip, but who found his way to the family's new home in Oregon where the dog had never been, three thousand miles away, crossing the Rocky Mountains and ice-choked rivers in the dead of winter to do so.

Thousands of similar cases have been reported. No doubt some can be dismissed as involving look-alike animals, but not all; often the returning animal has its original collar and name tag, and can be further identified by distinguishing marks and scars.

Particularly fascinating are those cases in which the returning animal appears to be responding to the physical and emotional needs of some remote person. An example is that of an Irish soldier in World War I, whose wife and small dog, Prince, took up residence in 1914 in Hammersmith, London, while he was sent with one of the earliest contingents to the battlefields of France. After a period of service he was granted leave to visit his family, but when he returned to battle, Prince was utterly disconsolate and refused all food. Then the dog disappeared. For ten days the wife tried desperately to trace him, to no avail. Finally she decided to break the news in a letter to her husband.

She was astonished when she heard from him that the dog had joined him in the trenches at Armentières, under heavy bombardment. Somehow Prince had made his way through the streets of London, seventy miles of English countryside, hitched a ride across the English Channel, traveled over sixty miles of French soil, and then "smelt his master out amongst an army of half a million Englishmen and this despite the fact that the last mile or so of intervening ground was reeking with bursting shells, many of them charged with tear-gas."

None of these cases prove that Oscar the cat has genuine premonitions of death. For all we know, he may be employing a highly developed sense of smell, as many of the experts suggested. On the other hand, in view of recent research we should remain open to the possibility that future knowing may be happening in Oscar's case alongside whatever physical senses he may be employing.

British biologist Rupert Sheldrake has made a compelling case for genuine premonitions in animals in his research on dogs that seem to know when their owners are returning.

Dogs may also know when their owners are *not* coming home. In their book *The Haunting of the Presidents,* Joel Martin and William J. Birnes report that just before President Abraham Lincoln was assassinated at Ford's Theatre in Washington, D.C., on the evening of April 14, 1865, the Lincoln family dog became frantic at about the same time as the curtain was rising at the theater. The pet, usually gentle and quiet, inexplicably started barking uncontrollably and running around the family quarters in a frenzy, as if looking for its master, the president. None of the White House personnel could calm the animal. The dog continued running through the hallways until it stopped, threw its head back, and began to wail. The thought on everyone's mind was that something terrible had gone wrong and that the president was in danger. There was no quieting the dog, whose yelps roused servants from all over the White House.

No event in recent history ignited the debate about premonitions in animals as the tsunami that swept the coastline of the Indian Ocean on December 26, 2004, which was triggered by a magnitude nine temblor off the coast of northern Sumatra. One of the areas that bore the brunt of the surging floodwaters was Sri Lanka's Yala National Park. Aerial photos could find no evidence of any dead animals that made the park famous—elephants, leopards, deer, wild boar, monkeys, jackals, and crocodiles. Just before the tsunami struck, the monkeys stopped accepting bananas from tourists, a nearly unheard-of behavior. On India's southern coast, flamingos left well before the tsunami hit. In Khao Lak, along Thailand's western coast, also hard-hit by the tsunami, a dozen elephants giving rides to tourists began to trumpet hours before the tidal wave struck. This behavior coincided with the time that the earthquake fractured the ocean floor, triggering the tsunami. An hour prior to the arrival of the tidal wave, the elephants again became agitated, and just before disaster struck they bolted for higher ground, some breaking free of their chains to do so. Just minutes before the tsunami, dogs were seen running inland from the same area.

The ensuing debate about whether or not the fleeing animals were using premonitions of impending disaster, or highly sensitive physical senses, duplicates the flap over Oscar the cat. The possibility they were using *both* sensory and nonsensory ways of knowing is rarely considered.

In 1981, biologist Ruth Buskirk, of the University of Texas at Austin, reviewed the unusual behavior of eels, frogs, snakes, turtles, sea birds, pigeons, chickens, cats, dogs, horses, cows, rats, and mice prior to thirty-six earthquakes on four continents. After exhaustive analyses of her data, she said, "Our main conclusion was, boy, the animals can sense anything, including very minor changes that happen before earthquakes, but there's so much background noise during an earthquake." It remains unclear, she concluded, just what stimuli—sound, vibrations, electrical or pressure changes in the atmosphere, or other physical microchanges—the animals are reacting to.

Some seismologists are skeptical of even physically based sensing. The U.S. Geological Survey, a government agency, maintains that a reproducible connection between earthquakes and animal behavior has never been made. Andy Michael, a USGS geophysicist, says, "What we're faced with is a lot of anecdotes. Animals react to so many things—being hungry, defending their territories, mating, predators—so it's hard to have a controlled study to get that advanced warning signal." In the 1970s, the USGS did a few studies on animal prediction, but nothing concrete came out of it, says Michael.

Those humans who paid close attention to animal behaviors fared best during the tsunami. The indigenous tribes of the Andaman and Nicobar Islands, near the quake's epicenter, are believed to have survived without a single death by retreating to higher ground because they noticed unusual changes in the behavior of dolphins, birds, and lizards.

It's not the first time lives were saved that way. When a massive earthquake hit the densely populated city of Haicheng in northeast China in 1975, the residents noticed abnormal behavior in animals, including snakes, which came out of hibernation a week before the event. With a week's notice, the populous city was warned, and thousands of lives were saved. Chinese researchers are now focusing on the behavior of pigeons, which are extremely sensitive to ground vibrations.

It isn't likely that skeptics will be convinced that animals have premonitions based on the case of Oscar the cat, or by changes in the behavior of animals prior to earthquakes and tsunamis. Hypersensitivity to scents, electrical discharges, or tremors may indeed explain these behaviors and should not be dismissed. In some cases, however, relying on sensory explanations may be clutching at straws.

Some skeptics also suggest that all so-called ESP events in humans can be explained by hypersentivity to physical stimuli such as scents, tremors, and electrical signals. These "explanations" appear inadequate for premonitions, however, because there are simply no accepted mechanisms by which information could be acquired from the future through physical stimuli.

Sheldrake has received dozens of accounts in which animals prevented their owners from entering situations that were dangerous or life-threatening. Many involve dogs who refused to walk along a path where limbs or trees fell where the person and the dog would have been. Others involve horses, dogs, or cats that delayed or prevented their owners from embarking on foot or by auto onto paths or roads where accidents later occurred, in which the owner might have been injured or killed. In one case, a dog refused to enter an underground pedestrian walkway, forcing the owner to turn back. At that moment there was a loud crash as the concrete ceiling fell down. In another case, a dog prevented its owner from boarding a boat that exploded soon afterward. Another dog saved his owner's life by pulling him away from the roadside just before a truck careened around the corner and crashed into the place they would have occupied.

Hyperacute hearing? Sensitivity to tremors or electromagnetic signals? Perhaps. But some cases make precognition nearly unavoidable, because the animals appear to have had no sensory clues about what was about to unfold. Consider, for instance, a case in which a woman was driving with her cat lying in the backseat of the car, its usual napping spot. Suddenly it awoke and became increasingly disturbed. She continued driving, when the cat jumped to the front, nudged her arm, and even gave her a slight bite on her hand that held the steering wheel. The woman eventually stopped the car, and at that moment a large tree crashed onto the road a few yards ahead, where she would have been if she had continued driving. In another case, an Austrian couple was driving along a steep mountain road when their poodle began to howl. The dog put her paws on the driver, as if to stop him. Then the dog's behavior "became mad." The driver slowed to a crawl, and when he slowly rounded the next corner he saw that the road had disappeared a few meters ahead, carried away in an avalanche. Only a precipice remained. The couple was convinced their poodle had saved their lives.

These cases, from Sheldrake's rich archives, illustrate the literal meaning of a premonition, a warning that comes before, except in these cases the warning is mediated by an animal and not experienced directly by a human.

Still, these cases do not absolutely prove that highly sensitive physical senses are not being employed by the animals in question. A new twist in research on premonitions, however, may change this limitation—so-called presentiment experiments, which we've explored. These sophisticated, computer-based studies appear to offer firm evidence that humans, and perhaps animals as well, can sense future events. In these experiments, hyperacuity of the physical senses cannot possibly explain the individual's reaction because the event causing the reaction *has not yet occurred*. One presentiment experiment, in earthworms, suggests that the same ability exists in lower forms of life. It would be surprising if animals, lying in-between in terms of complexity, were not also endowed with precognitive abilities. If this proves to be the case, millions of pet owners will say, "We knew it all along."

FIRST SIGHT AND MINDSIGHT

The ability to know distant or future events has long been called "second sight." Psychologist and consciousness researcher James C. Carpenter, of the Rhine Research Center in Durham, North Carolina, believes the term *second sight* is misleading. In two seminal papers published in 2004, Carpenter proposed calling the human ability for distant and future knowing *first sight*—a fundamental, innate ability that everyone has, and which transcends our visual sense.

First sight can be conveniently thought of as psychic antennae or mental radar that sweep our world in both space and time, acquiring information that we use every moment of our existence. First sight permits us always to exist "a little beyond ourselves in space and ahead of ourselves in time," as Carpenter puts it. First sight is not limited to short distances and brief durations, however; if the need arises we can significantly expand the reach of our knowing.

When you think about it, first sight resembles our other senses. You can't taste tasting, hear hearing, feel feeling, or see seeing. You just taste, hear, feel, and see without forethought or analysis. Once these senses kick in, we don't intellectualize about them by thinking, "I am touching something now." We aren't fully aware of them, even while they are operating. At this moment I am touching the keys on my computer keyboard while writing this sentence; and, although my touching the keys gives me neural feedback, it is so subtle I don't pause to register it consciously. In the same way, we usually don't think about premonitions as they happen. They just occur—as first sight, a knowing that is outside of full awareness. But there is, of course, a fundamental difference between first sight and our physical senses. Our physical senses are body-bound; first sight is not.

According to psychologist Kenneth Ring of the University of Connecticut and Evelyn E. Valarino, his research colleague, even blind people appear to possess first sight. Ring and Valarino report that congenitally blind individuals who have had near-death experiences (NDEs) or out-of-body experiences (OBEs) sometimes give detailed reports, later confirmed, suggesting that they have remotely *seen* a particular person, event, or scene during the NDE or OBE. But if they have been blind since birth, how is this possible?

This ability in the congenitally blind sounds like "blindsight," a condition that has been investigated extensively by neuroscientists in recent years. In blindsight, an individual responds to visual stimuli without consciously perceiving them. If a blindsighted person with no awareness whatsoever of any visual perception is asked to predict aspects of a visual stimulus, such as the location or movement of the stimulus, they are able to do so at levels significantly above chance. This is evidence that they are "seeing without seeing." Blindsight most often occurs following injury to the normal visual pathways in the brain following trauma, stroke, or some other medical condition.

In spite of the similarity, this is *not* the condition Ring and Valarino have uncovered. For one thing, their congenitally blind subjects do not have and have never had normal visual pathways that *could* be injured. Moreover, they perceive things at a distance, beyond the range of vision of normally sighted people.

Ring believes the congenitally blind who see things at a distance during near-death experiences (NDEs) do so because they have entered a distinctive state of transcendental awareness he calls *mindsight.*

This realm of transcendental awareness is barred to us during the normal waking state, Ring says. But as one nears death, conscious awareness is paradoxically expanded, according to typical reports of NDEers who have been there. In this state, says Ring, mindsight kicks in, making possible the acquisition of distant and future information, unrestrained by space and time.

Ring and Valarino contradict those who claim that remote knowing involves some subtle, highly sensitive exercise of normal vision. To emphasize, not only do Ring and Valarino's congenitally blind subjects not have normal visual pathways and have never had them, but in many instances *there is no visual stimulus,* because the things that are "seen" are out of sight for even normal individuals. In spite of this, conscious perception takes place anyway.

Carpenter takes things further. He believes that first sight—Ring and Valarino's mindsight—operates continually, 24/7, no letup—and not just during near-death experiences, but normally. Moreover, it functions so efficiently and subliminally that we are seldom aware of it.

Native tribes take first sight as a given. Josiah Gregg was an explorer, naturalist, and author who traded on the Santa Fe Trail during the 1830s. On one occasion he watched a Comanche arc an arrow that killed a prairie dog out of sight behind a hillock, a trick Gregg could not duplicate with a rifle.

When Victorio, the Apache leader, wished to know the location of the enemy, which often included the U.S. Cavalry, Lozen, his shaman and sister, would stand with outstretched arms, palms up, and pray. As she turned slowly to follow the sun's path, her hands would begin to tingle and her palms changed color when she faced the foe. The intensity of the sensation indicated the approximate distance of the enemy.

David Unaipon, an Aboriginal Australian, described in the early 1900s how the use of smoke signals depended on a nonlocal function of consciousness. Westerners who witnessed this custom assumed that some sort of code was involved in the signaling. Not so, said Unaipon; the function of the smoke signal was simply only to get everyone's attention so that distant, mind-to-mind communication might then take place.

If first sight is fundamental, why is it not as obvious to us moderns as it is to tribal peoples? Perhaps it is not surprising that first sight goes undetected. Human functions—and dysfunctions—sometimes exist unnoticed, right under our noses. An example is congenital color blindness.

English chemist John Dalton first described this condition in 1798 after recognizing his own colorblindness four years earlier. He discovered that, like his brother, he confused scarlet with green, and pink with blue, a tip-off that this was an inherited condition. Dalton supposed that the vitreous humor, the liquid inside his eye, was colored blue, causing him to selectively absorb longer wavelengths. He left instructions for his eyes to be examined after his death, but the vitreous humor proved perfectly clear. Years later, DNA extracted from his preserved eye revealed that he had a deficiency in certain photo pigments in the retina. After he published his famous paper "Extraordinary Facts Relating to the Vision of Colors," people woke up to the existence of a malady that occurs worldwide, including around 7 percent of males and 0.4 percent of females in the United States.

Why was the circulation of the blood throughout the body undetected by anatomists until William Harvey described it in 1628? Why was the rotation of the earth around the sun concealed for millennia? History is studded with "invisibles" that escaped notice, which, following their discovery, seemed obvious. These instances remind us of the folk saying "If you want to hide the treasure, put it in plain sight."

We see what we *can* see, and what we can see is determined largely by our beliefs. According to Lawrence Blair in *Rhythms of Vision: The Changing Pattern of Belief*, the natives of Patagonia could not see Magellan's ships when they arrived at the tip of South America in 1520. To the aborigines, the shore party appeared out of thin air on the beach. The shamans eventually discerned a faint image of the tall ships anchored offshore. After they pointed out the images and everyone concentrated on the concept of giant sailing ships for a while, the galleons materialized. Michael Polanyi reports a similar incident when Darwin's ship, HMS *Beagle,* anchored off Patagonia in 1831. The natives could see the tiny rowboats, but could not detect the mother ship. Their belief system had a place for small craft, but not for large vessels.

All of us, including scientists, have blinders built into our worldview. As astronomer and author David Darling puts it, "If science searches the universe—as it does—for certain kinds of truth, then these are inevitably the only ones it will find. Everything else will slip through the net." First sight and premonitions are cases in point.

Premonitions are among the most common expressions of first sight. They are a searchlight into the darkness of the future, alerting us to events lying just ahead. For this ability to function best, it needs to operate quickly and be acted on immediately. For this to happen, premonitions and other first-sight functions are unlikely to be processed by analytical thought, because rational analysis would delay action or prevent it altogether.

When we use first sight we don't reason, we simply act. History is filled with examples of individuals who have learned to rely seamlessly on this ability, which is often regarded as luck or intuition.

A combat pilot knows when to veer right or left to escape anti-aircraft fire before it arrives. A martial arts adept knows his opponent's moves before they happen. Great battlefield commanders know the enemy's moves ahead of time. A gifted running back sees holes open up in the defense before they occur. A skilled researcher "just knows" the right path to follow to produce results. These actions often take place without the interference of the rational mind, on the spur of the moment, for reasons that are obscure to the individual experiencing them.

First sight is not always correct. Sometimes it is embarrassingly wrong and misleading. This isn't surprising. No human faculty is perfect, including those autonomic processes that normally operate beyond our awareness. Our heart skips beats even when it is not stressed; our blood pressure gets out of whack, even without an external stimulus; our bowel can become sluggish or overactive, even without obvious provocation. But it's the overall pattern of activity—how a function serves us in the long run—that matters most, not whether a system functions perfectly all the time.

If I sail a boat from San Francisco to Honolulu, I will be off course nearly all the time, because it is impossible to steer my craft perfectly without deviation. I'll arrive at my destination not through perfect steering but by constant course corrections. Premonitions are like that. They don't need to provide us with a perfect picture of the future; a simple heads-up or gut feeling will often suffice, alerting us to pay closer attention than usual to what is about to happen. This may present itself as a general sense of foreboding, as a fragmentary image of a future event, as a symbolic or metaphorical picture, or in some instances a highly detailed vision of what lies ahead.

"The sky in the daytime," says Carpenter, "flooded with the sun's light, looks blue and empty, but at night without the sun, it can be seen filled with flickering starlight." Just so, the dazzling light of logic can obscure the presence of subtle premonitions and other first-sight manifestations. This means that if we want to become better at detecting first-sight operations in our life, we need to learn to "speak the language," which is often symbolic, not logical. Premonitions usually don't arrive with banner headlines announcing, "There is a road obstruction around the bend. *Slow down now!*" Instead, the slow-down message may, for instance, take the form of a snake with a belt around its middle or a rope tied in a knot—something curved, with a barrier or impediment. The symbols may be so subtle that we never actually figure them out, but we don't have to. A sufficient hint is delivered and we respond anyway—in this instance by slowing down and avoiding the road obstruction without knowing why. Afterward, we may speak of nothing more than a hunch, a feeling, intuition, or plain dumb luck.

Some persons are able to exercise control over their first-sight abilities and make constructive use of them, says Carpenter, such as persons who develop their sensibilities in art or music, or who cultivate their powers of memory or attention to detail. This commonly involves some mental discipline, such as meditation, that hones one's ability to relax, focus, and pay attention to what is happening not just in the world outside, but to one's inner emotional state as well.

I'm convinced that first sight is common in my profession of medicine. It is also vigorously denied. When I was in medical school, I was amazed by the diagnostic skills of three of my professors. They could arrive at diagnoses with only scraps of information. I often could not detect a trail of logic that led them to the right answers. When I asked them how they did it, they could not explain their reasoning, but would respond with references to "experience," "clinical judgment," or some other nonexplanation. These superb teachers were materialists to the core. They would have been embarrassed or angry if someone had suggested they were employing first sight as part of their professional skills. Particularly intriguing were CPCs—clinicopathological conferences—in which the case of a deceased individual would be presented. As the discussant, they would predict the correct diagnosis that would be revealed by the autopsy findings. They were almost always correct in exquisite detail in these predictions, for reasons, again, that often eluded me.

No doubt there are experts in many fields who are equally adept in deploying first sight in problem solving, and equally skilled at disguising it—not just from others, but from themselves as well.

PREMONITIONS AND THE BRAIN

No one has yet discovered a "premonition center" in the brain. But with the advent of sophisticated brain-scanning techniques, we're learning more about those areas of the brain that may be involved in future knowing.

Amnesia is a partial or total loss of memory. It is often caused by damage to a deep-seated area of the brain called the hippocampus, which is also involved with emotion and the workings of the autonomic nervous system. The damage can occur as a result of infection, trauma, stroke, or conditions such as Alzheimer's or Parkinson's disease.

Eleanor Maguire, of the Wellcome Trust Centre for Neuroimaging at University College London, studied five patients with classic amnesia, all of whom had suffered brain infections that damaged the hippocampus. Although they could remember names of relatives, they were unable to recall past events. But it was not just recall that was affected. The researchers asked them, along with a control group of subjects without amnesia, to visualize and describe in detail several *future* scenarios such as visiting a beach, forest, museum, castle, or pub, or a future Christmas party or meeting with a close friend, and to describe what the experience would feel like. The descriptions were disorganized and emotionless. The hippocampus-damaged subjects could not describe spatial relationships between objects that were part of the future scenarios, and they said little about what they felt like. They could not see the experience as a whole, but saw instead a collection of separate images. As one subject said, "It's not very real. It's just not happening. My imagination isn't . . . well, I'm not imagining it, let's put it that way."

"The results are actually showing that amnesia is really worse than we thought—patients are really stuck in the present," Maguire says.

Maguire's work sheds new light on an old subject. It shows that amnesia involves not just memory deficits but also an inability to imagine future events.

Other research supports these findings. In a study involving fMRI brain scans in normal subjects, Kathleen McDermott and her colleagues at Washington University in St. Louis found that memory processing centers in the brain are activated when individuals imagine potential future events.

The discovery that the hippocampus is involved in visualizing the future may be important in understanding premonitions. Brain function can vary dramatically in normal humans. For example, some individuals have prodigious memories, while others struggle to recall where they put their car keys or what they had for lunch. Do those individuals who possess a gifted memory have a "bigger and better" hippocampus than those with poor memories? Might those individuals who have a gift for premonitions have a "hippocampal advantage" that enables them to better see the future? Might those who deny that premonitions exist, and who insist that they've never experienced premonitions, be suffering from hippocampal dysfunction?

Maguire asked her subjects to visualize potential future scenarios. People who have premonitions also visualize possible future happenings. A major difference is that the individual having a premonition often experiences a certainty that the future event will occur, while the individual who is merely visualizing a possible future event considers it imaginary. The brain may not respect this difference. It has a way of responding as if the imagined event is real. If we vividly imagine or dream we're being attacked by a predator, the brain responds as if the imagined or dreamed event is actual, sending signals to the body that churn out stress hormones that prepare us for the real thing. Just so, the brain's hippocampal area may not distinguish between imaginary future events and premonitions that seem real. This suggests that it may be impossible to determine the validity of premonitions by focusing on what the brain is doing—but it's fun to speculate on what we might learn if we did.

For instance, I'd like a peek at the hippocampal function of skeptics who deny the validity of premonitions. Is their hippocampus on vacation? I'd also like to know whether people who are gifted at premonitions have super-ramped-up hippocampal function when compared with individuals who claim they are premonition challenged. A good place to look is a group of skilled visualizers of future scenarios: London's professional black-cab drivers.

It's not easy to become licensed to drive a black cab in London. Drivers have to learn "the knowledge," as it's called, which includes up to twenty-five thousand street names and the locations of all the major tourist attractions. Cabbies must know not only how to get somewhere, but they must know the most direct route possible. The bewildering labyrinth of streets in a six-mile radius of Charing Cross is particularly daunting. It generally takes three years of training to master "the knowledge," and three-fourths of those who enter taxi school drop out before finishing the course. During their training, something happens to the cabbies. By the time they finish, they no longer have ordinary brains.

Maguire and her colleagues performed fMRI scans on sixteen London cabbies and found that in all cases they were different from fifty control subjects. One particular area, the posterior or rear region of the hippocampus, was larger in all the taxi drivers. The longer they were on job, the larger the region became.

When Maguire's findings were featured on BBC News, they resonated with a lot of people on both sides of the Atlantic. One individual said that his experience as a cab driver made him better at business decisions—an acknowledgment of improved intuition and first sight? Another individual described how, when he drove a taxi to pay for college, he experienced a marked increase in mathematical skills, including the ability to visualize complex geometric patterns, shapes, and diagrams. Later in the military he scored very high on special tests for navigation, piloting, and cryptology. Cynicism surfaced as well. One American said that Maguire's study was clearly not done on New York cab drivers. Another agreed, saying he'd had cab drivers in the United States who appeared to have no hippocampus at all. One individual credited a rude New York City cabbie with a premonition. He described how he was assisting a ninety-year-old man who was extremely obese to get into the taxi to go to a hospital to have a cataract operation. The surly taxi driver would not assist in getting the elderly man into his taxi or out of it. Even so, he held out his hand for a tip. When the younger man refused, the taxi driver fumed and sped off. It turned out that the surgeon operated on the wrong eye. The young man credits the discourteous taxi driver—perhaps wrongly—with an unconscious premonition, doing what he could to prevent the elderly patient from getting to the hospital.

Maguire warns against the use of Global Positioning System (GPS) directional devices in London's taxis. "We very much hope they don't start using it," she said. "We believe this area of the brain increased . . . because of the huge amount of data they have to memorise. If they all start using GPS, that knowledge base will be less and possibly affect the brain changes we are seeing."

GPS devices may not be the only premonition inhibitors we should be concerned about. As we've become increasingly reliant on information technology, there is less need to rely on our first sense, our ability to be a little ahead of ourselves in space and time. Why should I need a premonition of the weather this weekend, when I can click on the Weather Channel's Web site and check the ten-day forecast for any city in the United States? I don't need to use my own intuition in judging the stock market's movement; financial gurus have already used *their* intuition and posted their predictions online and in newsletters. I can get forecasts on the rise of global temperatures and the melting of polar ice caps years in advance; on whether it's likely to rain on my vegetable garden this summer; on who's likely to win the Super Bowl, on and on.

Realizing this, I can almost feel my hippocampus shrinking. I feel Maguire's warnings should be taken seriously. Reliance on electronic gadgets to do our envisioning for us may indeed affect the brain negatively, dumbing down our first sense.

Can we fight back? We're not likely to disable all the electronic devices that have become an integral part of our lives, but there are antidotes to all these premonition surrogates. Let's recall McDermott's findings: when individuals purposefully imagine potential future events, their memory processing centers in the brain are activated. This suggests that envisioning the future might be good for the brain and our cognitive ability.

In one study involving thirteen thousand American women entering their later years, researchers found several activities that correlated with the preservation of their cognitive function as they aged. Among these was reading books. While reading a good novel, one is continually envisioning future scenarios, imagining upcoming twists and turns of the plot. It is impossible to read an engrossing novel without exercising this faculty. Whether or not we get it right, these mental exertions are essentially mini-premonitions, imagined microvisions of the future, and they appear to be good for the brain.

KNOCKED PSYCHIC?

Maguire's research deals with the effect of the *enhancement* of brain function on mental acuity. Sometimes it appears that brain *damage* might be good for premonitions.

A recurring Hollywood motif is the malfunctioning computer, engine, or spaceship that is set right when an exasperated operator delivers an angry swift kick or a blow with a crude wrench. This behavior is practically archetypal. When our watch, cell phone, or TV remote acts up, our instinct is to give it a good shake and, if that doesn't work, a firm whack. Sometimes this causes the stubborn object to come to its senses and begin operating normally once again.

Psychotherapist Sandra Ingerman has been "shaken up" by physically traumatic events that may have altered her perceptual abilities. Along with anthropologist Michael Harner, Ingerman has helped revive ancient shamanic techniques that typically involve clairvoyance and precognition. As the anthropological literature makes clear, individuals don't rationally decide to become a shaman, they are called to do so. The calling often involves life-and-death experiences such as serious illness, danger, and physical trauma.

Ingerman lives in my hometown of Santa Fe, which has led us to several interesting discussions about shamanism. On one occasion I asked her if she'd had any radical experiences that influenced her professional path. She revealed that she'd survived three near-death experiences, including being struck by lightning.

She described how she was once asked to speak to a group of Native Americans about shamanism. She felt awkward doing so, since Native Americans generally know infinitely more about shamanism than do whites. As she anticipated, her audience seemed completely bored and half asleep with what she had to say—until she casually mentioned that she had once been struck by lightning. At that moment her entire audience came alive and sat bolt upright, as if *they* had been lightning-struck. This single fact legitimized Ingerman in their eyes, and they were riveted by her remarks for the rest of her lecture. She had hit a nerve—their knowledge that potentially lethal physical trauma can presage profound wisdom and power, which in the shamanic tradition is nearly always associated with future knowing.

Harriet Tubman, the abolitionist who helped hundreds of slaves to freedom prior to the Civil War, is a classic example of the link between future knowing and physical trauma. At age twelve, Tubman was nearly killed when she was hit in the forehead by a two-pound lead weight, thrown by an angry overseer. It split her skull and left a hole in her forehead, which she later masked by wearing masculine hats. Tubman received no conventional medical care following her injury, which may have been a blessing, considering the state of the art at the time. When she recovered, she was different. She began to have "trouble with her head." She would experience what she called her "sleeps," the sudden need to lie down and take quick naps, often in the most awkward circumstances. She began to have visions of future happenings. She would sometimes hear music fill the air. She sensed that a window would open in her head, and she would see or fly through it and observe important things. Although these experiences occurred following her near-lethal injury, she also maintained that she had inherited special gifts from her father, who "could always predict the future."

Modern physicians would diagnose Tubman as having narcolepsy or temporal lobe epilepsy. Because her visions, out-of-body experiences, and premonitions followed so closely on the heels of her head trauma, it's tempting to conclude that the trauma caused them. This is not a stretch. History is peppered with famous people whose temporal lobe epilepsy was associated with seeing visions and hearing voices; Dostoyevsky is an example.

Was brain malfunction the catalyst for Tubman's precognitive ability? It's tempting to think so. Although she dreamed before her head trauma occurred, the blow seemed to ramp up her dreams to great clarity and power.

Tubman personally escorted three hundred slaves to freedom via the Underground Railroad without ever getting captured or losing any of the slaves she was helping. Her amazing feats were guided by specific dreams and premonitions, through which she learned about safe houses, river crossings, and friendly helpers she had never previously known. She has been called "one of the greatest dreamers of all time."

In a typical episode, while conducting a group of four slaves to freedom in November 1856, she was overcome by one of her "sleeps" and collapsed. While unconscious, she envisioned a ford in the river shallow enough to get across, as well as a cabin on the other side where they would be given food and shelter. She awoke in time to avoid the trackers and bloodhounds, cross the river at the place she had dreamed, and meet a black family who fed and sheltered them, just as she had foreseen.

Alas, not much is known about the connections between future knowing and traumatic brain injury. One looks in vain for "premonitions" or "precognition" in the indexes of current neurology texts. This is not surprising, because nearly all neurologists consider precognition to be impossible, nothing more than fantasy, hallucinations, a sign of mental illness, or the result of some pathological process loose in the brain.

A rare exception is neuropsychiatrist Vernon Neppe, of the Pacific Neuropsychiatric Institute in Seattle, Washington. He and psi researcher John Palmer examined the correlation between paranormal experiences, including premonitions, with temporal lobe dysfunction associated with epilepsy, drug use, and head trauma. These associations proved to be statistically significant in both normal individuals and in those seeking care for neuropsychiatric problems.

How might head trauma make the brain *more* functional, better able to perceive outside the here and now? No one knows. We can speculate, however, that head trauma might inhibit certain brain processes that, under normal conditions, screen out or block precognition. Brain mechanisms that are normally dormant might reemerge as heightened perceptual powers—shaking things loose, so to speak.

If Harriet Tubman were alive today, she might help us resolve the role of brain trauma in premonitions by submitting to brain scans and other tests. But for now, those secrets rest with her.

It isn't surprising that our precognitive abilities often lie outside conscious awareness. In the past, individuals who could see the future in detail were considered shamans, prophets, and oracles, and they occupied places of honor in their societies. Today, however, there aren't many attractive job opportunities for seers and visionaries. They are more likely to get medicated than hired. So the old powers have retreated to the security of the unconscious and the darkness of dreams, where the resistance of culture is temporarily suspended.

How can we nudge premonitions onto the stage of full awareness? Before confronting this question, let's explore more fully how they manifest, the purposes they serve, our attitudes toward them, and factors that influence our awareness of them.

THREE

PREMONITIONS: WHY, WHAT, HOW?

"There is really no before and after for the mind."

—Erwin Schrödinger, Nobel physicist

SPEAKING THE LANGUAGE OF PREMONITIONS

We often behave toward first sight like ugly Americans visiting a foreign country who demand, "If you want to talk to me, speak English." We want premonitions to speak our language; we want to be fully conscious of them; and we prefer that they appear in graphic, literal detail, no interpretation required. Give us the straight facts, we say to them, including the place, date, and time. Alas, first sight usually doesn't conform to these expectations. We have to learn *its* language, which more often than not resembles art, poetry, or music. As Carpenter describes the process, "An image comes to mind, the memory of a song occurs of its own volition, a mood descends or arises, a silly mispronunciation intrudes into everyday speech, one name is substituted for another, a shadow is misinterpreted as a snake, or in the depth of sleep a dream takes shape."

As a tourist, one doesn't have to completely master a foreign language to reap its benefits; a few phrases and a respectful attitude will work wonders in drawing out the locals. First sight follows similar rules. If we want it to emerge from its normally invisible level, we must learn its language, approach it with humility, and be grateful for whatever messages appear. A little respect goes a long way.

Symbolism erupted in the experiences of Susan Faludi, a Pulitzer Prize–winning journalist and social critic. In her book *The Terror Dream: Fear and Fantasy in Post-9/11 America,* she explores how the terrorist attacks led to an inflation of hypermasculine virtues, the denigration of women, and the call for greater domesticity in American society. In an interview she said, "There were articles . . . blaming feminists, saying feminists had weakened our military, had weakened our resolve, that feminism was unpatriotic. There was this whole message to women that they needed to sort of back off their demands for independence or . . . face being regarded as almost treasonous."

In the early-morning hours of 9/11, before the events of the day unfolded, Faludi had a dream that seemed to predict these developments, couched in the symbolism that so often characterizes premonitions. In her dream, she was sitting in an airplane next to another woman, and a young man came up to them and shot two bullets. "One went into my throat at a sort of odd angle, and one into her throat at an odd angle," she said. "And I realized that we were both alive, but we couldn't speak." Faludi believes the dream was prophetic. "Now, I don't pretend to be a psychic," she explained. "I don't know why I had this dream. But later it struck me that it had this remarkable metaphorical quality to it, because when I began to look at our response to 9/11, what repeated over and over was . . . the way that women were silenced and, more generally, the way our culture silenced any kind of questioning or examination of our reactions."

The symbolic language of premonitions also invaded the life of Dr. Kathleen Hall, a stress management expert and author with degrees in finance, divinity, and spirituality. Her advice has been featured widely on major TV networks and in major newspapers. She lives with her family on a horse ranch called Oak Haven, south of Atlanta, Georgia, where she maintains a bird sanctuary and rescues animals. In a series of unnerving events that took place on her ranch, she got a real workout in translating the language of premonitions.

One morning following a demanding road trip, Hall was sipping coffee on her back porch with her dogs and cats, contemplating the nearby shimmering lake. She suddenly became aware of around twenty huge black vultures perched on the fence near the lake. She had lived at Oak Haven for more than two decades and had never seen vultures.

Hall reminded herself that vultures play a valuable role in nature, cleaning up dead animal carcasses. But although there had been animal deaths on the farm before, vultures had never shown up. She was rattled by the experience and wondered if their presence was an omen. She recalled that within the past three weeks there had been several animal deaths on the farm—two dogs, one cat, and her horse. Had some sort of death energy settled over the farm? There might be more deaths to come, she thought;

three more of her dogs were twelve years old and two cats were eighteen. Could the vultures sense the life force draining from these creatures? Were they waiting for their demise?

Wanting the vultures gone, Hall fetched a .22 rifle and fired into the air to scare them away. They flew but continued to circle overhead, refusing to leave. Was the circling an omen of her own death, she wondered? "I don't feel as if I am going to die," she assured herself. "Maybe something, or some energy within me, is dying and they are making me take notice of some phase of my life. I believe in signs and so I don't take this lightly. . . . So I reluctantly thank you vultures for inviting me to reflect upon all facets of my life and connect with this death energy."

Two mornings later, while again sitting on the porch, she saw a dark shadow in the pasture by the lake. Investigating, she saw that it was the skeleton of an opossum—oddly, just a few inches from where she had found her dead cat's body the week before. At the same moment she saw a couple of dead fish floating along the water's edge. This was a first; never before had she seen dead fish in this pure, spring-fed lake.

Wanting to inspect the fish for clues of their death, she climbed a fence to remove them from the water. As she put her foot onto a sand bar, it kept going; she was being sucked down into the quicksand-like mud. Within seconds she was up to her waist, then up to her shoulders. "This is it," she thought. Every time she moved a hair, she sank a little deeper. Then she noticed a fence post she might reach, and, without moving her lower body she grabbed it. Slowly and methodically, she pulled herself out of the muck. When she fell breathless onto the bank, she was covered with mud from her toes to her chin.

This was the exact place the vultures were perched two days earlier, and three feet from where the other animals had been eaten the past week. "I was pretty freaked out for a few moments," she said. "Were the vultures the premonition of my own possible demise? Are we all sent premonitions of impending events, and maybe we are too busy in our chaotic lives to see the clues?"

Her husband was shaken by the event. He kept saying, "What if that post had not been there for you to grab? What if it would have sucked you down a few more inches? No one would have ever found your body."

Were the dead pets, a dead horse, a dead wild animal, dead fish, and vultures symbolic warnings of her own demise? They indeed stirred premonitions that she might die, and she came within inches of doing so. If she had taken the warnings—if that was what they were—more seriously, would she have avoided her near-fatal experience?

Dr. Hall's experience is a showcase of key features of premonitions—their symbolic nature and their frequent connection with life-threatening future events. Her experience suggests one of the most convincing reasons premonitions may have evolved: those humans who possessed this sense might have had a survival advantage over those who did not.

WHY ARE PREMONITIONS NOT MORE ACCURATE?

One of the linchpins of quantum physics is the uncertainty principle, elaborated in the early twentieth century by legendary physicist Werner Heisenberg. According to this venerable rule, it is impossible to determine both the position and momentum of a subatomic particle at the same time. Our knowledge of the attributes of a particle is fundamentally limited. When we focus on a particle's position, we distort its momentum, and when we focus on momentum, we cannot fix its position. Our knowledge is partial, and there is apparently no way around this barrier.

This situation bears a striking resemblance to premonitions. In one example after another, people may be stunningly accurate about the "what" of the event, but they can't come up with the "where" and the "when" of it. So when people report detailed images of impending disasters, as they did before the terrible events of Aberfan and September 11, but fail to specify the location and date of the happening, they may be demonstrating not flawed talents but a principle that penetrates much foreknowledge just as uncertainty permeates the world of atoms.

But if premonitions confer a survival advantage on those who have them, why should they be fragmentary? Why would they not fully reveal themselves? The partial nature of premonitions is surely a reason large numbers of people still succumb to disaster.

But the situation is not so simple. It's not easy to determine if premonitions are accurate or not, because it's difficult to distinguish between a premonition that arrives incomplete and one that is incompletely remembered. Premonitions commonly arrive in dreams, which are notoriously soon forgotten. Moreover, the premonition interval—the time that elapses between the premonition and its fulfillment—can be days or weeks. The longer the delay, the greater the chance the premonition may be misremembered. In many of the dream premonitions of 9/11 that have surfaced, individuals forgot they'd dreamed of the disaster until the events of the day jogged their memory. It would be difficult if not impossible for those individuals to know if they'd recalled everything exactly as they'd dreamed it, unless they'd written down the dream on awakening, or promptly revealed it to a friend.

Even if premonitions were accurate in every detail, this does not mean people would necessarily act on them. To have a premonition is not always to heed it. People often have hunches or suspicions they don't act on, later wishing they'd done so.

In the early morning hours of September 13, 2008, Hurricane Ike slammed into Galveston Island off the Texas coast. In spite of warnings of certain death if they stayed, many refused to evacuate. A week later, fifty-six bodies were pulled from the wreckage and hundreds of people remained missing. If individuals refuse to heed such clear warnings about a physically demonstrable hurricane bearing down on them, it's not surprising they'd snub a premonition.

Premonitions of a dreadful event can be swamped simply by lethargy. It can be more comfortable to persist in ruts, habits, and routines than run the risk of embarrassment if one's intuition doesn't pan out. In addition, there can be secondary gains to ignoring premonitions. For those individuals who decided to ride out Hurricane Ike, it might have added to their self-image as a tough Texan—if they survived.

What if there were no uncertainty in premonitions? What if they were infallible? If we could see the future with unfailing accuracy, life as we know it would be upended.

If warmongers knew with complete certainty they would be victorious, they would plunge ahead without any restraint whatsoever. If individuals knew for certain the future swings of the stock market, the entire system would be wrecked, because everyone would bet everything on a sure thing and withdraw funds from weaker companies, dooming them. Sporting events, whose appeal rests largely on the fact that we don't know their outcome, would cease to fascinate us; they might become extinct because of lack of interest. Species would vanish if hunters, trappers, and fishermen knew ahead of time where their prey was located. Human affairs would be transformed. Why assiduously court your lover if you know her decision in advance? Crime would become epidemic, since criminals would only commit crimes they knew would go undetected. For thousands of reasons, perfect precognition would be a disaster. We forget that human affairs require a high degree of uncertainty, messiness, and chaos to function smoothly. Yes, we are an oxymoronic bunch.

For all we know, nature may have experimented with totally accurate future knowing in the past, and subsequently "decided" it was better to gear us down to our present state of imprecision. Tadeusz Kawecki, an evolutionary biologist at the University of Fribourg in Switzerland, suggests that learning in general may have an evolutionary cost. In experiments with fruit flies, he found that the insects that learned the fastest died sooner than their slow-learning peers. "If it's so great to be smart, why have most animals remained dumb?" he asks. Just so, if totally accurate foreknowledge is an advantage, why have premonitions remained imperfect? Limited premonitions, it seems, may be a blessing in disguise. They keep the "ecosystem" in balance.

THE REPRESSION EFFECT

No event in modern times has evoked more talk of premonitions than the sinking of the mighty RMS *Titanic* on her maiden voyage in the early morning hours of April 15, 1912. The ship was considered the highest achievement of naval architecture and technical innovation, and was declared "practically unsinkable" by *The Shipbuilder* magazine. Who would have imagined it would carry 1,523 souls to their deaths?

The answer, it turned out, was lots of people. Hundreds of vivid dreams, hunches, forebodings, intuitions, and visions were reported from both sides of the Atlantic. Ian Stevenson, the late emeritus professor of psychiatry at the University of Virginia, collected many of them, eventually corroborating nineteen reports from England, America, Canada, and Brazil that occurred within two weeks prior to the tragedy.

Some left little to the imagination. One person who held passage dreamed twice that the *Titanic* was upside down in the ocean, with crew and passengers thrashing about in the water. Although his dreams did not prompt him to cancel, he eventually did so because of a change of business plans.

Not everyone disregarded their instincts. Among those holding passage who cancelled at the last minute was financier John Pierpont Morgan, one of the wealthiest men in the world. Morgan was said to be superstitious about sailing on a ship's maiden voyage. George W. Vanderbilt II, of the famous Vanderbilt family, also cancelled because of a premonition experienced by Mrs. Vanderbilt's mother. The ship's second engineer, Colin MacDonald, had a premonition that disaster lay ahead and opted to avoid the cruise. The wife of Luigi Gatti, manager of the ship's elegant A la Carte Restaurant, which passengers called The Ritz, also had a premonition that something was amiss and warned her husband not to sail, but he ignored her and perished with the ship. Others may have skedaddled for unconscious reasons. A group of twenty-two stokers was late and the captain made the decision to sail without them, which saved them from a watery grave.

Psi researcher Dean Radin has shed light on why people frequently don't heed premonitions of disaster. He designed a suite of Web-based games in September 2000 that allows individuals to test their psychic abilities online. One of these tests (or trials) assesses precognitive ability by gauging how well a user can describe a photo that the computer will select *after* the individual enters a description of the upcoming image. The user enters words or checks boxes to describe the future image—whether it will be an indoor or outdoor scene, whether it will feature people, water, and a host of other traits. The images are generally calming—there are no fires, explosions, or airplane crashes.

Radin was curious whether premonitions of September 11 might have spontaneously intruded into people's attempts to describe upcoming images, so he evaluated the words people used to predict the images that would randomly appear from September 9 through the morning of September 11, 2001, just prior to the terrorist attacks. Around 900 trials and over 2,500 words accumulated over this period. One person commented:

> airliner (seen from left-rear) against stormy cloud backdrop, flashes of streaky cloud, ovoids, two persons
>
> firstly a dragonfly? Then a log [or] branch suggestive of Everglades, then a fast dynamic scene of falling between two tall buildings, past checkered patterns of windows
>
> first tall structure like an industrial chimney, then flashes of rounded

crenulated form—peacock-like headdress of American Indian woman? Then surface like volcanic ash plume or cauliflower

Another individual entered these words:

It is of something falling; it will be a chaotic scene

Another online user contributed this description:

Intense . . . too hot to handle; blasting; is the coast clear? they were checking the coast!

Another said:

White House; gone in the blink of an eye; scald; man's folly; band red; surging; palace; not easily conned; US power base; flexing muscles; surprise.

Were these premonitions of 9/11? Radin examined the data from all the online precognition trials contributed from September 2, 2000, through June 20, 2003. During this period, around twenty-five thousand people participated in nearly half a million trials. From these, he selected only those trials that included word descriptions, not checked boxes. This narrowed the data down to about a quarter million trials and 841,000 words. Then he analyzed each trial to see if it contained any of nine words or their synonyms that applied to the chaos of 9/11: *airplane, falling, explode, fire, attack, terror, disaster, pentagon,* and *smoke.* He predicted that on 9/11 there would be a surge of trials in which these words appeared. To his surprise, the curve dropped to the lowest point in three years of data collection. The closer 9/11 came, the less frequently the key words showed up. A statistical test showed that the odds against chance of obtaining scores this low, and falling on 9/11, was 3,300 to 1. "Thus," says Radin, "the data didn't just indicate that premonitions intruded into people's thoughts just prior to 9/11. Rather it suggests that, on average, such thoughts were significantly *avoided.*"

If this isn't just a coincidence—and the odds against chance suggest overwhelmingly that it isn't—what would cause it to happen? "One possibility," Radin suggests, "is that in the days before 9/11 many people began unconsciously to sense trouble brewing, but there was no context for those feelings so they were repressed." Repression, he noted, is an unconscious psychological mechanism that permits us to avoid disturbing emotions or images. "No one wants to walk around with troubling images of disasters rattling around in their heads," Radin says, "so repression is expected. Only the rare individual can avoid personally identifying the negative thoughts without repressing them, and fewer still are willing to publicly admit such thoughts. This may be why verified premonitions of major disasters that are recorded before the fact are relatively rare."

In the video issued by Osama bin Laden following September 11, many of the terrorists revealed they had dreams and visions prior to the attacks that were highly suggestive of them, even though these individuals were kept in the dark about the specific nature of what was to happen until the very last minute. Fearing that these terrorists would discuss their premonitions publicly and expose his attack plan, bin Laden told the terrorists to disregard their premonitions. Following Radin's logic, perhaps the reason the terrorists consciously acknowledged their premonitions, and Radin's Web users did not, is that the terrorists had a context that permitted the fiery images to make sense: they were planning to kill as many Americans as they could; they *wanted* the chaos to happen.

This may help explain why many passengers on the *Titanic* who had premonitions of doom disregarded them. They did not want such an event to occur, and the prevailing belief that the ship was unsinkable erased any context in which sinking *could* happen.

Radin went further and asked whether denial is specific to premonitions of disaster, or whether it affects premonitions in general. From August 2000 through June 2004, people entered a whopping seventeen million trials on his online, precognitive card-guessing test. When he analyzed the results, he discovered a huge decrease in performance just prior to September 11, as mentioned in Chapter Two. The odds against chance of seeing a drop that deep, that close to 9/11, was 2,700 to 1. What are the odds that two tests— the photo description test and the card-guessing experiment—would show the same effect prior to 9/11? Radin calculated that the odds against chance were 1.8 million to 1, making coincidence highly unlikely.

All told, this evidence strongly suggests that people unconsciously repress premonitions of a looming disaster, and that the repression extends to premonitions in general.

People often tell me they want to be able to have premonitions of upcoming calamities, and that the more vivid the warnings are, the better. For some people this may be true. But Radin's work suggests that this view is often naive. His findings indicate that a glimpse of the future can scare us witless, and cause us to stick our heads in the sand about what we've envisioned.

Repressing premonitions may be a learned behavior that has been passed down through generations. In the Western world not so long ago, if premonitions were not hidden the consequences could be lethal.

Scotland's most celebrated witch trial was that of the North Berwick witches from 1590 to 1592. Seventy persons were implicated, of whom some were tortured into confessing and were burned alive. The "second sight"—knowing things beyond the reach of the physical senses before they happened—was considered particularly damning in the accused.

King James, of Bible-translation fame, was involved in the Berwick trials. In the spring of 1590, while returning to Scotland with his new wife, Anne, daughter of the King of Denmark-Norway, his royal fleet encountered fierce storms. One of the admirals felt the storms were the work of Danish witches. Suspects were rounded up. They confessed under torture that they had sent devils to climb up the keel of Anne's ship. James, who would later be called "the wisest fool in Christendom," decided to set up his own tribunal in Scotland. By autumn Scotland was aflame with witch hysteria.

One of the accused was Agnes Sampson, whom James examined personally at his palace. Although she was considered to have healing powers and served her community as a midwife, this did not save her. She was fastened to the wall of her cell by a witch's bridle, an iron instrument with four sharp prongs that was forced into her mouth, two prongs pressing against her tongue and the other two against her cheeks. She was not permitted to sleep and was tossed around with a rope around her head, "being a paine most grievous." After these and other ordeals and the discovery of the Devil's mark on her "privities," she confessed to all fifty-three indictments against her. On January 28, 1590, she was garotted, then burned to ashes. Her family was assessed the cost of her trial, which came to a little over £6.

King James felt he was doing God's work when he published his lengthy work *Daemonologie* seven years later in Edinburgh, a document that exemplifies the convoluted intellectual rationalizations of the witch hunts. Scotland was second only to Germany in the barbarity and number of its witch trials, with one estimate of between three thousand and four thousand witches executed overall. A confession was not required for burning; one's general reputation was considered sufficient proof for indictment and execution. Once an indictment was drawn up, the accused was not allowed to dispute its accuracy. Execution generally took the form of burning. The costs of the trial and execution were assessed to the victim or her family. Fear of witches died hard in Scotland. In 1727 Janet Horne was the last person to be burned as a witch.

What prompted such visceral fear and horrific recrimination toward individuals believed capable of premonitions and prophetic visions? Then, as now, the content of these visions was frequently of crop failures, natural disasters, illness, and death. This dire content could pose problems for the seer, for seeing a disaster was often equated with causing it.

One of the earliest precognitive dreams on record deals with disaster, in the form of crop failure and famine. As recorded in Genesis 41, Pharaoh had two dreams. In one, seven healthy fat cows were envisioned, followed by seven lean ones. The ugly lean cows then devoured the healthy ones. In a second dream, Pharaoh saw seven healthy ears of grain growing on one stalk, then a stalk with seven thin, weather-beaten ears. The thin ears of grain swallowed up the full healthy ears. None of the Egyptian sages could decipher the dream's meaning. Joseph, who had a reputation as a dream interpreter, clarified everything. The cows and grain had to do with alternating periods of plenty and famine, he said. During the first seven years of abundance, the country should harvest and store as much grain as possible, so they could endure the ensuing seven years of famine. Pharaoh was pleased, and Joseph became famous. Others, like the Berwick witches, have not been as lucky.

Because there has often been a price to be paid for announcing morbid premonitions, perhaps it is not surprising that so many of them are now unconscious, of which the exploding church in Beatrice, Nebraska, is an example. The social cost of premonitions may also help explain their brevity. It would be easier to repress a premonition lasting only three to five seconds, as in the presentiment experiments, than one lasting three to five hours.

EVOLUTION AND INSTINCT: STAYING AHEAD OF THE GAME

Several years ago, when psi experimentalist Richard Broughton was president of the Parapsychological Association, he gave an address at the annual convention titled "If You Want to Know How It Works, First Find Out What It's For," the "it" referring to psi. Broughton suggested that if psi in general is a human ability, then its function is probably the same as for all the other abilities with which evolution has seen fit to endow human beings: survival.

Although the premonition interval can be hours, days, or weeks, in the presentiment experiments it is typically three to five seconds. Can a three-second warning aid survival? Some say no. But how long does it really take to step out of the way of an oncoming auto that one "just knows" is headed one's way? To decide not to eat food or drink water that a hunch tells us is polluted? Decisions such as these can be made almost instantly. Pilots of jet aircraft can initiate countermeasures to missiles and swerve to avoid ground fire in split seconds. Automobile drivers can suddenly change course to avoid a road obstruction they "saw" around the bend. Instant decision making is particularly common in elite athletes. Basketball adepts can pass to where a player *will* be; great baseball hitters often know if the next pitch will be a curveball or fastball *before* it leaves the pitcher's hand. It's as if biological evolution has been generous in allotting us a mere three seconds for premonitions to unfold.

Intellectualizing about decision making eats up time. Perhaps that's why premonitions so often occur outside of our awareness. While three seconds is an eternity for reflexive, instantaneous, unconscious actions to be taken, it is not long enough for deliberation to occur. If premonitions are to aid survival, we cannot afford the luxury of thinking about them.

ENTROPY AND EMOTION

Why are premonitions of disasters, tragedies, and death so frequent?

Remote viewing pioneer Stephan A. Schwartz has taught thousands of individuals, and he finds that people are more adept at viewing certain types of images remotely than others. They are particularly good at describing targets in which some kind of energetic change is taking place. These targets demonstrate a high degree of entropy, a scientific term derived from a Greek word meaning "transformation inside." Entropy is a measure of the disorder, randomness, or chaos in a system.

During a series of remote viewing sessions that Schwartz ran in the early 1980s, one of the targets was a photograph of the USS *Enterprise*, the world's first nuclear-powered aircraft carrier. In several hundred remote-viewing sessions, this particular image was randomly selected twenty-seven times by Schwartz to be the target image, and was identified correctly by subjects twenty-three times. Many of the targets were aesthetically more compelling, yet it became obvious there was something about *Enterprise* that made her special in remote viewing.

The viewers commented again and again on the ship's nuclear reactor, even though this was not visible in the target photograph. This surprised Schwartz, who is a naval veteran who knows ships firsthand. How could civilians know this ship was nuclear-powered instead of petroleum-fueled? The viewers didn't identify the reactor as such, but they remarked over and over on the energetic transmutation that was occurring within the ship. Typical comments were, "There is a little star inside this target." Or, "Something very hot and fierce is inside this thing." Or, "It's like a sun inside a metal box."

In the hundreds of sessions, only one other target evoked similar results—a commercial solar generating station in Arizona. The solar station was a tall tower with a boxlike structure at the top, onto which a large array of mirrors on the ground focused the sun's rays, which turned water into steam. This energy transmutation captured the attention of the viewers with ease.

Nuclear physicist and consciousness researcher Edwin C. May, director of Cognitive Sciences Laboratory in Palo Alto, California, while doing research on remote viewing funded by the Pentagon, was occasionally asked to "look in" on suspected nuclear weapons-testing facilities, rocket tests or launches, or some other system requiring changes in energy. Like Schwartz, he also found that these kinds of targets seemed particularly easy for viewers to describe.

The similarity of this finding to premonitions is striking. Earlier we examined some examples of premonitions—the exploding church in Beatrice, Nebraska; the Aberfan disaster, in which a runaway mountain of coalmine refuse buried a school; and the fiery tragedies of September 11. In every one of them, dramatic sudden changes in entropy occurred as the "system" suddenly became highly disorganized, i.e., destroyed. Energy transmutation took place in each example—a gas explosion in the church, a mountainside giving way, jet fuel exploding when planes crashed into buildings, which then crumbled.

Physicist May wondered if entropy itself could be the information-carrying mechanism for successful remote viewing. To test this possibility he amassed a huge pool of target photographs and graded them according to the entropy present in the image, and how it changed spatially across the photograph. This resulted in a spatial gradient for each image, a technical term for how change moved across the face of the photo, independent of the actual nature of the entropy itself. According to his hypothesis, it should not matter if the photo was of a nuclear-powered ship, an exploding church, crashing skyscrapers, or an earthquake. The *rate* of entropy change or movement toward disorder was the crucial thing.

So far, five experiments with remote viewers have been conducted to test this idea, four by May and one by a different researcher. All five confirm May's hypothesis: the higher the entropy gradient, the better the remote viewing accuracy.

He found, too, that this correlation applied *to different parts of the picture.* People could correctly remote-view certain components of the image, and not others, depending on the entropy gradient involved.

May's discovery may help explain the "how" and the "what" of premonitions. Throughout history, *premonition* has taken on the connotation of something terrible, such as a disaster or life-threatening illness. A disaster always involves increasing disorder, disorganization, and chaos—things suddenly going from good, to bad, to worse. Thus people report premonitions of imminent automobile wrecks, earthquakes, explosions, plane crashes, sinking ships, incipient illness, or death much more frequently than pleasant things like pay raises, parking spots, or winning the lottery.

Death represents ultimate entropy for the body, and in *violent* deaths the entropic change is rapid. According to May's hypothesis, violent deaths might be expected to be a common theme in premonitions. And so they are.

Perhaps the largest deadly entropic event of the twentieth century was World War II, with its fifty million deaths and unspeakable horrors. Hile Wechsler, an Orthodox Jewish rabbi from Western Europe, seemed to foresee these events in a series of premonitory dreams. Wechsler published an anonymous account of his dreams in 1881 in a pamphlet entitled "A Word of Warning." The dreams foretold a genocidal fate for the Jewish people of western Europe. Wechsler saw that anti-Semitism would become extremely destructive, and that it would begin in Germany and march eastward across Europe to engulf most of the European states. He wrote, "One wants to destroy the Semitic element lock, stock, and barrel . . . one wants to rack and ruin the Jews so radically that their atoms will never be connected and re-synthesized." He saw that the big European powers would not save the Jews. They should rather go to Palestine, settle there, and take up agriculture. Rabbi Wechsler's dreams came true a half century later with Adolf Hitler's rise to power. They make chilling reading. They have been reprinted in *The Reluctant Prophet* by Jungian analyst James Kirsch.

In some dreams the entropic component is truly remarkable. In 1836, Robert Macnish, the Scottish author of *The Anatomy of Drunkenness,* recorded a premonitory dream of his own death that would occur a year later. In the dream, he is completely entropic: he has turned to stone. One senses entropy and disorganization virtually oozing from the pages of his book. "I dreamed that I was converted into a mighty pillar of stone," he wrote, "which reared its head in the midst of a desert, where it stood for ages, till generation after generation melted away before it. Even in this state, though unconscious of possessing any organs of sense, or being else than a mass of lifeless stone, I saw every object around—the mountains growing bald with age—the forest trees drooping in decay; and I heard whatever sounds nature is in the custom of producing, such as the thunder-peal breaking over my naked head, the winds howling past me, or the ceaseless murmur of streams. At last I also waxed old, and began to crumble into dust, while the moss and ivy accumulated upon me, and stamped me with the respect of hoar antiquity." Months later Macnish contracted typhus fever and died after a two-week illness. *Typhus* is derived from Greek words meaning "vapor" or "smoke," potent symbols of dissolution.

May's breakthrough idea may also explain why people have partially correct premonitions. In the Aberfan coal-mine disaster, many people reported the coal-mine tailings sliding into the town and the destruction of something, but they could not locate the time and place of the happening. It was the entropic aspect of the event they saw—something going from an organized stable state to chaos and disorder. Many people had premonitions of September 11 in which planes exploded after flying into something, somewhere. Again, they were identifying the energy transmutation or entropic aspect of the event.

A premonitory dream by Samuel Clemens, better known by his pen name Mark Twain, illustrates this partial, entropy-based pattern. In 1858, he and his brother, Henry, were working on steamboats on the Mississippi River. One night Sam had a terrifyingly vivid dream, in which he saw Henry's body in a casket that was balanced across two chairs. Atop the casket was a bouquet of white roses with a single red one in the middle. A few days later Sam received word that the boiler on Henry's boat had blown up, severely injuring him and killing or injuring 150 others. Sam rushed to his brother's side and sat with him during his final hours. The next morning, numb with grief, he went downstairs to the area where the bodies awaited burial. Henry's body was in a metal casket balanced across two chairs. One thing was missing: the roses. At that moment a volunteer nurse entered with a bouquet of white roses and laid them on Henry's casket. In the middle of the bouquet was a single red rose.

In Twain's dream, the dominant image is not the accident itself, but the death of his beloved brother. One might think that, if the entropy gradient is important, Twain would have dreamed of the explosion. But for Twain, who loved his brother deeply and blamed himself for his death for the rest of his life, it was probably Henry's death itself that was most entropic, not the boiler that blew up.

During the 1970s and 1980s, experimentalist Charles Honorton, of the Psychophysical Laboratory, then at Princeton University, reported that images that evoked strong emotional responses, such as those containing violent or sexual content, were quite easy for viewers to perceive remotely. Researcher Caroline Watt, at the University of Edinburgh, found that target images that carried an emotional wallop and contained movement, novelty, and incongruity were more likely to be identified as the distant targets in remote-viewing experiments. These factors also seem important in premonitions, as in Mark Twain's precognitive dream of his brother's death, and

Rabbi Wechsler's dreams of the tragedies that would befall Europe's Jews.

The key ingredient may be *meaning*. For an individual to acquire information via premonitions, it helps if the target embodies some emotional significance and personal importance. A friend of mine who is a nut about sports has dreams of who is going to win championship games in a variety of sports. He calls these dreams his "mental movies." When I suggested these weren't genuine dream premonitions, but inferences and predictions based on his extensive knowledge of sports, he was irritated. He continues to insist that his mental movies are premonitions, preferring to believe that he possesses "the gift."

But in the premonitions we've examined so far, such as Aberfan, September 11, Beatrice, avoiding doomed trains, and knowing when one's child is in danger, more is involved than the spectacle of landslides, explosions, and demolished buildings. There is a seriousness to these instances of foreknowledge that is not conveyed by the idea of a "mental movie." Premonitions do not exist for our entertainment or amusement. They are overwhelmingly related to survival—of ourselves and of those we love.

We will never understand how these phenomena operate without making a place for their subjective side, such as the elements of caring, compassion, love, and meaning that are so often embedded in the foreknowledge itself. These personal factors distinguish premonitions from meaningless, random events, and account for why they become seared into memory. The close connection of premonitions with these human traits reveal that they are not external or foreign, but innate and integral, as we saw in our examination of first sight. To have a premonition is as natural as breathing.

Now let's examine further why we should want to invite premonitions into our lives, and how we might do so.

FOUR

WHY SHOULD WE WANT TO CULTIVATE PREMONITIONS, AND HOW DO WE DO IT?

"[R]ather than forming its experiences in the 'here and now,' consciousness may choose to sample the 'there and then.'"

—Robert G. Jahn, Ph.D., Princeton Engineering Anomalies Research Laboratory

CULTURE AND PREMONITIONS

Because most premonitions occur spontaneously and unbidden, many people believe it is impossible to purposely cultivate our ability to know the future. Premonitions and precognitive dreams, they say, are immune to our wishes and intentions. They skitter away if we focus on having them, and therefore should be left alone.

Among those interested in this question was Samuel Johnson, England's great essayist, poet, biographer, and lexicographer. In 1773 Johnson, with his biographer and boon companion James Boswell, visited the Hebrides or Western Isles of Scotland.

This breathtakingly beautiful jumble of islands remains relatively unspoiled, with unique flora and fauna. The native Gaelic language contributes to the islands' exotic charm. The Hebrides were settled early in Britain's history; the standing stones at Callanish may date to 3000 B.C.E. The first written mention of the Hebrides is by the Greek historian Diodorus Siculus in 55 B.C.E. Later, Pliny the Elder and the Egyptian astronomer Ptolemy mentioned the islands, suggesting contact with the Roman world. In the sixth century A.D, St. Columba brought Christianity to the islands and founded several churches. Later, Viking raiders dominated the islands until the Scots won a decisive battle and ultimate control in 1275.

Johnson was one of the great informavores of his day. He was fascinated by reports from the Western Isles of "the second sight," the alleged ability to know things beyond the reach of the senses. "The Second Sight," he wrote, "is an impression made either by the mind upon the eye, or by the eye upon the mind, by which things distant or future are perceived, and seen as if they were present." The islanders simply took this ability as a natural—even expected—part of life. Visions, voices, and premonitions were in the air; people were likely to be considered odd if they did *not* believe in them.

Johnson was determined to give the reports of second sight a fair hearing. He wasn't the first investigator in the Hebrides. The physician Martin Martin of the Isle of Skye had written of these matters in his treatise "Account of the Second-Sight" in his classic 1703 book *A Description of the Western Islands of Scotland.* Martin believed that the most common version was a premonition of impending death. The vision could be symbolic, such as a shroud or an empty chair. Some said the visions were made possible by the local whisky. No, said Martin; a drunk man never has second sight. Martin was diligent in his reportage; he not only set down the stories he was told, but he interviewed all the witnesses to these events, interrogating them mercilessly.

Ten years before Dr. Johnson's trip to the area the Rev. Donald MacLeod collected forty examples of second sight and published them in 1763. Most of them were premonitions of death that turned out to be true. But not all concerned fatalities. In one case, a seafarer from Skye was returning home unannounced, and decided to test his mother-in-law's reputation for second sight. He was bringing her a haunch of venison as a present, and decided to "send" the information to her. When he arrived home, she said she had despaired of his return, fearing the worst, until she had suddenly "seen" him holding something in his hand that looked like flesh.

Johnson certainly knew about Martin and MacLeod's accounts of second sight. He had planned to expand on these reports by gathering more of them, but he could not; the native islanders did not speak English and he did not speak Gaelic. He did discover, however, that everybody from the islands, "except ministers from the mainland," accepted the existence of second sight.

Johnson summarized his views in his classic 1775 work *Journey to the Western Isles of Scotland.* He concluded that second sight could not be controlled or manipulated, but was something of a blessing that was bestowed. As he explained, "This receptive faculty, for power it cannot be called, is neither voluntary nor constant. The appearances have no dependence upon choice: they cannot be summoned, detained, or recalled. The impression is sudden, and the effect is often painful. . . . By pretension to second sight, no profit was ever sought or gained. It is an involuntary effect in which neither hope nor fear are known to have any part. Those who profess to feel it do not boast of it as a privilege, nor are considered by others as advantageously distinguished. They have no temptation to feign; and their hearers have no motive to encourage imposture."

Johnson would have known that some individuals who possessed the faculty of second sight considered it not a blessing but a curse. The best-known example was Henri IV, called Henri the Great, king of France from 1589 to 1610. Henri was one of the most popular rulers in French history, much loved by his people because of his compassion and kindness. Several unsuccessful assassination attempts were made on his life during his reign, and he had the macabre premonition that he would be murdered in his coach during the coronation ceremonies for his second wife. "Oh, this cursed coronation, it will cause my death," he told his confidant Maximilien de Béthune, duc de Sully, who recorded it in his memoirs. His vision came true when François Ravaillac stabbed the king to death while he rode in his coach during the coronation.

Nevertheless, Johnson concluded that belief in second sight was irrational and basically useless, saying, "This faculty . . . is . . . without any visible reason or perceptible benefit. It is ascribed only to a people very little enlightened; and among them, for the most part, to the mean and the ignorant."

Although Johnson is to be admired for his openness toward "the Second Sight," he got it wrong on many counts. Traditional cultures the world over would find laughable his contention that these events are "commonly useless," "have no dependence upon choice," and "cannot be summoned, detained, or recalled." In many cultures people invite precognitive dreams on a nightly basis, and they recall and analyze them the following morning. Dismissing these societies as "mean and ignorant" says more about our ignorance than theirs. Yet in other ways Johnson was an accurate judge, conceding that in the end "we must be content to yield to the force of testimony" in deciding the validity of these matters.

If Johnson had traveled only 517 miles to the northwest from the Outer Hebrides, he would have reached a country that probably would have demolished nearly all his conclusions. Here he would have reached the easternmost tip of Iceland, a country in which the great majority believes in "psychic dreams." Since the island was permanently settled in the ninth century, dreams have abounded in its sagas, literature, biographies, letters, articles, books, and folklore. A Gallup Poll in 2003 of twelve hundred Icelanders aged eighteen to eighty-five found that 72 percent found meaning in their dreams. Around 70 percent believed that dream precognition is real, and more than 40 percent said they'd personally had precognitive dreams. Interestingly, more than half said they dream in color. One of the first psychological research studies ever conducted in Iceland, published in 1915, was about precognitive dreams. Books on dreams and dream interpretation have been published continually for decades and are read widely. Academic philosophy and psychology in Iceland are closely linked to the study of dreams. "Icelanders always were and still are great dreamers!" proclaims the Skuggsjá Dream Center in Akureyri, in northeast Iceland.

One of the most highly esteemed researchers in the international psi community is Professor Erlendur Haraldsson of the University of Iceland. Professor Haraldsson has tracked the psychic experiences of Icelanders for three decades. In 1974 he found that nearly 40 percent of his countrymen said they'd experienced psychic dreams; nearly 90 percent believed precognition in dreams is possible, likely, or certain; and only 3 percent considered them unlikely or impossible. These findings have remained consistent over the years.

One of the enduring Icelandic legends in modern times is that of "Dreaming Joe," a farmer and shepherd who was famous for his ability to see in his dreams the location of lost or stolen property and ships at sea.

Iceland is a fishing nation, so premonitions, not surprisingly, often involve fish. "Dreaming the fish" is part of the mystique of the Icelandic skipper, who is often a heroic, legendary figure. Generally known to his crew as The Man, the skipper employs any means that work to find fish. This often involves precognitive dreams. Eggert Gíslason, who claimed the ability to see the future in dreams since childhood, was a popular skipper because of his reputation for finding fish when others could not. On his very first outing, he dreamed the boat's course and saw the compass needle. On waking, he set the exact course and was rewarded with a bountiful catch. He encouraged his entire crew to participate in dreaming the fish. One season, one of Eggert's crew dreamed they found the body of a giant cow that was spangled with bright, shining fish scales, near a village in the east. Although most of the fishing fleet was heading west, Eggert honored the dream and sailed east. His crew landed a huge catch.

Sailors in Iceland's coast guard have made use of precognitive dreams. Capt. Eiríkur Kristófersson, of the coast guard cutter *Thor,* dreamed that an unfamiliar man gave him fifteen human jawbones that had been weathered for a long time. The horrified captain threw them back at the man. He interpreted the dream as a foreboding of something "very dark and bad" and imminent danger. Putting out to sea, the captain was haunted by the dream. He prayed to be spared a disaster that might claim fifteen lives. Believing danger was at hand, the crew prepared for calamity. Soon the dream began to play out. A terrible storm arose and wrecked the *Thor,* but fifteen men boarded the lifeboats in heaving seas and landed safely on shore.

Iceland is not the only country that can serve as a corrective to Johnson's premature and condescending conclusions. Haraldsson's international surveys show that two other Western countries compare almost equally with Iceland in the percentage of the population reporting psi experiences: Italy and the United States.

WHY WE WANT TO CULTIVATE PREMONITIONS

Throughout history people have coveted precognitive abilities for both honorable and ignoble reasons. Often they've wished to exert power over others by manipulating and controlling them. *Why do you want to cultivate premonitions?* If you cannot provide an honorable, ethical reason, it is best that you not proceed.

I'll elaborate on my reasons. I did not choose the few precognitive events I've experienced; they chose me. They did not happen through any deliberate attempt on my part to experience them. They seemed to be a message about how the world works. They came unbidden, as if a blessing or a grace.

This happens to a great many people because, I believe, human beings are naturally endowed with the capacity for premonitions. This is simply how our consciousness operates normally, before we learn to narrow its function because of social pressures and expectations. Premonitions are our birthright. We know this not only from the oral and written records of millennia past, but also from the presentiment experiments that recently have been conducted and replicated by scientists around the world. As a result,

we now know that if we choose to cultivate premonitions we are not struggling to acquire a foreign ability, but one that is innate and natural. We are
trying to recover who we are, not to become something we are not. We are at-
tempting to become better knowers, as some people try to become better
musicians, artists, or athletes.

Even so, this side of the psyche can be a minefield and is not for everyone. "Humankind cannot stand very much reality," T. S. Eliot reminded us.
That goes too for premonitions. There's a reason some people's minds are
narrowed so as to admit only a fraction of the information that is available to
us. Too much knowledge can overwhelm. It can be disconcerting, frightening, or threatening to glimpse the future or to share thoughts with someone
at a distance. This is not a criticism; we all differ in our tolerance for reality,
and it is no disgrace to admit our limitations. People's differences should be
respected. As the aphorism has it, "The psychotic drowns in the same water
in which the mystic swims." And you don't have to be psychotic to experience psychological difficulties as you swim in the premonition sea.

If you decide to invite premonitions into your life, I urge thoughtful-
ness in how you go about doing so. You may encounter monstrous figures
as did a young woman from Cincinnati, Ohio. While her husband was out
of town on a business trip, she looked out the window and saw, as if in a
daze, a sinister vision of the Grim Reaper running madly across her lawn.
It was gone in a flash, but was so vivid and menacing it left her shaken,
cold, and terrified, and with the certainty that something horrible had happened.

She expected her husband to return by three P.M., but he did not arrive.
She was distraught and pacing the floor when the phone rang at seven. The
hospital was calling to tell her that her husband was injured and unconscious.
At approximately the same time she saw the Grim Reaper, his car had been
hit by another vehicle traveling at high speed, crushing him against the
windshield. Fortunately, her husband survived.

I don't want to leave the impression that all the characters that inhabit
the nocturnal landscape are monstrous. Some are benevolent and divine,
even when they herald death—as the following case, though not a premonition, reveals.

A Minnesota woman who was hospitalized for major surgery heard a patient groaning and crying continually in the room across the hall. Later that

night she awoke and saw the door to the room open. As she watched, the figure of Christ emerged from the room, dressed in white, flowing robes. He walked slowly and silently to the woman's bedside. Smiling, he said, "I have come for him. Everything is all right." Then he left, closing the door behind him. Her bedside clock said 2:40 A.M.

When her nurse entered her room the next morning, the woman said, "The man across the hall died last night, didn't he?"

"Yes," the nurse answered. "But how did you know?"

She told the nurse of the night's events. When pressed, the nurse volunteered that the patient had died at 2:40 A.M.

PERSONALITY AND TEMPERAMENT

The computer-based presentiment experiments of Dean Radin involving the viewing of calm or violent images suggest that perhaps everyone has a built-in capacity to sense the future, although some are more adept than others. What sort of person is best cut out for premonitions?

One approach to this question is through the Myers-Briggs Type Indicator (MBTI), a questionnaire that probes psychological patterns.

The MBTI is based on the theories of psychologist Carl G. Jung in his 1921 book *Psychological Types*. The "Myers-Briggs" is said to be the most frequently used psychometric test in the western world. Its primary use is in identifying general trends in an individual's personality that might indicate the occupations for which they might be suited. Indeed, the originators of the test, Katharine Cook Briggs and her daughter Isabel Briggs Myers, developed it during World War II to help women who were entering industrial jobs for the first time find the sort of wartime tasks in which they would be "most comfortable and effective."

Research using the MBTI has shown that intuition and extroversion correlate with psi abilities in general. As you read about these factors below, the natural tendency is to ask yourself how well you measure up to them. That's fine, but bear in mind that the MBTI is not definitive. No personality test can put you under the microscope and tell you how well you have integrated all the known premonition-prone factors into your life, such as meaning, transcendence, a sense of unity with others, and a tolerance for chaos, mystery, complexity, and ambiguity, to mention only a few. None of these factors is absolute; all of them can be shaped and influenced by our behaviors, choices, beliefs, and even the company we keep.

No matter what your MBTI profile is, cultivating premonition-promoting qualities is the business of a lifetime. Essential to this task is a discipline or practice that helps us be present in each moment, pay attention, and notice the minute happenings of our existence. For some, this may involve a discipline that emphasizes spirituality, meditation, prayer, reverie, silence, or solitude. Immersion in art, music, or nature may fill this need for others. Some may prefer a more robust engagement with the world, as in dedication to charity or involvement in the helping professions. As many wisdom traditions tell us, there is more than one path up the mountain. The lesson is that the qualities that make one premonition-prone are not off-the-shelf, on-demand items. They come through invitation, discipline, and practice.

Now to some of the main factors that make us premonition-prone.

If you'd like to read further about the following characteristics and the research documenting them, I recommend a scholarly volume already mentioned in the Introduction: *Varieties of Anomalous Experience: Examining the Scientific Evidence* by researchers Etzel Cardeña, Steven Jay Lynn, and Stanley Krippner, and *Parapsychology: The Controversial Science* by researcher Richard Broughton.

Absorption. People who are premonition-prone tend to be comfortable with fantasy and the world of the imagination. A premonition, after all, is a what-if, a maybe, that lies in the future and has not yet happened. The imagination is required to entertain its possibility. The ability to fantasize is related to what psychologists refer to as absorption, the capacity to become totally engrossed in what one is doing. During absorption one's sense of self diminishes and one becomes identified with the task at hand. Boundaries between self and other soften, and the distinctions between past, present, and future recede. The flow of time gives way to a sense of an all-at-once, timeless now. In this state of awareness, there is nothing particularly odd about a premonition, because "pre" ceases to have meaning.

Belief in the transcendent. The transcendent may be conceived as a supreme being or as a vaguely defined otherness that is not connected with the idea of deity. But however conceived, a sense of the transcendent involves a certainty that the here-and-now does not constitute all of reality; there is something more than the mundane, everyday, see-touch-feel world. This belief suggests a greater wisdom or intelligence from which premonitions might arise.

A sense of the unity of all life. Foreknowledge often involves the certainty that something dreadful is about to happen to another person or group of individuals—an impending plane crash, earthquake, tsunami, or other disaster. Often these warnings involve not humans, but animals or some other life form. Sometimes the fate of an ecosystem or the earth itself is the object of concern. Individuals who sense their connectedness with others or to nature do not find it strange that this information might enter their awareness, because they do not consider their separation from "the other" to be fundamental.

Compassion and empathy. These traits are associated with premonitions for the same reason that a sense of connectedness with others keeps company with foreknowledge.

Intuition. Individuals who are highly intuitive are premonition-prone. They seem to know things instinctively, without having to filter them through reason and analysis. They are comfortable with the possibility of spontaneous, innate knowing. They easily tolerate ambiguity and the unknown. When premonitions emerge suddenly and unannounced, they do not resist them out of hand, but examine them with a sense of openness.

Comfort with chaos and disorder. People who are premonition-prone typically have a high tolerance for capricious, unexpected, and unpredictable patterns in life, a trait that is also typical of highly creative poets, musicians, and artists. Some actually court disorder as a way of experiencing unusual and inspiring insights. This means that their need for control is relaxed; they "go with the flow."

External locus of control. Those who shy away from premonitions and other psi-type occurrences tend to believe that they can control what happens in their lives. They shape events, events don't shape them; choice, responsibility, and control depend overwhelmingly on factors inside themselves. Psychologists call this attitude an internal locus of control. In contrast, those who honor premonitions tend toward an external locus of control. They don't sense the need always to be in charge. Compared to the "instrinsics," their counterparts, they are more likely to trust the workings of the world and the inherent goodness of others. They see themselves as part of a web of relationships that has no end, in which they are inextricably linked with all other persons and things in the world. While they accept responsibility for their actions and choices, they recognize that a complex array of factors always influences these decisions. As such, they place less emphasis on the notion of the rugged individual than do those with an internal locus of control.

Meaning. Premonition-prone individuals typically find meaning in life-happenings. Events, no matter how minor, are seen to represent and symbolize something; they have a significance that extends beyond the event itself. By paying attention they may comprehend patterns previously unseen, thereby adding depth and richness to life.

Interest and positivity. Premonition-prone persons aren't casual bystanders waiting to be clobbered by an experience of future knowing. They expect such events to occur simply because this, they believe, is how the world works. They tend toward trust, optimism, and positivity because they sense that the world, on the whole, is benevolent.

Respect for the unconscious. Those individuals who are most likely to experience premonitions honor the contributions of their unconscious mind to their mental life. They cultivate opportunities for the unconscious to manifest, as in dreams and reverie, or in activities such as hiking, painting, needlework, gardening—any activity in which the rational mind is parked in neutral with the motor turned off. This does not mean that premonition-prone persons are anti-intellectual. These individuals do not defy reason, but they complement it with activities that deepen and expand their range of knowing.

Personality type. Premonitions occur to every type of personality that has ever been described. But individuals who are especially premonition-prone are those having intuitive feeling (NF) personality types on the MBTI. As psychologist David Keirsey puts it, NF individuals aspire "to transcend the material world (and thus gain insight into the essence of things), to transcend the senses (and thus gain knowledge of the soul), to transcend the ego (and thus feel united with all creation), [and] to transcend even time (and thus feel the force of past lives and prophecies)."

Common sense. Premonition-prone individuals employ common sense especially in remembering premonitions. Many premonitions are fleeting and they often occur in dreams, which may not be remembered. Thus many individuals adopt the common-sense practice of taking pen and paper to bed to record their dreams immediately on waking, before the dream fades and becomes irretrievable.

Again, a word of caution. Even though certain personality patterns correlate with psi performance and premonitions, we should take personality tests with a grain of salt.

There are times in my life when I have identified with various Myers-Briggs combinations. Some days I feel so roaringly extroverted I can take on the world; on other mornings I feel so introverted I want to retreat to my study and never emerge. Which personality am I? My answer is: both.

The MBTI is a snapshot in time. But we're not frozen creatures; we're capable of growth, change, and flexibility. I've known people who forgot this. After taking the MBTI they became so intrigued with their personality pattern that they became slaves to it. They conformed to their MBTI pattern; they let their pattern live them. So let's use personality inventories as a rough guide, realizing they aren't the final word on who we are.

And even if we possess all the above twelve personality traits, that doesn't mean we can call up premonitions on demand, like songs in a jukebox. Premonitions require a way of relaxing into the world, in which we rely more on ways of *being* than on ways of *doing*.

Though not specifically about premonitions, a charming example of the being/doing relationship that favors them is related by the sinologist Richard Wilhelm. Wilhelm translated many Chinese philosophical texts into German, such as the *I Ching* and *The Secret of the Golden Flower*, which were subsequently translated into the major languages of the world.

Wilhelm was once in a remote Chinese village that was suffering from a severe drought. The villagers had invoked every kind of prayer for rain, but nothing worked. In desperation they sent for a well-known rainmaker who lived in a distant area. Wilhelm was on hand when the rainmaker, a wizened old man, arrived in a covered cart. He alighted, sniffed the air with disdain, then asked for a cottage on the village outskirts. He gave instructions not to be disturbed, and that his food was to be left outside his door. Nobody saw or heard anything of him for three days. Then the villagers awoke to a downpour of rain mixed with snow, which was unheard of for that time of year.

Wilhelm was greatly impressed. He approached the old man, who was no longer in seclusion. "So you can make it rain?" he probed. Of course he could not, the old man scoffed. "But there was the most persistent drought until you came," Wilhelm objected, "and then—within three days—it rains?" "Oh," the old man responded, "that was something quite different. You see, I come from a region where everything is in order, it rains when it should and is fine when that is needed, and the people also are in order and in themselves. But that was not the case with the people here, they were all out of Tao [the perfect way of nature] and out of themselves. I was at once infected when I arrived, so I had to be quite alone until I was once more in Tao and then naturally it rained!"

The villagers, the rainmaker explained, were trying to beat the climate into submission when they should have been looking inside themselves.

"Just being," as the rainmaker realized, can outperform muscular, aggressive action. The reward of inner quiet may be rain. It may be premonitions. It may be nothing at all—or everything.

THE IMPORTANCE OF BELIEF

One of the hallowed tenets of classical science is that one's beliefs should not affect the outcome of an experiment. The physical world doesn't care what we happen to think about it; it follows the so-called blind laws of nature, which are immune to our likes and dislikes.

All physicians know, however, that this view is incomplete. It may hold true in a chemistry experiment, but not in healing. One's attitude toward a particular therapy—whether you believe it will work or not—can exert a powerful influence over its effects. Everyone has heard of the placebo response, which is the positive effect that expectations, suggestions, and beliefs have on the effects of nearly all therapies. The placebo response has a flip side called the nocebo response, which is the inhibition of therapeutic effects resulting from negative attitudes or disbelief toward a particular treatment.

For more than half a century it has been known that one's beliefs affect performance in various ESP tests. The trailblazer in this research was Dr. Gertrude Schmeidler, who did the original testing on the effect of belief on psi performance in 1945 at Harvard University. She divided students into two groups: "sheep," who believed ESP effects might occur during the experiment, and the "goats," who did not believe ESP existed. She found highly significant differences between the sheep and the goats, with the sheep having an increased ability to predict events, and the goats having a decreased ability.

Between 1947 and 1993, a total of seventy-three sheep-goat experiments were done. When the results of these studies were pooled and examined in what researchers call a meta-analysis, the results showed a profoundly consistent effect of belief on the occurrence of psi. There was only one chance in a trillion that these findings were due to chance.

In 2007, researchers Kevin Walsh and Garret Moddel of the University of Colorado at Boulder examined whether the sheep-goat effect could be intentionally influenced. They recruited twelve students—six believing sheep and six nonbelieving goats—and asked them to guess the symbol on the hidden face of one hundred Zener cards, a type of card deck that has been commonly used in psi experiments since the 1940s. Before the guessing began, however, they attempted to shape the belief of the participants by providing them "fact" sheets that contained either pro-psi or anti-psi arguments.

The results showed that believers in psi, whose beliefs were supported by pro-psi fact sheets and verbal reinforcement, performed significantly better than any other group.

Walsh and Moddel concluded that innate psi ability alone cannot explain why some subjects perform better on psi tasks. Belief in psi is also highly important, and belief can be enhanced or diminished by arguments to which one is exposed.

In a related study, researchers Lance Storm and Michael A. Thalbourne attempted to change the attitude of skeptics toward psi in a computerized Zener card-guessing experiment. They found a significant correlation between success in card guessing and belief after "conversion" attempts were made to change the skeptics' minds.

This study, as well as scores of prior sheep-goat experiments, suggests valuable lessons in cultivating premonitions. Do you believe they are possible? Are they a part of the natural order, or are they prohibited by nature's laws? The answers you give to these questions may be more important than whether you have "the gift."

The influence of written and verbal arguments in these experiments suggests further questions. Do you expose yourself to pro-psi or negative-psi literature? Do you read authors who provide a comprehensive view of the thousands of psi studies, or do you confine your attention to the skeptical literature, which rarely if ever gives a balanced view of psi research? Do you associate with individuals who can provide positive reinforcement for the existence of psi, or do you surround yourself with skeptics? Anyone wishing to cultivate premonitions should consider these issues carefully.

I've made use of these lessons all my life. I have accumulated a sizeable library dealing with psi. I have immersed myself in the history of psi and the research that's been done in this field. I subscribe to psi research journals. I belong to a professional organization that is psi friendly and I attend its annual conferences. I correspond with individuals who share these interests. I hang out with psi researchers, many of whom I count as close friends. I find these friendships nourishing, and after I'm around these individuals I discover that I become more premonition-prone. I find that my dreams are more likely to be precognitive, my intuition sharpens, and new ideas come more easily.

RESPECTING CHAOS

Cultivating premonitions involves cleansing our "doors of perception," as William Blake and Aldous Huxley advocated, entering a state of awareness in which the world is accepted on its own terms. This requires paying attention to the tangle of events that arise in everyday life, without censoring, editing, or sorting our experiences according to what we think they *ought* to be.

One of the personality traits favoring premonitions is a respect for chaos and disorder. This doesn't mean that we never make our beds or clean our bathrooms; it simply means recognizing the world for what it is.

When nineteenth-century Victorians journeyed through the hinterlands of Switzerland as part of their Continental tour, they were often advised by clerics to avert their eyes. The disorderly jumble of mountains, they said, was evidence of the Devil's handiwork and were blasphemous. They were certain that God would never create such chaotic landscapes, a belief they expressed back home in their preference for manicured lawns and geometrically designed gardens. But any backpacker into wilderness knows that healthy forests and mountains are always a lovely mess, with tall, strong trees growing amid fallen, rotting ones, and rock-strewn slopes, valleys, and canyons of immense complexity.

Respecting chaos and disorder involves a tolerance for ambiguity (*ambiguous* is derived from Latin words meaning "to drive both ways"). Rejecting ambiguity can narrow people's lives and lead to intolerance. It can also extinguish premonitions.

One of my friends, who is a prolific creative writer, experienced foreknowledge on a regular basis. His wife, who was a member of a fundamentalist religious sect, considered his premonitions satanic. In the interest of domestic tranquility he stopped sharing his experiences with her, thinking this would silence her objections. She continued to berate him, however, doubly resenting him because he had now shut her out of a part of his life she knew he valued. Torn between his wife's hostility and his outside-the-box experiences, his premonitions dried up. So did his writing. One day he told me, "I'm dying." He divorced his wife "to save [his] soul," as he put it. Free to court weirdness and ambiguity in his life following his divorce, his precognitive experiences returned and his writing flourished once again.

What if we could see the world through the eyes of a lover? Couples who are deeply in love do not dwell on each other's faults; they accept each other totally and even glory in whatever imperfections may exist. Each enters the other fully; everything is shared and nothing is barred. Courting premonitions is like that.

So here's my advice for those who wish to be premonition-prone: court difference, variety, and ambiguity in your life. Relax and let go. Don't try too hard. Give up your pet ideas of how the world *should* work. Dabble in poetry; play with metaphors; shun literalism. Avoid habits, ruts, and routines. Make a place for variety, risk, novelty, playfulness, generosity, and mystery in your life. As Rumi advises, "Sell your cleverness and buy bewilderment." Don't be too attached to results, because this will lead to an attempt to control and manipulate outcomes, which is toxic to the openness and flexibility you are seeking. If you do these things, you will probably discover that the universe meets you more than halfway, perhaps with premonitions as its calling card.

One of the most universal admonitions in spiritual traditions is nonattachment—setting aside one's ego-based desires and preferences, and letting life flow and unfold on its own.

Some of my best teachers of nonattachment have been healers. They almost always describe healing not as some muscular effort to make it happen, but as a "non-effort" in which they set aside their personal desires and seek simply to be a conduit or channel for a power greater than themselves. They often don't ask for anything specific to happen, only that the best outcome prevail in any situation, without specifying what that outcome should be.

This is the "controlled accident" spoken of so frequently in the traditions of the East. It is Aldous Huxley's Law of Reversed Effort. It is "following the Tao," the way of nature. It is the willingness in Christianity to let "thy will be done." It is relying on wisdom greater than one's own.

In recent years, psi researchers have begun to explore this effortless, non-manipulative stance. Walter von Lucadou, a German physicist, psychologist, and psi experimentalist, advanced the so-called model of pragmatic information (MPI).

Lucadou, like most researchers in the field, maintained that psi experiences such as premonitions are unrestricted by space and time. They are analogous to the uncertainty principle in modern physics, he says. This rule, also known as the principle of indeterminacy, says we cannot determine the location and the velocity of a subatomic particle at the same time. The extent of our knowledge is always limited, because when we seek to define one characteristic, our probing disturbs the other value to an unpredictable degree. There is therefore a restriction on what we *can* know.

Lucadou saw an analogous situation in psi experiences. When we put them under the microscope, we hinder their appearance. This is precisely what most psi researchers have found: as psi experiences are increasingly scrutinized in the lab, they start to fade away. This doesn't mean they don't exist, or that the prior experiments documenting their existence lied, but that we have hounded them into hiding with our petulant demands.

This phenomenon is known as the decline effect, and it has been the bane of psi researchers since serious laboratory investigations began in the 1930s. Skeptics say the decline effect proves that nothing was happening in the first place. But the effect is so consistent that serious researchers consider it an intrinsic feature of psi phenomena, just as indeterminacy and uncertainty are built-in features of the subatomic world.

The implications are enough to drive researchers nuts, because it suggests that if we want a psi phenomenon to flourish we must *leave it alone.* If we insist on fencing it in with stringent lab conditions, it will skitter away like an electron. If we back off, there's evidence that the phenomenon may recover and reappear.

Decline effects should be seriously considered by anyone who wants to cultivate their capacity for premonitions. The best way to banish premonitions may be to systematize methods for having them and slavishly apply them without letup.

My paternal grandmother was precognizant. She was able to predict changes in the weather, which was a valuable asset to our farm family. She was the personification of patience. One of her favorite sayings was, "A watched pot never boils," which used to drive us grandkids to distraction. She was truly gifted at waiting on things, paying attention, noticing what most people would consider irrelevant. Never do I recall her hurrying about anything. I am certain my grandmother's patience and her premonitory abilities were related. She was the embodiment of the controlled accident. She awaited premonitions without expectation, and they came.

WHEN SHOULD WE PAY ATTENTION TO PREMONITIONS?

When premonitions are accompanied by physical symptoms, they should be listened to.

One of the most famous premonitions in modern history took place in a meeting between two titans of twentieth-century psychiatry, Sigmund Freud and Carl Gustav Jung.

In 1909 Jung visited Freud in Vienna. Although Jung had been Freud's student and confidant, things were not going smoothly; their collaboration would end three years later. One point of disagreement involved psychic phenomena; Jung was open to them and Freud was not, perhaps because he did not want his fledgling psychosexual theories further burdened by association with yet more controversy. In their meeting, Jung pressed Freud for his opinion on psychic happenings. Jung described what happened as their meeting drew to a close: "While Freud was going on this way, I had a curious sensation. It was as if my diaphragm was made of iron and was becoming red-hot—a glowing vault. And at that moment there was such a loud report in the bookcase, which stood right next to us, that we both started up in alarm, fearing the thing was going to topple over us. I said to Freud: 'There, that is an example of a so-called catalytic exteriorisation phenomenon.' 'Oh come,' he exclaimed, 'that is sheer bosh.' 'It is not, Herr Professor. And to prove my point I now predict that in a moment there will be another loud report!' Sure enough, no sooner had I said the words than the same detonation went off in the bookcase. To this day I do not know what gave me this certainty. But I knew beyond all doubt that the report would come again. Freud only stared aghast at me."

Whether we experience an extreme sensation like Jung's red-hot diaphragm, or something as minor as a headache, physical symptoms can alert us that lurking premonitions should be seriously considered.

Pay attention to premonitions if they are intrusive and insistent, as if clamoring for attention.

Again, an example from Jung's rich experiences.

During World War II, as he was returning home by train, he opened a book but could not focus on it because he became overpowered by the image of someone drowning. He attributed the mental image to the memory of an accident that had occurred while he was in military service. Try as he might, he could not put the memory out of his mind. This seemed so weird that he began to wonder if there could have been an accident. On reaching home and walking into the garden, he saw some of his grandchildren looking upset. They told him that one of the boys had fallen into the deep water in the boathouse. He could not swim and almost drowned, having been saved by his older brother.

Pay attention to a premonition when it indicates death, no matter how fuzzy the details may be.

In a dream of Jung's, he was attending a garden party and saw a woman he knew well, who lived in Basel, Switzerland. He knew instantly she was going to die. On waking, however, although he remembered the dream in detail, he could not manage to recall her name no matter how hard he tried. A few weeks later he received news that a friend of his who lived in Basel had been killed in an accident. He knew at once it was the woman in the dream who had been marked for death, but whose name he could not recall.

Jungian psychologist Jerome S. Bernstein, who has described many premonitions that preceded the tragedies of September 11, agrees. He suggests that when a dream premonition is extraordinarily vivid and deals with the body, physical health, and life or death, we would be wise to regard it as a literal message and take action, for we may not have a second chance.

Pay attention to premonitions when they seem intensely real.

This happens particularly during premonitory dreams, as opposed to waking premonitions. The dream premonition may "light up with glowing significance," as one individual put it, as if it is "realer than real." The dream can seem so important that one has the urge to record it, or to wake one's spouse or partner and share it.

In addition to these criteria, many people simply develop an intuitive feel for when to pay attention to a premonition and when to ignore it. Their sensitivities become refined and calibrated with increasing experience.

I've found, too, that reading about others' premonitions speeds the learning process, such as those described in *The Gift,* a compendium of cases from the files of the Rhine Research Center.

Moreover, there are Internet discussion groups where people can share and compare their premonitory dreams, such as the Web site of the International Association for the Study of Dreams (IASD).

ETHICS

During the 1990s I wrote three books on the role of prayer, healing intentions, and spirituality in healthcare. The final book in this trilogy was devoted to the harmful or negative uses of prayer. I never gave much thought to this issue until I came across a 1994 Gallup Poll that found that 5 percent of Americans have prayed for harm to come to others. I immediately thought, "That's only the one in twenty who will admit it." If this percentage is correct, fifteen million of us have prayed or are praying for ill to befall someone else—a virtual epidemic. If people are willing to use prayer to manipulate, control, or harm others, we can be reasonably sure that a great many individuals would use foreknowledge to do the same.

There's a tendency to attribute only lofty motivations to the use of future knowing. For instance, we'd like our physician to be capable of it, because she'd know ahead of time our diagnosis and how we are going to respond to a particular therapy. We'd want our national leaders to be precognitive as well, because future knowing could be used in diplomacy and might avert war. But what about the thief who would use his premonitory sense to know when you are going to leave home, so he could plan the perfect burglary? Or the torturer who would "just know" ahead of time how much pain he could inflict on his victim without killing him? Or the despot who knows he can commit genocide without interference from other nations?

The interplay of the lofty and debased sides of foreknowledge can be seen in premonitions surrounding September 11, where we see two types of premonitions at work—those that tended to be life-saving warnings, and those that were murderous.

About a week before September 11, an individual in New Zealand dreamed he was running through a building trying to escape something terrifying. In the dream he was surrounded by people with very dark eyes. Everything is in a state of collapse. An Arab man came toward him and sliced his finger slowly and deliberately with a cardboard-box cutter. It was a senselessly cruel and unexpected act. The dreamer awoke uncharacteristically early on September 11, turned on the radio to hear the news, and was stunned.

On July 29, a man in Michigan dreamed an earthquake hit New York City. He was watching Katie Couric on the *Today* show doing a remote hook-up from a television truck. She was talking about ten thousand people dying in a building, which the dreamer knew was either the Empire State Building or the World Trade Center. He knew the quake was devastating because Couric could barely control her emotions. In the background were huge open spaces where tall skyscrapers once stood. One building still standing had smoke billowing from all its broken windows.

You can read hundreds of similar dreams that are now posted on the more than 18 million Web sites devoted to "dreams of September 11." Most cluster in the days immediately preceding September 11. Some are chillingly reminiscent of actual events. They made no difference in the course of events; they were considered "just dreams."

We may not have taken precognitive dreams of 9/11 seriously, but our enemies did.

Three months after the carnage, on December 13, 2001, the U.S. Department of Defense released the transcript of a one-hour videotape of Osama bin Laden talking with others about the attacks. In one segment, bin Laden and his lieutenants are speaking with a group of individuals in a guesthouse in Qandahar, Afghanistan. The conversation turns to dreams and visions.

Bin Laden says, "Abu Al-Hasan . . . told me a year ago: 'I saw in a dream, we were playing a soccer game against the Americans. When our team showed up in the field, they were all pilots! . . . So I wondered if that was a soccer game or a pilot game? Our players were pilots.' He [Abu Al-Hasan] didn't know anything about the operation until he heard it on the radio. He said the game went on and we defeated them. That was a good omen for us."

An unidentified man says off camera, "Abd al-Rahman . . . said he saw a vision, before the operation, a plane crashed into a tall building. He knew nothing about it."

An unidentified shaykh adds, "The plane that he saw crashing into the building was seen before by more than one person. One of the good religious people has left everything and come here. He told me, 'I saw a vision, I was in a huge plane, long and wide. I was carrying it on my shoulders and I walked from the road to the desert for half a kilometer. I was dragging the plane.' I listened to him and I prayed to Allah to help him." The shaykh continues, "Another person told me that last year he saw . . . '[P]eople who left for jihad . . . and they found themselves in . . . Washington and New York.' He told me the plane hit the building. That was last year. . . . I have another man . . . my god . . . he said and swore by Allah that his wife had seen the incident a week earlier. She saw the plane crashing into a building . . . that was unbelievable, my god."

Bin Laden then describes his concerns that the terrorists might compromise the September 11 operations by talking about their dreams and visions, and how he took measures to prevent those potential leaks. As he explains, "The brothers, who conducted the operation, all they knew was that they have a martyrdom operation and we asked each of them to go to America but they didn't know anything about the operation, not even one letter. But they were trained and we did not reveal the operation to them until they are there and just before they boarded the planes. . . . We were at a camp of one of the brother's guards in Qandahar. This brother belonged to the majority of the [9/11 terrorist] group. He came close and told me that he saw, in a dream, a tall building in America, and in the same dream he saw Mukhtar teaching them how to play karate. At that point, I was worried that maybe the secret would be revealed if everyone starts seeing it in their dream. So I closed the subject. I told him if he sees another dream, not to tell anybody, because people will be upset with him."

Talk of premonitions continues on the videotape, as another person describes his dream about two planes hitting a big building. There is a sort of childish excitement in the taped conversations. Everyone is eager to tell his particular dream. Why?

Sigmund Freud said, in *The Interpretation of Dreams,* that "writers of antiquity who preceded Aristotle did not regard the dream as a product of the dreaming psyche, but as an inspiration of divine origin." Just so, if the terrorists can establish the connection of their actions with dreams, this will mean that Allah is on their side. They are therefore not crass murderers, but jihadist warriors situated in the glorious march of Islamic history. Their dreams establish that they are not acting on their own, but following divine orders. Thus bin Laden says, "I was *ordered* to fight the people until they say there is no God but Allah and his prophet Muhammad [emphasis added]."

Many individuals have a rose-colored view of premonitions. They believe they are always beneficent, warning people of approaching danger or incipient health problems. People who hold this view have difficulty accepting the fact that premonitions may aid terrorists, murderers, and despots.

It is easy to make a case for a sunny upbeat view of premonitions. Educator Alfred S. Alschuler has assembled 150 significant individuals in history who heard voices that provided healing, worthy information, and inspiration. They include persons such as Martin Luther, Saint Teresa, and Winston Churchill.

Churchill's experiences are typical. During World War II, his life was likely saved when he heard an inner voice telling him to sit on the opposite side of his staff car instead of the one to which he was accustomed. After driving a few blocks, a bomb landed near the car—on the side the voice had told him to avoid. On another occasion during the London Blitz, Churchill had a premonition, interrupted dinner, and sent his kitchen staff down to the bomb shelter. Minutes later a bomb struck the house, demolishing the kitchen.

But, as the bin Laden video shows, premonitions are not limited to the good guys. During World War I, a voice told a young Adolf Hitler to move down a trench just before a shell exploded, killing everyone in the group where he had been sitting. If Hitler's premonition had not occurred, the course of the twentieth century might have been significantly altered.

Little attention has been devoted to the ethical issues surrounding the intentional uses of future knowing. This must change. Focusing only on the bright side of foreknowledge is like recognizing the positive actions of a medication while ignoring its potentially lethal side effects.

As we've seen, research studies in the financial markets strongly suggest that using premonitions to make money doesn't work when greed and selfishness get the upper hand. In the field of remote viewing, which contains a strong element of future knowing, protocols seem to work best when they are used for a noble purpose. Perhaps there is an intrinsic factor in future knowing that limits negative applications.

We may be seeing this limitation being played out on a national scale. As I write, credit markets, lending institutions, and banks are failing in the United States and many stocks are in free fall. Analysts are calling this the most colossal financial crisis since the Great Depression. Lawmakers are meeting around the clock to come up with a rescue plan for Wall Street. While no one has a completely satisfactory explanation for why this meltdown happened, the most common cause being offered is greed.

America's investment markets themselves are a massive, national exercise in future knowing. Highly successful investment gurus are known for their uncanny intuition, which is the socially acceptable term for the ability to see the future. The very name, the "futures" market, is an indirect acknowledgment of the role of future knowing in the investment world.

The financial markets may contain feedback loops that prohibit greed from getting the upper hand, as in actual experiments in which precognition has been used to make profits in silver futures, as we saw earlier. When greed became excessive in these experiments, they failed. Perhaps this is what is happening in the collapse now taking place on a nationwide scale.

The Greeks had a word for this limiting factor. They called it *hubris*— excessive pride or self-confidence. The cousin of hubris is greed, the intense desire for wealth and power. The warnings about hubris are universal. As we read in Proverbs 16:18, "Pride goeth before destruction and a haughty spirit before a fall."

According to a Zen saying, "When the wrong man uses the right methods, the right methods work in the wrong way." The solution is to become the right man, the right woman, whose spiritual and moral development embodies empathy and compassion for others. Only then will the right methods work in the right way—including our "first sight," our ability to be beyond ourselves in space and ahead of ourselves in time.

Nearly all the individuals I know who have a highly developed premonition sense conform to this caution. They are well-balanced persons who lead creative, productive, harmonious lives. They tend to be generous, outgoing, and compassionate. They want to make the world a better place and relieve the suffering of others. Often they are healers. Those who are blessed with the capacity for future knowing often do not actively seek it, but find that it arises naturally in the course of spiritual maturation. But the natural co-arising of future knowing and a benevolent, selfless spirit can be overridden. When it does, disaster often follows. Just ask Wall Street.

QUESTION THE SOURCE

Premonitions can be grossly misleading, and they can be used as an excuse for irresponsible, reckless, or criminal behavior. Napoleon's megalomaniacal premonitions are classic examples. "I always had an inner sense of what awaited me . . . ," he boasted. "Nothing ever happened to me which I did not foresee, and I alone did not wonder at what I had accomplished." Really? What about the Battle of Waterloo and his exile and death on St. Helena?

Premonitions can be especially treacherous when authoritarian figures use them to influence the lives of others. In 1997, sixty-five-year-old Marshall Herff Applewhite, the leader of a group called Heaven's Gate, acted on his longstanding premonition that planet Earth was about to be "recycled," wiped clean of human life. Applewhite believed the earth was only a stepping-stone to a greater destiny he called the Next Level. The physical body was only a vehicle to get there. The only chance he and his followers had of surviving the earth's cleansing was to leave immediately by boarding an alien spacecraft he believed was hiding behind the comet Hale-Bopp, which had recently appeared. The ticket onto the spaceship was suicide. Thus on March 26, 1997, thirty-eight group members and Applewhite were found dead in a rented mansion in Rancho Santa Fe, California, an upscale San Diego community. Before killing themselves, they drank citrus juices to ritually cleanse their bodies. On suicide night they all ate an identical final meal and packed a small overnight bag with lip balm, clothing, spiral notebooks, and five dollars and change. They dressed identically in black shirts and sweat pants, new black-and-white Nike athletic shoes, and donned their Heaven's Gate Away Team arm patches before reclining on their individual bunk beds, ingesting a lethal amount of phenobarbital mixed with pudding or applesauce, chasing it with a shot of vodka, and placing plastic bags over their heads. The suicides were orderly; the members "shed their containers" in three shifts over three days. They were considerate of those who would discover their bodies; before the last two members killed themselves they took out the trash. They mailed two videotapes to former members, who realized what had happened and called the police. The victims included twenty-one women and eighteen men, all white, from ages twenty-six to seventy-two. Within a few months, two former members of the group, regretting they had missed the mass departure, killed themselves in copycat suicides. It remains the largest mass suicide in the history of the United States.

There were numerous warning signs of serious psychopathology, such as the fact that six male members of the group, including Applewhite, had undergone voluntary castration as a way of adhering to their ascetic, celibate lifestyle.

Marshall Applewhite could be the poster child for the dangerous combination of mental instability and wacky premonitions. In 1970 he checked himself into a psychiatric hospital after hearing voices and because he wanted to cure himself of "homosexual urges." After discontinuing psychiatric treatment, he had himself castrated. He believed he had once been Jesus. He advised his followers that if they believed in him, he would be their link to a higher level of human evolution. The videotapes of his final statements were shown to Louis Jolyon West, professor of psychiatry at the University of California at Los Angeles School of Medicine, who concluded that Applewhite was "delusional, sexually repressed and suffering from clinical paranoia."

The Heaven's Gate tragedy raises serious questions about how to distinguish valid premonitions from hallucinations and imaginary beliefs. This conundrum is ancient. In biblical times, people struggled with how to identify false prophets. Was the seer a genuine visionary or a raving lunatic?

Should the ancient Greeks trust the prophecies of the sibyls at the Oracle of Delphi? These questions still exist for us. If I have a premonition that involves you, how do you know *I'm* not crazy?

Common sense helps. Some anomalous experiences would be considered unreal by nearly everyone, such as thinking that one is Jesus, Elvis, or a unicorn. On the other hand, there are experiences that, while not explainable by accepted versions of reality, are nonetheless experienced by a significant proportion of the population, such as premonitions, clairvoyance, telepathy, or near-death experiences. Again, common sense can help sort which of these experiences are pathological and which are not. Talking with an angel may be innocent enough, but if the angel advises you to purchase an assault weapon and shoot kids on a school ground, the anomalous experience has crossed into psychopathology.

Some anomalous experiences occupy a middle ground where it's difficult to decide whether they are pathological or not. Consider hearing voices, which is widely regarded as a sign of schizophrenia. In one survey of fifteen thousand people living in Baltimore, two thousand of them, or 13 percent, said they hear voices. All these individuals are obviously not schizophrenic, unless something weird is going on in Baltimore, because schizophrenia is believed to affect no more than 1 percent of the population. Moreover, highly educated, creative, functional individuals sometimes hear voices. Nursing scholar Barbara Stevens Barnum, Ph.D., R.N., researched nurses' experiences of what she calls "expanded consciousness"—events that can't be explained rationally and that appear to transcend the physical senses. In a survey of 121 nurse leaders, all of whom held doctorates or master's degrees, she found that 41 percent of them described such experiences, which occasionally involved hearing voices. Not one of these nursing leaders mentioned fear or dread as part of the event.

An obvious criterion for judging the validity of premonitions is the psychological balance of the individual. Marshall Applewhite notwithstanding, anomalous experiences in general appear to be good for people's mental health. This upbeat view was affirmed by researchers at the National Opinion Research Center (NORC) at the University of Chicago. When sociologist, Catholic priest, and author Andrew Greeley and his colleagues at NORC examined people who had profound mystical experiences, those persons scored at the top on standard tests measuring psychological well-being. In fact, no other factor had ever been found to correlate so highly with psychological balance as did mystical experience.

THE COST OF DENYING PREMONITIONS

While on tour for my 1999 book *Reinventing Medicine,* in which I first divulged my precognitive dream about Justin (which is included in the beginning of this book), I was invited onto a live national radio talk show. Unbeknownst to me, the host had also invited a well-known cardiologist, whose role was to debunk my book. While waiting for the show to begin, the physician turned to me and said coldly, "I must tell you that I disagree with nearly everything you've written." I took a deep breath and tried mentally to prepare myself for the onslaught.

The host, wanting to stir up disagreement as quickly as possible, immediately asked me to relate my precognitive dream. After I finished, he turned to the cardiologist and said, "Now, Doctor, what do *you* think about this dream stuff?" Then he leaned away from the microphone and waited for the fireworks to begin.

Instead of attacking, however, the cardiologist lapsed into an awkward silence—"dead air" in radio terminology, which is not a good thing. I had no idea what he was thinking and neither did the host, who appeared near panic. Finally the physician said thoughtfully, "I think there may be something to Dr. Dossey's dream." The host nearly fainted; this was not what he had in mind. After another long pause, the cardiologist said meekly, "I think I'd like to relate a dream of my own." Then he said, almost tenderly, "I've never told this to anyone before."

While the show host wiped the sweat from his brow, the cardiologist described how he once had an elderly female patient in the hospital who required a cardiac catheterization. The night prior to the procedure the doctor dreamed that while he was performing the cath the patient became speechless, paralyzed on one side, and unconscious—indicators of a severe stroke. Upon waking, he was rattled and wondered whether he should cancel the test in view of the nightmare. Assuring himself that dreams mean nothing, he decided to go ahead. Later that day, during the actual catheterization, the woman experienced a stroke in precisely the same pattern he dreamed the night before. Although the woman recovered totally, the experience shook him profoundly.

For the rest of the radio program, the cardiologist and I found nothing on which we disagreed. We had a delightful chat, to the chagrin of our host.

It was a moving experience for me and for the cardiologist as well. When I returned home, I received a couple of e-mail messages from him, which dealt with similar experiences he'd had. "Nice touch," I teased him, "waiting until you had a national radio audience before going public! Great sense of timing!"

I wondered why he did it. Why not continue to keep those experiences buried? I believe he needed to unburden himself by sharing this highly meaningful event, and he felt safe in doing so with me, a professional colleague. He knew I wouldn't shame him, but would support him in his revelation.

How many people, I wondered, long to do the same? The answer, I believe, is thousands.

Psychoanalyst Elizabeth Lloyd Mayer describes a patient of hers whose premonitions helped make him famous. He was seeking help because of severe intractable headaches, for which no physical cause could be found. He was seeing Mayer as a last resort.

By the time he came to her, he was a world-renowned neurosurgeon. He was summoned when heads of state, dignitaries, and the wealthy needed their brains operated on. The man's fame was well-deserved; he never seemed to lose a patient. His life seemed to click on all fronts: not only was he at the peak of his profession, but he enjoyed a loving marriage and wonderful children as well. He was unable to identify any psychological cause of the headaches that were destroying his life.

Mayer probed here and there, searching for leads and clues. Because he was an eminent authority and was on the staff of a large university hospital, she inquired about his teaching duties. Sadly the man said that he did not teach any longer.

"I had to stop," he said.

"You *had* to?" Mayer asked.

He went on to explain how he could not keep up his teaching and had abandoned it, although he loved it as much as surgery itself. He disclosed to Mayer what he'd never told anyone—that he stopped teaching because he no longer believed he could teach what he actually does.

He told Mayer why his patients don't die on him. As soon as he learns that someone needs surgery, the doctor goes to the patient's bedside and sits at his or her head, sometimes for thirty seconds, sometimes for hours. He waits for a distinctive white light to appear around the patient's head. This was something he couldn't possibly admit to surgery residents, much less teach them. Until the white light appears, he knows it's not safe to operate. Once it appears, he knows he can go ahead and the patient will survive.

"How, he asks me, could he possibly reveal that?" Mayer said. "What would the residents think? They'd think he was crazy. Maybe he *is* crazy. But crazy or not, he knows that seeing the white light is what saves his surgeries from disaster. So how can he teach and *not* talk about it? It's a horrible dilemma. He's adopted the only possible solution: he's quit teaching."

When Mayer asked him when his headaches began, he was startled by his own response. "*That's* interesting," he said. "The headaches started two years ago. And I remember when I noticed the first one. It was the day I resigned from teaching, right after I told the dean."

So what *is* that white light that guides this world-class neurosurgeon? Putting myself in the place of one of his patients, it would not matter to me what the light was. I wouldn't care if it was an angelic presence, sprites, or pixies. I'd get down on my knees and thank the high heavens that I had the best surgeon operating on me, even if he were crazy as a loon.

What kind of system would pressure our best and brightest healers to clam up, stuff their wisdom inside, and turn mute about the things that matter most to them? What kind of profession would cause its most talented practitioners to live a lie?

Mayer didn't reveal whether the neurosurgeon's headaches improved, or if he owned up to his experiences and went back to teaching. Instead, she painted a vivid picture of his dilemma. She concluded, "The neurosurgeon with his headaches was an emphatic demonstration of how the fear of appearing credulous or crazy leads many people to disavow their reality, which can paralyze their creativity, conscience, and freedom to be themselves."

Not every physician hides unusual experiences of this sort. An admirable example is the courageous obstetrician-gynecologist Larry Kincheloe, who went public with his premonitions and bodily sensations that alerted him to impending deliveries in his obstetrical patients.

Truth be told, we don't actually know how common these experiences are, because most of those who experience them just aren't talking.

Jeffrey S. Levin is an outstanding pioneer in consciousness-related medical research. Jeff is a social epidemiologist whose landmark research was funded for many years by the National Institutes of Health. He founded a new field of study in the 1980s called "the epidemiology of religion."

Jeff's passion is unraveling the role of religious and spiritual practices in health and longevity. When he began researching this field, it was considered scientific heresy, not exactly the best way to advance your career as a young scientist. He persevered, however, and others followed. As a result, there are now thousands of studies in this field, and they reveal a consistent picture: those who follow some sort of spiritual path in their life—it does not seem to matter greatly which one they choose—live longer and are healthier than those who don't. They have a lower incidence of all the major killers of our day, including heart disease and cancer.

At one stage of his career, Jeff was recruited to join the faculty of a medical school on the East Coast. By this time his accomplishments were widely known. His reputation had preceded him, and his new colleagues regarded him as someone who was open to unconventional ideas.

As soon as he was settled in his new position, his colleagues began to drop by his office to share things they'd never told anyone else. They'd quietly enter, close the door, and often speak in a whisper, as if the walls had ears. They revealed weird premonitions that came true, "funny coincidences" that had shaken them up, and visions and revelations that came out of the blue. They always did so with a sense of secrecy, as if they might have to pay a price if anyone discovered they harbored thoughts such as these. Jeff would listen patiently, assuring them of complete confidence.

Eventually it came time for Jeff to present a talk at grand rounds, the weekly gathering at which some faculty member presents research in his or her area of expertise. At the conclusion of his talk, Jeff chose to go out on a limb. He reminded his faculty colleagues that, over the previous months, most of them had unburdened themselves of their private experiences in his office. "The person on your right has told me things he is unwilling to reveal in public," he said. "The person on your left has done the same. Over the past year, nearly all of you have told me things you won't tell each other. We all know these things are possible, because we've lived them. We are all in the same boat. *So can we drop the pretense and be honest with one another?"*

They could not do it. They were unwilling to speak out. Their concern about their public persona formed a mental obstruction to the flow of their own experience and absorbed their courage. They opted instead for a make-believe version of reality in which weird things don't happen—or, if they do, you make a secret of them—a faux world in which everything is well behaved, orderly, and, importantly, professionally acceptable. Their visits to Levin's office ceased as they put their masks back on, and once again became mute about some of the most meaningful experiences of their lives.

Denying premonitions may sometimes be fatal. Freud did not believe that dreams reveal future happenings. As dream researcher Robert Moss says, "On the contrary, he insisted, dreams stem from the dreamer's past, starting with the day residue and extending back—under veils of repression—into early childhood. Dreams are not predictions; they are psychosexual biographies."

In 1895 Freud had a dream about "Irma," a patient he had been treating for hysteria. The dream proved historic; it led him, he said, to invent psycho-analysis.

There is a tragic side to the dream, however. Dr. José Schavelzon, an Argentinian cancer surgeon and psychoanalyst, reviewed Freud's personal medical history and concluded that his Irma dream contained a nearly identical preview of the oral cancer that would kill him twenty-eight years later.

The evening prior to the dream, Freud received a visit from a junior colleague, "Otto," with whom he stayed up playing cards and smoking cigars. In the course of the evening they discussed Irma's case. Otto managed to irritate Freud by saying, "She's better, but not quite well."

In Freud's dream that night, Irma arrived in a large hall where he was receiving guests. Immediately taking her aside, he told her, "If you still get pains, it's really only your fault." Irma looked sick and told Freud she was suffering terrible pains, particularly in her throat. "It's choking me," she said. Thinking he may have missed something in his evaluation of her, he led Irma to a window and looked into her mouth. She resisted and had trouble opening her mouth, but Freud finally got a good look and found something alarming: "a big white patch" inside her mouth on the right side, an "extensive whitish grey scab" that reminded Freud of the turbinate bones inside the nose.

Still dreaming, he called for a second opinion from two colleagues. One said there was indeed an infection, but that "the toxin will be eliminated." The other specialist was not as positive; he stated that the infection had spread to the patient's left shoulder. Another doctor arrived. All four agreed on the origin of Irma's illness, and she was given an injection from a syringe. In the report Freud wrote up later, he said that the injection was thoughtless and that the syringe had probably not been clean.

What did it all mean? In his commentary on the dream, Freud noted that in real life Irma had no symptoms like those in the dream. Could she be a substitute character for some other patient who had choking sensations? He'd been miffed the evening before by Otto, who had said Irma was not yet fully cured. His dream, Freud eventually concluded, represented wish fulfillment on his part—the symbolic attainment of an often unconscious desire. It expressed his revenge on Otto, indicating indirectly that Irma's pains were Otto's fault, not his. The dream was essentially an attempt to exonerate himself from blame for Irma's ongoing physical symptoms.

Freud interpreted the syringe in the dream, used to give Irma an injection, as representing a penis, and concluded that the cure for her symptoms was sexual intercourse.

Freud knew that substitution occurs commonly in dreams, in which a dream character may represent another individual or several persons, but he seemed not to seriously consider that Irma might represent the dreamer himself.

Perhaps he should have. Twenty-eight years later, in 1923, oral surgeons removed a whitish lesion from Freud's mouth like the one he'd dreamed about in Irma's mouth—same appearance, same location. Thus began a series of radiation treatments and surgeries that would continue for fifteen years. The surgeries would leave further "scabs" resembling those in the Irma dream. By 1936 an actual carcinoma developed. Like Irma in the dream, Freud developed trouble opening his mouth as a consequence of his multiple surgeries and had to wear a removable prosthesis. The turbinate nasal bones Freud saw in his dream may have also been a preview of his state, because the surgical procedures left the nasal cavity visible from inside the mouth.

Moss concludes, "The evidence suggests that Freud's dream gave him a rather exact picture of both the origin and the histology of the oral cancer that subjected him to a painful and protracted death." Although Freud became interested in the idea that dreams can contain messages from the body, he missed this one—unlike Jung, who gave up smoking because of a dream.

Freud referred to the Irma dream as his "specimen dream," the center-piece for his theory of psychoanalysis. He was not modest. He considered the dream a validation of his creative powers, and an achievement on par with the conquests of military leaders such as Alexander the Great, Oliver Cromwell, or Napoleon Bonaparte. He wanted a marble tablet to be placed at the house where he had analyzed his dream about Irma with the inscription: IN THIS HOUSE, ON JULY 24, 1895, THE SECRET OF DREAMS WAS REVEALED TO DR. SIGM. FREUD.

A premonition-based explanation for the Irma dream really had no chance. It lost out not only because the alternative explanation was more flattering, but also because, if a premonition, the dream portended a morbid event that was not pleasant to dwell on. Besides, Freud had become convinced that dreams and psychoanalysis are about the past, not the future.

Did Freud ever weigh the potential cost of denying precognitive dreams? It's difficult to know. Late in life he wrote, "I am not an out and out skeptic. . . . If I had my life to live over again, I would devote myself to psychical research rather than to psychoanalysis."

One biographer has suggested that Freud had a deep and abiding interest in the paranormal, but disguised it for pragmatic reasons. He feared that until psychoanalysis was well-established, endorsing the paranormal would provide his enemies a weapon with which to ridicule and discredit the fledgling movement. Freud's caution may have benefited psychoanalysis, but it may also have cost him his life. Had he not been locked into his belief system about psychoanalysis, he might have used the Irma dream to give up his heavy cigar smoking, which was almost certainly the cause of his fatal oral cancer.

Premonitions are often called anomalies, which by definition are things that deviate from what is standard, normal, or expected. *Anomalous* comes from Greek words meaning "not even," which suggests a bump in the road. Premonitions are often ignored for this reason. Scientists who follow this practice believe it is entirely justified. If they paid attention to all the wild intuitions and predictions people have, science would grind to a halt. The practice of tossing out things that don't fit has been formalized in science, and elaborate guidelines have been developed to guide scientists in doing so.

Suppose I want to know my average body temperature. I measure it in the same way at the same hour for a week. All the measurements cluster around 98.6° F, except a few readings of around 110° F. I know that a sustained body temperature of 110° is incompatible with life, and I haven't been sick, so there must be some mistake. Perhaps I misread the thermometer or made an error in my recording, or maybe the thermometer transiently malfunctioned. Should I include the high readings? If I retain them they will skew the rest of my data. I decide they are unlikely to be valid and I discard them.

Scientists and statisticians do something similar with things that don't fit their expectations. The observations that get tossed out are called outliers, meaning that they lie far outside what's predicted. Sometimes outliers should be ignored. Instruments do malfunction, data transcription or transmission can go haywire, protocols can break down, samples can become contaminated, and so on. But sometimes outliers—including premonitions—don't lie. Sometimes it's one's expectations and theory that are wrong, not the outliers. By calling outliers anomalies and ditching them, it is possible to conjure a false view of things.

In 1985, Joe Farman, an obscure British geophysicist working at a remote outpost in Antarctica, stunned the scientific world with a paper published in the prestigious journal *Nature*. Farman and his little team had been quietly measuring the ozone layer at the bottom of the world since 1957, using an old-fashioned, low-tech instrument called a Dobsonmeter that had been assembled fifty years earlier in a shed outside Oxford. In 1982 their measurements began to drop; in 1983, Farman said, "It just went haywire; the levels really fell away." Farman realized that half the ozone had vanished. Thinking their ancient Dobsonmeter might be acting up, he obtained a replacement, which showed even lower readings.

The discovery was ominous. The high-altitude ozone layer protects life on Earth from the damaging effects of ultraviolet radiation coming from the sun. Biologists believe that life on land would probably not have evolved and could not continue without protection by ozone.

Farman not only documented the huge ozone hole that had opened up, but he also specified the cause: ozone-eating chemical reactions in the stratosphere, triggered by manmade chemicals called chlorofluorocarbons or CFCs.

Many of the world's scientists could not believe it. For years, NASA's satellites had been monitoring ozone levels around the world 24/7, taking 140,000 readings a day. If the ozone was disappearing, why hadn't NASA been the first to spot it? Opinions varied. Some experts said the software analyzing the data recognized the low readings as outliers and dumped them. Others said the anomalous data was not deleted but flagged as unreliable and therefore ignored. One expert said the data was misread because of "a clerical error."

In any case, it was a humbling moment for NASA. A tiny, unheard-of research team, using a clunky, hand-held instrument wrapped in a quilt, had beaten them to the punch on a very important matter. Farman's discovery was made the old-fashioned way: through dogged attention to detail and open-mindedness toward things that don't fit in.

It wasn't just the folks at NASA who were red-faced. In the early 1980s scientists were getting concerned about the potential problems posed by CFCs, but the problem was being minimized. In 1984, the U.S. National Research Council reported that the rate of ozone depletion was far less than anticipated and there was no cause for alarm. *The Wall Street Journal* trumpeted, "The ozone layer isn't vanishing after all."

Farman found not only a hole in the ozone layer, but also a hole in the way that outliers were being handled. This was not just a hairsplitting argument among the experts. Unless Farman had paid attention to the anomalies, the truth about ozone destruction might not have been discovered for years. The 1987 Montreal protocol, which led to drastic reductions in the manufacture of CFCs, would have been delayed, with almost certain increases in skin cancer and other health problems around the globe.

The ozone-hole story symbolizes the costs of discarding premonitions. Denying ozone depletion put human health at risk; denying premonitions does the same, because they so frequently warn us of impending dangers. And when premonitions are rejected as anomalies and outliers, we misconstrue the nature of our own consciousness. The result is a mangled, cheapened, narrowed concept of who we are—which, at our species' precarious state of existence, we can ill afford.

WOULD HISTORY HAVE BEEN DIFFERENT?

The costs of denying premonitions often go beyond individuals to involve whole nations. So it's not only our self-concept that can be damaged when we ignore premonitions; history can be distorted as well.

Throughout history many cultures have taken premonitions, dreams, and prophecy seriously. Cuneiform-script clay tablets from the great library of Nineveh, dating to around 5000 B.C.E., reveal that the ancient Babylonians and Assyrians treated dreams with respect and had methods of decoding them. Around fifteen prophetic dreams are recorded in the Old Testament, such as Pharaoh's famous dream in Genesis 41. Hannibal is said to have had a prophetic dream that encouraged him to cross the Alps with his war elephants and invade Italy in 218 B.C.E. A similar dream is said to have prompted Julius Caesar to cross the Rubicon in 49 B.C.E. Calpurnia, Caesar's wife, is said by Plutarch to have dreamed of his assassination the night before it happened and tried to warn him in vain. St. Thomas Aquinas, in *Summa Theologica*, affirmed that dreams have a precognitive character.

Most precognitive dreams are warnings of dire events that may happen to one's self or loved ones; only a small percentage are about happy portents. It is understandable that most are ignored. Aside from the fact that they are often imprecise, it is human nature to shy away from premonitions that are frightening. Even the great and wise have been known to turn away from grim intimations of the future. If these individuals happen to be national leaders, their country may pay a price along with them.

A well-recorded example involved Abraham Lincoln, who dreamed of his assassination shortly before it occurred. Lincoln related the dream to Ward Hill Lamon, his friend and former law partner in Illinois. Lamon, a big man, often served as Lincoln's bodyguard. He supervised security at the White House, often sleeping on the floor outside Lincoln's bedroom wrapped in a blanket and armed to the teeth. Even though Lincoln dreamed of a corpse lying in state in the East Room of the White House, heard mournful sounds, and saw the casket surrounded by soldiers standing guard, one of whom told him that the president was dead, Lincoln was not convinced his dream was relevant. When he told his wife, Mary, and Lamon about the dream, he downplayed its significance. "Hill," Lincoln said to Lamon, "your apprehension of harm to me from some hidden enemy is downright foolishness. For a long time you have been trying to keep somebody—the Lord knows who— from killing me. Don't you see how it will turn out? In this dream it was not me, but some other fellow, that was killed. It seems that this ghostly assassin tried his hand on some one else." About two weeks later Lincoln was fatally shot by the actor John Wilkes Booth in Ford's Theatre.

One can only wonder how history might have been different if Lincoln had taken his premonitory dream seriously. Although the Civil War had just ended, America was at a precarious stage. Many in the North were poised to wreak revenge on the South. Without Lincoln's steady, compassionate hand at the helm, the country descended into Reconstruction, which created odium among conquered Southerners that persists in some areas a century and a half later.

Consider the trigger event that plunged Europe into World War I—the assassination of Archduke Franz Ferdinand of Austria in Sarajevo. If the premonitions of Bishop Joseph Lanyi of Grosswardein, Hungary, had been given more weight, the blood bath of the Great War might have been prevented.

Early on the morning of June 28, 1914, Bishop Lanyi arose from bed and recorded his dream about Archduke Franz Ferdinand, whom he had once served as a tutor. In the dream the bishop had gone to his desk to look through some letters. The one on top was bordered in black and bore a black seal with the coat of arms of the archduke. Recognizing the handwriting as that of the archduke, Bishop Lanyi opened the letter. On the upper part of it was a postcard-like picture, showing a street and a narrow passage. Sitting in a motorcar were the archduke and his wife with a general facing them. Another officer sat beside the chauffeur. Suddenly from the throng leapt two young men who fired at the archduke and his wife. The following text accompanied the picture:

Dear Dr. Lanyi,

I herewith inform you that today, my wife and I will fall victims to an assassination. We commend ourselves to your pious prayers.

Kindest regards from your
Archduke Franz,
Sarajevo, the 28th of June,
3:45 A.M.

The startled and tearful bishop jumped from bed and noted that the clock read a quarter to four. He went immediately to his desk and wrote down everything he had seen and read in the dream. Around two hours later a servant entered and noticed the bishop saying his rosary. He asked the servant to call the bishop's mother and a houseguest because he wanted to offer mass for the archduke and his wife. He then drew a sketch of the assassination scene because he felt there was something strange about its imagery. He had this drawing certified by two witnesses, then sent an account of the dream to his brother Edward, who was a Jesuit priest. Appended to the letter was a drawing of the motorcar, the narrow passage, the throng, and the assassins leaping toward the car and firing. When photographs were published in the press a few days later, the drawings were in close agreement, except that there was only one assassin, instead of two.

When word of the bishop's experience surfaced, doubts naturally arose. A reporter from Vienna's *Reichspost* immediately investigated the matter, examining the drawing and talking to the two witnesses, who confirmed the story. In addition, the bishop's brother Edward was questioned immediately by the editor and writer Bruno Grabinsky, who stated that the priest confirmed receiving the letter and the sketch.

If premonitory dreams were always as accurate as Bishop Lanyi's, there would be little debate over their usefulness. But there is a spectrum of accuracy in premonitions, ranging from those that are precise in every detail, to those that are completely wrong. In between are dreams that may be partially accurate and blurred with frustrating symbolism, such as the following examples.

Barbara Garwell, an English housewife from Hull, dreamed in early March 1981 that she was riding in a car with two Germans wearing Nazi SS uniforms. A limousine approached and came to a halt, out of which stepped a well-known actor. The two SS men got out of their car, and one fired a pistol at the actor, who fell. Three weeks later, President Ronald Reagan, the former movie star, stepped out of a limo and was shot and severely wounded by John Hinckley, Jr. Were the SS uniforms relevant? Hinckley had been a member of a neo-Nazi group, but was expelled in 1978 because of his violent ideas.

Garwell had another vivid dream later that same year, in September 1981, in which a single row of men was seated in a stadium. They were wearing dark suits and had "coffee-colored skins." Garwell knew only that the site was somewhere in the Middle East. Then two soldiers, also with "coffee-colored skin," charged the seated individuals and sprayed them with automatic-rifle fire. Three weeks later, on October 6, 1981, President Anwar Sadat of Egypt was shot dead when four Egyptian soldiers leaped from a vehicle in a military parade and sprayed seated dignitaries on a reviewing stand with automatic-rifle fire. Garwell was careful to document that she experienced both these dreams before the event in question occurred, and she had witnesses sign statements to that effect.

Should anyone have listened to Garwell? Did her premonitions occur by chance? Did she report only those premonitions that may have been valid and ignore those that didn't pan out? Are they too general to be of use, as critics charge?

Psychologist Keith Hearne, a pioneer in the field of lucid dreaming, collected every single premonition Garwell had in 1981. She described each one on a form as soon as they occurred and mailed them to Hearne. Over the course of the year, she reported fifty-two in all. These were submitted to two blind judges, who rated the correlation of each premonition with events that happened in the twenty-eight days that followed. They also mapped the premonitions onto a control year—i.e., an arbitrary year other than 1981, the year the premonitions actually occurred. This tested whether Garwell's premonitions were so general they'd match up with events in any year. The premonitions for the correct year had significantly higher specificity than when the premonitions were applied to the control year. They were *not* so general that they'd match up with events in any year. One of most interesting aspects was a consistent twenty-one-day latency period or precognitive interval between her premonitions and their apparent fulfillment, as in the Reagan and Sadat premonitions. Although no one knows why that particular interval exists in Garwell's case, it might prove useful, because it could provide authorities time to act on Garwell's premonitions should they wish to take them seriously.

On October 11, 1982, *Time* reported a dream of George Wallace, Jr., that took place in 1972. In the dream, his father was shot and killed. This occurred a few nights before his father was shot by Arthur Bremer, though not fatally, while campaigning as a presidential candidate in Maryland.

Strong national leaders are never loved by everyone. It is likely that, all the time, there is someone somewhere who is willing to do them great harm. To be helpful, therefore, it's not enough for someone to announce they've had a premonition that "someone is going to assassinate the president." Specificity as to time and place, and identifying characteristics of the assailant, are required if the premonition is to prove helpful. Unfortunately, these factors often go missing, even in premonitions that later prove true.

To compound the problem, some individuals such as John Williams, who do experience highly specific premonitions of assassinations, can be loathe to reveal them, lest they be thought mad or actually part of the plot. Williams, who foresaw the assassination of British Prime Minister Spencer Perceval in 1812, was persuaded to remain silent by his wife and close friends even though he dreamed about the assassination three separate times.

A friend of mine who considers himself psychic has been asked by police departments around the country to help locate missing people. On one occasion he led them to the victim's body, only to be placed under investigation for murder. How else, they said, could he possibly know where the body was hidden?

Amid the myriad false premonitions that get reported, a few gems always lie buried. This situation is little different from conventional intelligence. Will history be different for societies and nations willing to wed these dual sources of information?

IF WE CAN SEE THE FUTURE, CAN WE CHANGE IT?

In Pharaoh's precognitive dream in the Old Testament in Genesis 41, Joseph not only interpreted his dream, but he gave Pharaoh an action plan to prevent the approaching famine. He should appoint a wise viceroy, Joseph said, and impose a new tax during the seven bountiful years to fill the granaries as a hedge against the upcoming famine—a job opening Pharaoh filled with Joseph himself. This reveals how some cultures see premonitions: a glimpse of a future that is flexible and subject to change. Joseph, thus, in one version of the story, says to Pharaoh, "It is not to distress men that God foreshadows to them what is to come, but so that forewarned they may use their sagacity to alleviate the trials announced when they befall."

The idea that everything that is foretold in "bad" dreams can be dispelled through ritual practices is ancient. In the New Kingdom Dream Book of ancient Egypt (also known as the P. Chester Beatty III papyrus), dating to the thirteenth century B.C.E., a two-part ritual is recommended. First, the dreamer is cleansed by rubbing his face with bread soaked with beer, herbs, and myrrh. Second, the dreamer must tell his dream to the goddess Isis, addressing her as "Mother." A Mesopotamian practice to dissipate the evil of a precognitive dream was to transfer it to a lump of clay, which was then allowed to dissolve in a flowing river. Similar practices date to the eighth century B.C.E. in central Asia, where rituals were used to transfer the negative energy of morbid precognitive dreams to bits of earth or pieces of wood, which were then destroyed or scattered. All of this was done so bad dreams wouldn't come true.

The Iroquois believed they could modify the course of foreseen events by partially enacting a dream under controlled conditions. In one example, a Mohawk warrior dreamed he was captured and tortured to death with fire. He had his fellow villagers bind him and burn him with red-hot knives and axes, as in the dream—but not to the point of death.

Capt. Robert S. Rattray, an anthropologist in the employ of the British government in the African Gold Coast before and after World War I, became fascinated with the Ashanti people. He describes how the Ashanti would dispose of a "bad" dream by confiding it in whispers to the village rubbish dump or the communal latrine.

Among Hispanics in central Texas where I grew up, the power of an ominous premonitory dream could be annulled by placing an egg yolk in a glass of water, then placing the glass under the dreamer's bed the following night. The yolk was believed to absorb the negative energy of the dream, and was disposed of the following day.

The question of whether we can change a future scenario we've seen in a premonition involves that Gordian knot of philosophy: free will. If we see the future, are we locked into it, slavishly required to act out the preview? And if not, and we do act to change the future that we've glimpsed, was it really the future, since what we foresaw did not actually happen?

Cultures around the world believe that the outcome of events foreseen can be changed, and modern analysis affirms these beliefs in our culture as well. In 433 reports of precognition gathered by the Rhine Research Center, in which there was enough threat of danger to merit intervention, in two-thirds of the cases the individual never took any action. But in the one-third of cases in which the individual did try to intervene to change the future they'd foreseen, successful attempts outnumbered the unsuccessful ones two to one.

Not all attempts to intervene are successful. In one report a woman in

New York State experienced a premonition in a dream that a plane would crash at the shore of a lake and that the roof of the third cottage on the dirt road leading to the lake would catch fire as a result. There was only one man involved, and he would be burned alive. She tried to write two warning letters the morning following the dream, but found herself saying that the fire engine would try to reach the site by the canal road, which was the wrong route, making them arrive at the crash site too late. The dream was so vivid that she was aware of every plane that flew over that day. In the late afternoon while cooking she said to her husband, "That's the plane—the one that's going to crash! Robert, stop the firemen before they try the canal; they have to take the basin road and they don't know it." Her husband went outdoors and said, "That plane's all right," only to hear his wife shriek, "It is *not!*" Within seconds the plane crashed. The firemen could not reach the site in time, having taken the canal track instead of the basin road. The single pilot was burned to a crisp. The cottage she saw in the dream was slightly damaged. The woman was a wreck for weeks, wondering how she could have prevented it.

What should one do if a premonition points to an imminent tragedy? Louisa E. Rhine, who gathered and analyzed thousands of such reports, offered some down-to-earth advice. If the premonition leaves the individual with a strong conviction that it is a valid warning, it should be handled as such by taking reasonable steps to prevent it. However, since we lack foolproof criteria for distinguishing false premonitions from valid ones, and since cranks and fanatics abound, she advised against issuing public warnings. Moreover, some premonitions involve so many people and elements that it's difficult to act effectively on them even when one wishes to do so, as in the premonition of the plane crash. Then there are cases in which people try to intervene, only to make matters worse, or actually contribute to the occurrence of the event.

Consider, for example, an Oregon woman who awoke one morning with an inexplicable fear that that her three-year-old son was in danger of being killed in an auto accident. To thwart any such possibility, she decided to take her son to her mother's house, several miles distant. After arriving, she felt such relief that she'd done the right thing that she burst into tears. These soon changed to tears of sorrow, however, when a policeman suddenly arrived at the door with a crowd behind him, holding her son's limp but alive body in his arms. The little boy had somehow left the house unnoticed and gone to sit quietly under a tree in the yard, where he had been run over and severely injured by a runaway car.

Far more typical are premonitions that are successfully acted on, as when Amanda rescued her baby from its crib before the chandelier fell onto it.

Sometimes action to avert danger is only partially successful. A man bought a building for a car dealership in Georgia, and installed a plate-glass window with a large electric sign in front. His wife dreamed that a tornado blew the sign into the window, demolishing it. Taking his wife's premonition seriously, that very day he purchased tornado insurance. A few days later, a tornado blew the sign into the window, shattering it, just as his wife had dreamed.

Instances like this could be called "just in case" examples. The man did not anchor the sign or board up the plate-glass window, but he did take measures to ameliorate damage just in case his wife's premonitory dream proved true. Similarly, people who have premonitions of a plane crash may not actually cancel their travel plans, but they may change the hour or day of their reservation just in case.

J. B. Rhine, who pioneered lab-based psi research, suggested that the critical issue in changing the future was the "efficiency" of the precognition— i.e., how detailed it was. Premonitions rarely provide a picture of the future in exotic detail. Rhine suggested that the paucity of details indicates that the future is fundamentally fuzzy and imprecise, not fixed; it contains enough "wiggle room" for the insertion of actions that can make a difference in how events unfold.

On balance, a solution to this question that would satisfy everyone seems as far away as ever. The problem, of course, is that we don't know enough about the nature of space, time, and consciousness to untie this knot. In Walter Bagehot's famous phrase, daylight has not been fully let in upon the magic.

"Nobody can convince anybody of the actuality of precognition," psychoanalyst Stephan Kierulff says. Or, perhaps, that they can change the future.

DANGERS

A question that should always be asked about premonitions—and almost never is—is, "Is this stuff safe?" There are reasons to be concerned, because problems can arise when people devote themselves to concentrated, prolonged efforts to see the future.

An example was the CIA-sponsored remote-viewing research conducted in the 1970s, 1980s, and 1990s at Stanford Research Institute (SRI) and elsewhere by physicists Harold E. Puthoff, Russell Targ, Edwin C. May, and others. Some of the results of this work were declassified following an executive Order by President Clinton in 1995. At one point in the project, Targ was asked by Soviet psi researchers engaged in similar remote-viewing activities, "What do you do to keep your subject from cracking up or going crazy during the experiments?" Nuclear physicist Edwin C. May, who was the director of the CIA project at the time of its termination in 1995, affirmed the psychological hazards. May said, "I believe RV [remote viewing] can be psychologically dangerous. . . . I have had to dismiss otherwise sane people from the project because they 'went off the deep end' after doing too many RV's [remote viewings]. . . . I have a hard rule that I act as a subject once in each new experiment. I want to experience the protocol to see if it *feels* right. I think that in general, and for sure in my own case, it is too easy to become overwhelmed by ego after successful trials. I do well and it scares me. So I don't do it in general."

Do concerns about remote viewing apply to premonitions? A premonition is essentially a remote view of the future. If intense efforts to remote view involve psychological hazards, protracted attempts at premonitions are also likely to be risky.

As we've seen, one of the most common themes of premonitions is events that pose a physical danger, such as natural or manmade disasters, or impending health problems. We are innately primed to detect these kinds of happenings before they occur. In the presentiment experiments it was the violent images that would later be shown to people, not the pleasant, calming ones, that elicited an unconscious bodily reaction *before* they were selected and shown by the computer. And in surveys of premonitions, it's also the violent, danger-laden warnings that predominate. Is there a downside to these premonitions? Worrying about future problems can cause psychological stress. But are there physical consequences as well?

Alison Holman, a professor in nursing science at the University of California at Irvine, and her colleagues published a study in 2008 of the long-term effects of acute stress reactions to the terrorist attacks of September

11, 2001. Their study involved 2,729 Americans nationwide. Their article, "Terrorism, Acute Stress, and Cardiovascular Health: A 3-Year National Study Following the September 11 Attacks," appeared in *Archives of General Psychiatry,* one of the nation's leading psychiatry journals.

Although nearly all the people surveyed lived outside of New York City and Washington and didn't know anyone who'd been involved in the attacks, more than one-tenth of them reported acute stress symptoms such as nightmares and insomnia immediately following the attacks. In the next three years, more than 40 percent said they continued to worry that a repeat terrorist attack would harm themselves or a member of their family. The results: the most fearful individuals were three to five times more likely to be diagnosed over the next several years with cardiovascular problems such as heart disease or stroke.

These individuals weren't different from most Americans. Many of us are still living on edge. About a third to one-half of our citizens continue to tell pollsters they're worried about becoming a terrorist victim, and that an attack is very likely or somewhat likely to occur within the next several months.

These fears don't make rational sense. The statistical risk of dying from a terrorist attack in America is comparable to being struck by an asteroid or drowning in a toilet, and there has not been a repeat attack in the United States since September 11, 2001. In spite of this, the apprehension lingers.

A main reason for the increased level of fear is that the national alert level, determined by the Department of Homeland Security, has never dropped below yellow, the third of the five levels, since September 11. In-your-face reminders of impending disaster are always present. Each time someone boards one of the approximately thirty thousand daily commercial flights in the United States and passes through a security checkpoint barefoot and partially undressed, the old worries are stoked. New Yorkers have been particularly exposed to terrorism warnings. Ubiquitous advertisements have appeared on the city's subways urging people to report suspicious observations to a counterterrorism hotline. In 2007, 1,944 New Yorkers saw something and phoned in tips. The result: the number of terrorists arrested as a consequence of the tips was zero.

Holman's study strongly suggests that this hypervigilance comes with a physical cost: increased risk of stroke, high blood pressure, and heart attack. These findings prompted science journalist John Tierney seriously to ask,

"Which is more of a threat to your health: Al Qaeda or the Department of Homeland Security?"

A flood of premonitions occurred prior to September 11, documented by clearinghouses such as the Rhine Research Center in Durham, North Carolina. What is the effect of these premonitions on those who experience them? Do premonitions of impending crises carry the same physical risks of cardiovascular disease as the acute and chronic stress reactions following September 11? No one has answered this question so far. But there's no reason to think that the stress triggered by premonitions of disaster is any different from the stress from worrying about terrorist attacks that might lie ahead. The heart and other organs presumably can't distinguish the source of the stress; they only sense that it's happening.

Might premonition-prone individuals be comparatively *less* susceptible to the stress caused by the fear of looming crises? Psychological tests of people who have had profound mystical experiences showed that these events correlated with psychological balance and well-being. So perhaps those blessed with future-knowing skills are more resistant to the stresses that degrade the health of chronic worriers.

Indulging in psi-type experiences has carried red flags for a very long time. The warnings have often reflected spiritual, not physical concerns. An example is St. Teresa of Ávila, who, in a letter written in January 1577, said, "I've had raptures again. They're most embarrassing. Several times in public . . . during Matins, for instance. I'm so ashamed, I simply want to hide away somewhere!"

A student of Zen Buddhism reported to his master that during meditation he had experienced visions of Light and True Buddhahood. The master soberly responded, "Keep meditating. It will go away."

In a comparable story, one day it was announced by Zen Master Joshu that the young monk Kyogen had reached an enlightened state. Much impressed by this news, several of his peers went to speak with him. "We have heard that you are enlightened. Is this true?" his fellow students inquired. "It is," Kyogen answered. "Tell us," said a friend, "how do you feel?" "As miserable as ever," replied the enlightened Kyogen.

Yet, these cautions are not absolute. Transformative epiphanies, prophecies, foreknowledge, future knowing, premonitions—the sacred scriptures of all great religions contain myriad examples. Now, as then, personal discernment and wise guidance can make the difference between whether these experiences are a hazard or a blessing.

CAUTIONS

Nonetheless, caution is wise for anyone who wants to cultivate premonitions or any other anomalous experience.

Two personality traits, absorption and openness to experience, are known to contribute to both psychopathology and anomalous experiences. Absorption is the tendency to become engrossed in an experience. Openness to experience is the disposition to be responsive to, and to explore, new and unconventional ideas and experiences. A certain degree of absorption and openness to experience is healthy, and is found in all creative individuals. But these traits can become extreme; people can become so absorbed and open that they lose their critical faculties. When this happens, they may have trouble distinguishing valid premonitions from hallucinations, or be taken over by delusions.

Some things don't mix well with premonitions. There is firm evidence that traumatic life events, such as childhood maltreatment and post-traumatic stress disorder, can contribute to anomalous experiences and distorted reality testing. Persons with a history of substance abuse, schizophrenia, and mood disturbances such as major depression and neuroticism, in which a person is abnormally sensitive, obsessive, tense, or anxious are also more likely to have anomalous experiences. Some brain conditions, such as damage to the left temporal lobe and dysfunction in the right cerebral hemisphere, can cause hallucinations and delusions. Individuals experiencing any of these problems should think twice before intentionally cultivating premonitions.

What about the aftermath of psi-related experiences? Almost any type of anomalous experience can lead to unpleasant aftereffects. Psi researcher Ian Stevenson found that the most common emotions following telepathic experiences were anxiety and depression. But in larger surveys of extrasensory experiences in general, the most commonly reported emotions are anxiety and happiness.

Fear often follows psi experiences. This is usually due not to the experience itself, but to the prevailing attitude toward these phenomena in the surrounding culture. This is particularly true in America. As one survey respondent said, "My belief was and is that if I had talked about this experience, I should have been treated as insane or deluded. . . . [M]y career prospects might have been seriously damaged."

The aftereffects of psi experiences are clearly culturally dependent. In Brazil, for instance, where psi experiences are widely considered in a favorable light and as an indicator of spiritual progress, 80 percent of college students in one survey said the experience had a positive and tangible effect on their life, and some believed the experience had either saved their lives or made it possible for them to save someone else's life. In contrast, in the United States there is a much lower tendency to interpret anomalous experiences positively. Concerns center on what one's peers will think, whether one can control the psi ability, being incapacitated by becoming overloaded with the thoughts of others, or too much responsibility should one's psi ability become known.

Most anomalous experiences aren't invited; they occur spontaneously, out of the blue, and they can be disorienting. If you experience psychological difficulties following premonitions or other psi-type experiences, I advise seeking help from a mental-health professional. I recognize the sad truth, however, that exposure to the psychiatric profession can be hazardous following a psi experience. Many psychiatrists can't tell a valid premonition from a hallucination, and their therapy can make matters worse. Many consider all psi experiences pathological by definition. If they go by the book when faced with someone who claims they have glimpsed the future, they may diagnose them as crazy. "The book" is the *Diagnostic and Statistical Manual of Mental Disorders,* the venerable *DSM,* which lays out the recognized categories of mental illness and how to diagnose them. Under "schizotypal personality" there are several diagnostic criteria, two of which could be construed as applying to premonitions: magical thinking and unusual perceptions. So should someone who has had a disturbing premonition trust a psychiatrist or not? This is a serious question, because of the likelihood of being placed on an antipsychotic medication. This can be a disaster because, as the saying goes, "Normal people do not tolerate crazy drugs."

Consider what happened to Anna Martínez (not her real name), a middle-aged Hispanic woman, following a premonition. Anna moved from Mexico to Los Angeles when she was five years old. She had a hard life, including an abusive father and an alcoholic, chronically unemployed husband. She would frequently dream of her grandmother in Mexico, who always said Anna had "the gift." Anna often had precognitive dreams that were so specific they amazed her family members. Two months before seeking help at the county hospital's psychiatric unit, Anna awoke from a frighteningly vivid dream in which her husband of twenty-three years stepped off a downtown curb during rush hour and was hit by a bus. Although the dream haunted her, she could not bring herself to tell her spouse. Two weeks later, Anna's husband was killed by a bus not far from his workplace. A devout Catholic, she sank into depression, guilt, and the fear that she had caused her husband's death as a result of her "bad thoughts." She stopped eating and sleeping, and kept repeating that she was going to be punished by God.

Her daughter took her to the emergency room of a large metropolitan hospital. A second-year psychiatry resident diagnosed her with "complicated bereavement with psychotic features." He reasoned that her dream and the bus accident were merely a coincidence, and that it played into her unconscious, ambivalent emotions toward her abusive husband. Her guilt over the loss had triggered a depression in a woman whose history pointed to a tendency toward psychosis according to his standards. The psychiatrist's focus on Anna's "flawed reality testing" made her feel even more anxious and isolated. But Anna knew there was no coincidence; she'd experienced these "coincidences" all her life.

She wanted to know things her doctor was not concerned about, because they had no place in his worldview. How could she have known the future? Did her vision cause her husband's death? Was there something she could have done to prevent his accident, some way she could have warned him before it happened? How could she live with herself knowing that her thoughts might have killed him?

Anna's visit to the psychiatrist could have turned out differently. All psychiatrists are not cut from the same cloth. There are monumental differences in their attitudes toward psi, and some are quite knowledgeable and open. So if I were distressed following a premonition and wanted professional help, I'd first make sure the counselor is open to psi. I would also consider consulting someone trained in the Jungian tradition. Carl G. Jung experienced premonitions often during his life, and respect for them is inherent in the school of psychiatry for which he is known. I would also follow a rule that would have been helpful to Anna: if your doctor consistently makes you feel worse, find another one.

Premonitions convey warnings of impending events and can be life-saving, yet this may not be the most important way they impact our lives. If we engage them and take them seriously, they can also rearrange our view of the world in the most fundamental ways, as we will now see.

FIVE

PREMONITIONS AND OUR WORLDVIEW

"[C]onsciousness must be part of nature,
or, more generally, of reality."

—Niels Bohr, Nobel physicist

PATHS TOWARD PREMONITIONS

If premonitions are real—if we really can know something before it happens—we find that we have parachuted into two of the most intractable, contentious debates in human history: the meaning of time and the nature of consciousness.

If premonitions are valid, our commonsense beliefs about time—that it flows inexorably in one direction and that we're locked into knowing only the past and present—can't be correct, because this view prohibits premonitions.

How else might we proceed? What concepts of time might permit premonitions?

One option is to consider that the past, present, and future are simultaneously present, laid out in what physicists call a block universe that resembles an eternal present. In such a world there would be nothing surprising about premonitions. In fact, "future knowing" would be a misnomer, because the future and the present would exist at the same time. As physicist David J. Miller of the Centre for Time at the University of Sydney in Australia says, "If you have the block universe view, the future and the past are not any different, so there's no reason why you can't have causes from the future just as you have causes from the past."

Or perhaps, as some physicists suggest, time can curve back on itself via "closed time-like loops," permitting information from the future to crop up in the present.

Perhaps we might revision time by changing our perceptions. Time flowing one way, most physicists say, is a psychological illusion. Can we give up the illusion? Can we "change time" by changing the way we think? The answer appears to be yes. Many meditative practices teach practitioners to step out of time, as it were, and experience it as an eternal now. The result is a premonition-friendly version of reality.

But there is a problem, and it has to do with the nature of consciousness. Nearly all the novel approaches to time that are currently circulating within science assume that consciousness is confined to the brain and body. But maybe consciousness is not like that. Perhaps it can range freely in space and time. If so, it might escape the present, zoom forward in time, snatch a vision, and scurry back to "now," resulting in what we experience as a premonition. Or perhaps consciousness is already present everywhere in space and time. If so, there would be no necessity for it to travel anywhere at all. In this case, consciousness would have access to all the information that exists, has ever existed, or shall exist. This would mean that premonitions would occur as a matter of course, because no information would be shielded from consciousness. We could know information from the future and the past as readily as from the present. There would be nothing radical or special about premonitions, and we would not make a fuss about them.

So we can work our way toward the possibility of premonitions by readjusting our vision of time through new models in physics; by giving up the illusion of a flowing, one-way time through meditative approaches; by rethinking the nature of consciousness, or by some combination of these alternatives.

There is one other way: the way of evidence. This way is not speculative, theoretical, or philosophical. It does not rest on argument, but on fact.

J. B. Rhine, the legendary founder of experimental parapsychology in the United States, exemplified this approach. Like many philosophers and scientists today, he had great difficulty in contemplating the idea that precognition *could* happen, for this would mean, he said, that an effect comes before its cause. "It is hard to understand how the act of perception, which is the result, could occur before its cause," he said. "If there were ever an occasion in science on which it would appear proper to use the word impossible, it would be when the hypothesis of prophecy is advanced." But Rhine added that theory must conform to evidence and that, in his opinion, since future knowing had been demonstrated experimentally, science should modify its worldview to accommodate precognition.

That's how the evidence game should be played in evaluating premonitions: theory must yield to fact. Sentimentality must be set aside, and our favorite shoulds and oughts discarded, no matter what violence this may do to our personal views and cherished theories. As Thomas Henry Huxley, Darwin's great defender, described this process, "The greatest tragedy of science—the slaying of a beautiful theory by an ugly fact."

OUR BELOVED TIME

Our personal lives and our civilization are built around the notion of flowing, one-way time.

Consider our legal system. Our concept of justice and graded punishment assumes unidirectional, linear time. This version of time tells us that a one-year sentence for a crime is more severe than a sentence of six months, and that a ten-year sentence is harsher still. If time did not flow uniformly in one direction, these calibrated, variable sentences would make no sense. If time were otherwise, parking violators might as well be punished with a life sentence and rapists given a day in the pokey.

The Western ethos of hard work, optimism, and progress requires one-way time. We say that if we labor we can build a better future for our children and ourselves, and make the world a better place. These beliefs embody yet-to-come possibilities, a tomorrow, a future over the horizon.

In Christianity there is a temporal thread running in one direction from the moment of Creation to Armageddon and the Rapture. As in our judicial system, the doctrines of sin and salvation, guilt and punishment, demand a view of linear, unidirectional time.

If time were not linear and one-way, capitalism would be threatened. Savings, loans, investments, and the accumulation of interest assume that the future is always ahead of us. If time worked differently, banks, credit institutions, and the stock market could not work the way they do. Payment deadlines and foreclosures would make no sense. The insurance industry would collapse, because aging and death would not convey the urgency they do now. Insurance policies would not mature; neither would human bodies, which might even get younger.

Democracy and free elections would be spurious unless time flowed into the future. Elections assume accountability and the replacement of officials who don't measure up. Unless time's arrow pointed to the future, the notion of electoral change, like the idea of progress, would be nonsensical.

The rituals of daily life would be upended if time didn't behave itself. Punctuality would go out the window. No one could be late for work; we couldn't burn dinner by cooking it too long; prevention of illness would make no sense; aging would not occur; tooth decay would be a fiction; the coffee in your cup might get hotter instead of colder.

Is it any wonder we so doggedly defend our belief in flowing, one-way time? This view is so ingrained and integral to our lives that we react strongly when anyone questions it. When those time specialists, the physicists, begin to tamper with our cherished beliefs about time, we feel threatened and condemn them as geeks and nerds and turn away. What do *they* know? We protect our view of time as if it were our beloved child.

TIME IN A MUDDLE

Time means different things to different people. As poet and essayist Henry Van Dyke said, "Time is too slow for those who wait, too swift for those who fear, too long for those who grieve, too short for those who rejoice, but for those who love, time is eternity."

There's no getting around it: understanding premonitions requires understanding time. Unfortunately science can't give us final answers about what time is. "Time," says physicist Paul Davies, "is Einstein's unfinished revolution."

Sixteen centuries ago St. Augustine expressed his frustration with time, saying, "What, then, is time? If no one ask of me, I know; [but] if I wish to explain to him who asks, I know not." Not much has changed. Nobel physicist Richard Feynman said essentially the same thing as St. Augustine: "What is time? We physicists work with it every day, but don't ask me what it is. It's just too difficult to think about."

While it's true that most people live their lives untouched by these time troubles, others discover that there's no way to paper over the Great Time Debate. I recall my own encounter with these problems as an undergraduate student at the University of Texas at Austin. I was enrolled in a course in classical physics. Several students convinced Professor Hutchinson to depart from the lecture schedule and devote one hour to Einstein's theory of special relativity. He agreed, and crammed as much as he could into the hour, including the mind-boggling paradoxes for which Einstein and his brainchild are famous. The professor explained, for example, that if a twin travels on a rocket into deep space at a significant fraction of the speed of light, when he returns to earth he is younger than his twin who stayed behind. As they near the speed of light, clocks run slower and the mass of an object increases; at the speed of light time stops and the object's mass becomes infinite. The length of measuring rods shortens as they accelerate to light-speed. By the end of the hour, all of us sat in stunned silence—except one of my classmates, who was pushed over the edge. Unable to restrain himself, he threw his notebook to the floor, stood up, waved a clenched fist, and in his best Texas drawl shouted angrily, "Dr. Hutchinson, *do you really expect us to believe this shit?*"

I have often wondered what my skeptical, agitated classmate thought when space travel became a reality. Would he have continued to deny, among other things, that moving objects age more slowly than stationary ones? Cosmonaut Sergei Avdeyev, who orbited the earth for 748 days in three space flights, is about one-fiftieth of a second younger than he would have been had he stayed at home. "In other words," says Princeton astrophysicist J. Richard Gott, "he has time-traveled about one-fiftieth of a second into the future. It's not much, but with faster rockets it could be more."

The paradoxes involving time in modern physics "are enough to make your neurons misfire, then sizzle and explode," says science writer Amanda Gefter. "Physicists have long struggled to understand what time really is. In fact, they are not even sure it exists at all. . . . [S]ome researchers increasingly suggest that time is not a fundamental feature of nature, but rather an artifact of our perception." Summing up these views, Gefter suggests that "the greatest trick the universe ever pulled was convincing us that time exists." As physicist Davies describes this trick, "Notions such as 'the past,' 'the present' and 'the future' seem to be more linguistic than physical. There is none of this in physics. . . . No physical experiment has ever been performed to detect the passage of time."

Einstein agreed. In a letter of condolence to the wife of his best friend, he wrote, "For us faithful physicists, the separation between past, present, and future has only the meaning of an illusion, though a persistent one."

No event in recent years illustrates the unsettled state of affairs surrounding time better than a gathering of around two-dozen top physicists, historians, and philosophers at the Seven Pines Symposium in Stillwater, Minnesota, in 2001. The purpose of the meeting was to debate the nature of time. To say there was no agreement is an understatement. Opinions varied so wildly that one professor of physics reported, "I don't see any evidence that they're talking about different parts of the same elephant." The director of the meeting closed it by referring not to mathematical equations or experimental findings but to the ancient Chinese sage Lao Tsu's view of time and space:

> These two spring from the same source but differ in name;
>   this appears as darkness.
> Darkness within darkness.
> The gate to all mystery.

When physicists tinker with time, people can be horrified. Consider the end-of-the-world fear triggered by the startup of the Large Hadron Collider (LHC) in September 2008 by scientists at the European Organization for Nuclear Research (CERN) near Geneva, Switzerland. The LHC is a $6 billion particle accelerator that sends beams of protons careening around a seventeen-mile ring, crashing them into one another to re-create the aftereffects of the Big Bang, then monitoring the debris in hopes of learning more about the origins of the universe. This retreat in time to the earliest beginnings of the universe triggered lawsuits in Europe and the United States. Critics feared the experiment would create a mini black hole that might expand to suck the earth out of existence in an instant. Headlines around the world predicted disaster of biblical proportions. One British newspaper, *The Sun,* trumpeted, END OF THE WORLD DUE IN NINE DAYS. Physicists were accused of playing God, and some critics dubbed the experiment the Doomsday Test. The lawsuits were not successful, and on September 10, 2008, the largest and most expensive science gadget in world history was turned on. No black holes gobbled up the earth, but something unexpected did happen. It broke. A few days after startup, the LHC was out of commission, CERN said, due to the failure of a single, badly soldered electrical connection.

Many factors fed the dread of the LHC startup, including a credibility gap surrounding high-energy physics. After all, nuclear bombs capable of ending all life on earth are the most tangible result of the past half-century of atomic research. But re-creating the creation—"fooling around with time," as one observer put it—also stoked fears.

PREMONITIONS DO NOT CONTRADICT
THE LAWS OF NATURE

Skeptics have long argued that premonitions cannot happen because they violate the laws of nature. Because there is no consensus on the nature of time, it's not clear what laws premonitions might be violating. It's not the laws of nature that are being violated so much as the assumptions we make about how things are supposed to be. Time appears to flow in one direction. But as we know, not everything is exactly as it appears.

Some scientists have come around to the idea that premonitions are compatible with contemporary physics. They believe that the future may commingle with the present, opening the door for future knowing. An example is Brian Josephson, a Nobel physicist at Cambridge University. Josephson is intrigued with researcher Dean Radin's computer-based presentiment experiments showing that people can sense the future. "So far," Josephson says, "the evidence seems compelling. What seems to be happening is that information is coming from the future. In fact, it's not clear in physics why you can't see the future. In physics, you certainly cannot completely rule out this effect."

Physicist Richard Shoup, of the Boundary Institute in Los Altos, California, believes we are surrounded by backward-acting influences, in which the future causes the present. The reason we don't see most of these backward-caused effects is that they are often small and subtle, and because we are looking in the wrong places for them. In order to see them we have to be more attentive; we must *want* to notice them. And we must lure them out of hiding and give them a nudge to show themselves, as Radin and others have done in their presentiment and online precognition experiments. Shoup believes it's difficult to overstate the importance of this research. It may demand a re-interpretation or reformulation of quantum theory, and even a reconsideration of the scientific method.

Others insist there's plenty of room within current physics to accommodate premonitions, and that no further tinkering is required. For instance, the eminent physicist Gerald Feinberg, discussing psi events, said, "If such phenomena indeed occur, no change in the fundamental equations of physics would be needed to describe them." Feinberg is referring to the well-known fact that in classical physics Newton's laws of motion work equally well in either direction, forward or backward, and Maxwell's equations do the same where electromagnetism is concerned. The same can be said of Schrödinger's famous equation in quantum physics. Physicist O. Costa de Beauregard agreed with Feinberg, observing, "Today's physics allows for the existence of so-called 'paranormal' phenomena of telepathy, precognition, and psychokinesis. . . . The whole concept of 'non-locality' in contemporary physics requires this possibility." Physicist Henry Margenau concurred, saying, "Strangely, it does not seem possible to find the scientific laws or principles violated by the existence of [psi phenomena]."

For more than a century, the main objection from skeptics is that premonitions violate natural laws. This objection is hollow on two counts. First, as the comments of the above scientists show, current science *permits* premonitions, it does not prohibit them. Second, even if skeptics could scrounge up a natural "law" that appears to be violated, that so-called law would need to be modified to accommodate stubborn facts—that in exacting experiments now replicated around the world, foreknowledge has been documented beyond reasonable doubt.

CAN WE AFFECT THE PAST?

If we can know the future and take action to change it—choosing not to travel on a train or plane, say, after we've seen it crash in a dream—might we also be able to change the past as well? Common sense says no; past events have already happened and are therefore fixed and unchangeable. But as the views from modern physics on the nature of time show, common sense is not always a reliable guide to how things work.

William Braud, research director of the Institute of Transpersonal Psychology in Palo Alto, California, reviewed twenty-four published experiments in which people try to "reach back" in time to influence events mentally that presumably have already happened.

Studies of Inanimate Objects. Five of these experiments involved inanimate objects, such as electronic random event generators. People were able successfully to influence their output *after* the machine had run, *if* the earlier output of the machine had been recorded but not actually observed by an individual. There was less than one chance in ten thousand that the successful results could be explained by chance.

Let's consider a typical experiment of this type, which involves a computer-like random event generator designed to spit out a random chain of ones and zeros. A recording is made of its output, which no one observes. Because its output is truly random, the recording should contain equal numbers of ones and zeros over an extended period of time. Later, after the machine has run and the recording has been made, someone tries mentally to influence the machine's output, moving the sequence either to more ones or more zeros. Then when the recording is examined, it is found to demonstrate not equal numbers of ones and zeros as predicted, but a preponderance of one or the other, according to the choice of the individual who attempted mentally to influence it. This has been replicated in dozens of experiments. It's as if the individual's intentions reached back in time and influenced the random process.

Why can't this happen if the recording was actually observed? According to the most widely accepted interpretation of quantum physics, events at the subatomic, quantum level are not real until they are observed. Before they are observed they exist as an array of possibilities, not actualities. It's the act of observation that collapses all the possibilities into a single, recognizable event. Psi experimenters suggest that, if quantum events aren't fixed prior to observation, they are susceptible in this state to the intentions and wishes of observers in the present. Observing them following observation is ineffective, however, because they've been rendered unchangeable by being observed.

Studies in Living Systems. Braud also reviewed nineteen experiments in which individuals tried mentally to influence random processes in living systems, both human and nonhuman, after they had happened and been recorded, but prior to anyone's observation of the records.

For example, in 1998 Dean Radin and his colleagues recorded the disorderly fluctuations of electrodermal activity, a measure of sweating, in subjects located in Las Vegas, Nevada. The recordings of these sessions were stored without being observed. Two months later, healers located in Brazil, six thousand miles away, attempted to influence the recordings in a specified direction. They were successful in doing so; there were only 1.6 chances in a hundred that the results could be explained by chance.

In three experiments, the patternless entry of cars into a tunnel in the center of Vienna during rush hour was recorded by photo-beam monitoring. The record was converted into click sounds, which influencers tried to change in a specified direction thirty to forty-five days later. In two of three experiments, they were successful in doing so.

In other studies, influencers tried to modify random, prerecorded activities of gerbils running in activity wheels, the multiplication of blood parasites in rats, the random rates of entry of shoppers into a supermarket, and the breathing rates of humans, prior to the observation of these recordings. The combined results of all nineteen of these studies were hugely positive; the odds against chance were more than three million to one. How large were these effects? Braud found that the average effect size was ten times as great as those that were obtained in the medical studies establishing the effectiveness of aspirin in reducing heart attacks.

Again, a key factor is the lack of observation of the recording of the prior event. Observation seems to fix the outcome in an unchangeable state. But if observation has not occurred, the events remain indefinitely as "seed moments," in Braud's graphic language, meaning that they can germinate into outcomes that are chosen by someone at a later time.

RETRO-PRAYER: PRAYING FOR THE PAST

Our attempts to influence the past may have large-scale effects on human health. In 2001, Leonard Leibovici, professor of medicine at Israel's Rabin Medical Center, tested this possibility. He performed a randomized, double-blind experiment in which prayer was offered in the present for adult patients who had been hospitalized for sepsis (bloodstream infection) four to ten years *after* they had been hospitalized. Roughly half the 3,393 patients were retroactively prayed for and half were not. On examining their hospital records after the prayer was offered, he found that the length of hospital stay in the prayed-for patients was significantly shorter, as was the duration of fever, compared to the patients for whom prayer was not offered in the present.

I should add that Leibovici is an avowed skeptic of the notion that people's intentions or prayers can affect another person remotely, whether in the past, present, or future. He interprets the outcome of his study *not* as evidence that healing intentions or prayer changes the past, but as proof that research in this field produces such strange outcomes that it can't be trusted, including his own carefully constructed study.

How might the results of Leibovici's experiment be explained? It is unlikely that the prayers and intentions of individuals in the present reached back in time to change the hospital course of patients after it was a matter of record. It is more likely that the change was effected while the course of the disease was still forming, before the various forms of medical observation were brought to bear on it—exams, probes, blood tests, X-rays, scans, and so on. All illnesses have a beginning, presumably including a stage in which subatomic, quantum-level processes are at play as a collection of mere possibilities that can be influenced in various directions. Like a shirt that has been laundered but not ironed, the patient's physiological processes have not taken on any permanent creases. Disease has not yet formed; healthy function remains possible. Braud, as mentioned, suggests that these earliest pre-observation states are "seed moments" in which the disease process is susceptible to thoughts, intentions, and prayers.

Leibovici's bold experiment suggests that for certain operations of consciousness, "earlier" and "later" may have no meaning. Our thoughts and intentions may operate forward in time, as in premonitions, or backward as well, as in retroactive prayer and other forms of retro-intention. Our *premo*nitions may be symmetrical with *retro*monitions.

QUANTUM POSSIBILITIES

One of the simplest, yet most profound and puzzling, experiments in the history of physics is the so-called double-slit experiment. This historic discovery is usually attributed to the English scientist Thomas Young, who around 1800 tried to determine whether light was made up of particles or waves. Young's startling conclusion was that light could be either, depending on how one went about the experiment.

Imagine a stream of light particles called photons (or electrons or any other subatomic particle) being shot at a barrier with two small slits in it. On the far side of the barrier is a screen or video camera that registers when it is hit by the photons. If only one of the slits is open, the screen or camera will see a scattering of hits that are clustered directly opposite the open slit—just what one would expect if the photons were individual particles. But when both slits are open, a different pattern is seen. In this case one sees an interference pattern, which could only be produced if the photons were behaving like waves that overlap with one another.

In a different twist, you try firing not a stream of photons but single ones at the barrier when only one slit is open. Again, as you'd expect, you see the cluster pattern behind the slit, as before. Now you open both slits and fire single photons. You'd expect to find two cluster patterns, one directly behind each slit. But you'd be wrong. Instead, you find the interference pattern, which is producible only if the single photon is passing through both slits at the same time, as would a wave, with the emerging waves interfering with each other after passing through the two slits.

But how does the single photon know whether to behave like a particle or wave? How does it know, on its path toward the slits, whether one or both will be open? Is this future knowing?

Suppose you try to trick the photon in what is called a "delayed choice" experiment proposed by physicist John A. Wheeler. You place a shutter in front of one of the slits, a shutter that is so fast you can open or close it *after* the photon has passed through the slits in the barrier, but before it is registered on the screen or camera. The result is that if you closed one slit after the photon passed through it, the pattern that's registered indicates particles; if both slits remain open, the pattern looks like the interference pattern produced by waves. In some way, the photon "knows" that one of them would be closed or both open *after* it has gone past the slits.

Psi researcher and theorist Dean Radin says, "Somehow the photon 'knows' *after* it had already gone past the slits that one of them would be closed *later.*" Radin is not saying that a subatomic particle knows something in the same sense that a human being does. It presumably doesn't go through processes of reason, analysis, inference, intuition, or any other process that's involved in human cognition. But even if we strip the photon's behavior of all these human attributes, a kind of future knowing remains. This apparent foreknowledge of whether a slit will be open or closed is a dead ringer for a premonition.

Or perhaps the subatomic particle knows nothing in the delayed choice experiment, and it is the human experimenter who is causing its strange behavior. In this view, the particle is merely following orders, which are the experimenter's choice to open or close the shutter after the particle passes through the slit. This decision acts backward in time, "telling" the particle .to behave either as a wave or particle. This amounts to backward causation, shaping an event that has already happened by taking action in the present. This represents a cause coming after the effect, and violates our customary idea of one-way time, in which things always happen into the future.

The double-slit and delayed-choice experiments defy reason. Physics professors know this, and they use them as rites of passage to tease young physics students out of their rational habits of thinking. Nobel physicist Richard Feynman, who will forever be known as the wizard who solved the mystery of the 1986 Space Shuttle *Challenger* disaster by uncovering the flawed O-rings, was a much-adored master teacher who warned his students to loosen up in the face of the mysteries of quantum physics. "There was a time," he said, "when the newspapers said that only twelve men understood the theory of relativity. I do not believe that there ever was such a time. . . . On the other hand, I think it is safe to say that no one understands quantum mechanics. . . . Do not keep saying to yourself, if you can possibly avoid it, 'But how can it be like that?' because you will get 'down the drain' into a blind alley from which nobody has yet escaped. Nobody knows how it can be like that."

The double-slit experiments suggest that a photon knows that an open or closed slit is coming, and behaves accordingly. Thus we see premonition operating all the way down, from the large to the smallest scale in nature.

Most scientists insist that at some stage of evolutionary complexity consciousness somehow emerged from matter. Perhaps, in seeing hints of premonitions at the subatomic scale, we are bumping into the earliest evidence of consciousness in matter—premonitions as a kind of proto-mind. Or, rather than emerging from matter, perhaps, like matter, "consciousness was there in the first place," as historian-philosopher Willis Harman believed.

This view has been taken seriously by philosopher David J. Chalmers, director of the Centre for Consciousness at the Australian National University in Canberra. Chalmers proposes that consciousness may be fundamental in the world, produced by nothing more elemental and reducible to nothing more basic. Premonitions at the quantum level may count as evidence for this pervasive, elemental stuff we call consciousness.

Physicist Freeman Dyson also thinks consciousness is loose in the world and is distributed throughout the universe, down to the smallest dimensions. As he says in his book *Infinite in All Directions*, "The universe shows evidence of . . . mind on three levels. The first level is the level of elementary physical processes in quantum mechanics. . . . The second level at which we detect . . . mind is the level of direct human experience . . . [There is] a third level of mind, a mental component of the universe."

CONSCIOUSNESS

Dyson believes the cosmos is suffused with consciousness, from the grandest level to the most minute dimensions. If it is, why aren't we aware of it?

"We don't know who first discovered water, but we can be sure that it wasn't a fish," the old saw reminds us. Continual exposure to something reduces our awareness of its presence. Over time, we become blind to the obvious. We swim in a sea of consciousness, like a fish swims in water. And like a fish that has become oblivious to his aqueous environment, we have become dulled to the ubiquity of consciousness.

In science, we have largely ignored how consciousness manifests in our existence. We've done this by assuming that the brain produces consciousness, although how it might do so has never been explained and can hardly be imagined. The polite term for this trick is "emergence." At a certain stage of biological complexity, evolutionary biologists claim, consciousness pops out of the brain like a rabbit from a magician's hat. Yet this claim rests on no direct evidence whatsoever. No scientist has ever observed consciousness emerging from matter. As Rutgers University philosopher Jerry A. Fodor flatly states, "Nobody has the slightest idea how anything material could be conscious. Nobody even knows what it would be like to have the slightest idea about how anything material could be conscious. So much for the philosophy of consciousness."

In spite of the complete absence of evidence, the belief that the brain produces consciousness endures and has ossified into dogma. Many scientists realize the limitations of this belief. One way of getting around the lack of evidence is simply to declare that what we call consciousness is the brain itself. That way, nothing is produced, and the magic of "emergence" is avoided. As astronomer Carl Sagan expressed his position, "My fundamental premise about the brain is that its workings—what we sometimes call mind—are a consequence of its anatomy and physiology, and nothing more." Nobelist Francis Crick agreed, saying, "[A] person's mental activities are entirely due to the behavior of nerve cells, glial cells, and the atoms, ions, and molecules that make up and influence them."

This "identity theory"—mind equals brain—has led legions of scientists and philosophers to regard consciousness as an unnecessary, superfluous concept. Some go out of their way to deny the existence of consciousness altogether, almost as if they bear a grudge against it. Tufts University cognitive scientist Daniel Dennett says, "We're all zombies. Nobody is conscious." Dennett includes himself in this extraordinary claim, and he seems proud of it.

Others suggest that there are no mental states at all, such as love, courage, or patriotism, but only electrochemical brain fluxes that should not be described with such inflated language. They dismiss thoughts and beliefs for the same reasons. This led Nobel neurophysiologist Sir John Eccles to remark that "professional philosophers and psychologists think up the notion that there are no thoughts, come to believe that there are no beliefs, and feel strongly that there are no feelings." Eccles was emphasizing the absurdities that have crept into the debates about consciousness. They are not hard to spot. Some of the oddest experiences I recall are attending conferences where one speaker after another employs his consciousness to denounce the existence of consciousness, ignoring the fact that he consciously chose to register for the meeting, make travel plans, prepare his talk, and so on.

Many scientists concede that there are huge gaps in their knowledge of how the brain makes consciousness, but they are certain they will be filled in as science progresses. Eccles and philosopher of science Karl Popper branded this attitude "promissory materialism." "[P]romissory materialism [is] a superstition without a rational foundation," Eccles says. "[It] is simply a religious belief held by dogmatic materialists . . . who confuse their religion with their science. It has all the features of a messianic prophecy."

The arguments about the origins and nature of consciousness are central to premonitions. For if the promissory materialists are correct—if consciousness is indeed identical with the brain—the curtain closes on premonitions. The reason is that the brain is a *local* phenomenon—i.e., it is localized to the brain and body, and to the present. This prohibits premonitions in principle, because accordingly the brain cannot operate outside the body and the here-and-now. But consciousness *can* operate beyond the brain, body, and the present, as hundreds of experiments and millions of testimonials affirm. Consciousness cannot, therefore, be identical with the brain.

These assertions are not hyperbolic, but conservative. They are consistent with the entire span of human history, throughout which all cultures of which we have record believed that human perception extends beyond the reach of the senses. This belief might be dismissed as superstition but for the fact that modern research has established its validity beyond reasonable doubt to anyone whose reasoning has not clotted into hardened skepticism. To reiterate a single example—the evidence supporting foreknowledge, our concern in this book—psi researchers Charles Honorton and Diane Ferrari examined 309 precognition experiments carried out by 62 investigators, involving 50,000 participants in more than 2 million trials. Thirty percent of these studies were statistically significant in showing that people can describe future events, when only five percent would be expected to demonstrate such results by chance. The odds that these results were not due to chance was greater than 10^{20} to 1.

During the past decade a flood of scholarly work has appeared supporting the premise that consciousness is not equatable with the brain, such as the exemplary book *Irreducible Mind,* by University of Virginia psychologists Edward F. Kelly, Emily Williams Kelly, and colleagues. Hundreds of additional books and studies supporting this view are provided in the references section of this book. In addition, books are now available that are specifically devoted to the objections of skeptics, such as Cambridge philosopher Chris Carter's admirable *Parapsychology and the Skeptics.*

But what if the "promissory materialists" were correct? What if consciousness is indeed identical to the brain, as they contend? One result, never admitted by the materialists, is that there would be no reason to believe their arguments. For if they are merely "brains being brains," their decisions are unlikely to have been arrived at by careful reasoning and thoughtful decision-making. Because they were following the dictates of their brain, they could not have arrived at a different conclusion, in which case their views lose any claim to objectivity and may therefore be ignored.

But of course the brainiacs don't *really* think their consciousness is the same as their brain. For example, they lobby funding agencies to obtain research grants. In doing so, they assume that the funders have the freedom to decide where the money goes, which must mean the granters are not simply brains whose decisions are predetermined by the biochemical fluxes in their gray matter. Moreover, in their scientific papers the materialists say, "We have shown" such and such, not, "Our brains have shown." And when they kiss their kids good night they say, "I love you," not, "My brain loves you."

No society could function successfully according to the materialists' views. The notion of self-responsibility and freedom of choice underlie the justice systems and international codes of conduct of all civilized nations. The brain-equals-consciousness perspective is one in which no one is responsible for anything, in which case the very concept of justice makes no sense.

Of course there is *some* relationship between the brain and the *contents* of consciousness. If I sip a glass of merlot, my thoughts and feelings change as the chemicals do their work. But how should this connection be understood? *Can* it be understood? Some suggest no, such as British philosopher Colin McGinn: "The problem is how to integrate mind with the physical brain—how to reveal a unity beneath this apparent diversity. That problem is very hard, and I do not believe anyone has any good ideas about how to solve it."

I suggest that throughout history many great thinkers have indeed had good ideas about how to understand the mind-brain connection, including Plato, Friedrich Schiller, William James, Henri Bergson, Thomas Edison, Carl G. Jung, Aldous Huxley, C. D. Broad, and many others. The general idea they have proposed is that the brain, rather than producing consciousness, receives it from the outside. It then filters and modifies what is received, thereby shaping the thoughts and feelings that make up our mental life. British neuropsychiatrist Peter Fenwick, a leading authority on near-death experiences, calls these ideas "transmission theories" of mind-brain interaction.

A key feature of this view is that the brain restricts consciousness by acting as a "reducing valve," as Aldous Huxley put it. The brain is like a dirty prism that cannot collect all the light to which it is exposed. It is like a tourniquet on consciousness, choking our perceptions down to a trickle. Thus physicist David Darling suggests that we are conscious not *because* of the brain, but *in spite* of it.

One of the first modern thinkers to endorse an outside-the-brain view of consciousness was William James, who is considered the father of American psychology. In his 1898 Ingersoll Lecture at Harvard University, James took a courageous stand against what he called "the fangs of cerebralistic materialism" and the idea that consciousness is produced by the brain. He acknowledged that arrested brain development in childhood can lead to mental retardation, that strokes or blows to the head can abolish memory or consciousness, and that certain chemicals can change the quality of thought. But to consider this as proof that the brain actually makes consciousness, James said, is irrational.

Why irrational? Consider a radio, an invention that was introduced during James's lifetime, and which he used to illustrate the mind-brain relationship. If one bangs a radio with a hammer, it ceases to function. But that does not mean that the origin of the sound was the radio itself; the sound originated from outside it in the form of an electromagnetic signal. The radio received, modified, and amplified the external signal into something recognizable as sound. Just so, the brain can be damaged in various ways that distort the quality of consciousness—trauma, stroke, nutritional deficiencies, dementia, etc. But this does not necessarily mean the brain "made" the consciousness that is now disturbed, or that consciousness is identical to the brain.

British philosopher Chris Carter endorses this analogy. Equating mind and brain is as irrational, he says, as listening to music on a radio, smashing the radio's receiver, and thereby concluding that the radio was *producing* the music.

To update the analogy, consider a television set. We can damage a television set so severely that we lose the image on the screen, but this doesn't prove that the TV actually produced the image. We know that David Letterman does not live behind the TV screen on which he appears; yet the contention that brain equals consciousness is as absurd as if he did.

America's greatest inventor, Thomas Edison, was a contemporary of James, and he held a similar view. "People say I have created things," he wrote in 1911. "I have never created anything. I get impressions from the Universe at large and work them out, but I am only a plate on a record or a receiving apparatus—what you will. Thoughts are really impressions that we get from the outside."

If we damage a lung our breathing ability is reduced, but we do not assume on this basis that our lungs make the air they breathe. If our stomach is diseased our digestion suffers, yet this does not prove that the stomach makes the food it digests. Yet the mind-equals-brainiacs insist that damage to the brain and the resulting diminution of brainpower proves that the brain makes consciousness.

The radio and TV analogies can be misleading, however, because consciousness does not behave like an electromagnetic signal. Electromagnetic (EM) signals display certain characteristics. The farther away they get from their source, the weaker they become. Not so with consciousness; its effects do not attenuate with increasing distance. For example, in the hundreds of healing experiments that have been done in both humans and animals, healing intentions work equally well from the other side of the earth as at the bedside of the sick individual. Moreover, EM signals can be blocked partially or completely, but the effects of conscious intention cannot be blocked by any known substance. For instance, sea water is known to block EM signals completely at certain depths yet experiments in remote viewing have been successfully carried out beyond such depths, demonstrating that the long-distance communication between the involved individuals cannot depend on EM-type signals. In addition, EM signals require travel time from their source to a receiver, yet thoughts can be perceived simultaneously between individuals across global distances. Thoughts can be displaced in time, operating into both past and future. In precognitive remote-viewing experiments—for example, the hundreds of such experiments by the PEAR Lab at Princeton University—the receiver gets a future thought before it is even sent. Furthermore, consciousness can operate into the past, as in the experiments involving retroactive intentions. Electromagnetic signals are not capable of these feats. From these differences we can conclude that consciousness is not an energetic signal.

Then what is it? My conclusion is that consciousness is not a thing or substance, but is a *nonlocal* phenomenon. *Nonlocal* is merely a fancy word for *infinite*. If something is nonlocal, it is not localized to specific points in space, such as brains or bodies, or to specific points in time, such as the present. Nonlocal events are *immediate*; they require no travel time. They are *unmediated*; they require no energetic signal to "carry" them. They are *unmitigated*; they do not become weaker with increasing distance. Nonlocal phenomena are *omnipresent*, everywhere at once. This means there is no necessity for them to go anywhere; they are already there. They are infinite in time as well, present at all moments, past, present, and future, meaning they are *eternal*.

This picture is not arbitrary. It is the image of consciousness that is required in order to accommodate the evidence for premonitions we've reviewed.

Nonlocality can be a shocking notion when encountered for the first time. No apologies are necessary for this; some things are simply that way. As the great physicist Niels Bohr said, "Anyone who is not shocked by quantum theory has not understood it." No one is immune. Einstein was so shocked by the possibility of nonlocal events in physics that he denounced nonlocality as "spooky action at a distance." But nonlocal events are no longer a matter of debate in physics; numerous experiments prove their existence.

The best-known studies are those of physicist Alain Aspect and his colleagues at the Institut d'Optique in Orsay, France, reported in 1981 and 1982. The researchers sent photons flying from a common source in opposite directions to separate detectors located several meters apart. The arrangement allowed a characteristic of the photons called polarization to be changed during flight. When the polarization of one photon was changed, the polarization of the opposite-moving photon also changed immediately. Because the changes were simultaneous, and because the photons were moving in opposite directions at light-speed, there was no possibility that a time-requiring signal could inform one photon what was happening with its twin. How was this possible? Most physicists conclude that the distant particles behaved as if they were "entangled" as a single particle; what was done to one affected the other immediately.

In 1998, Nicolas Gisin and his team at the University of Geneva provided additional evidence that nonlocality is an inherent aspect of nature. They set up detectors eleven kilometers, or roughly seven miles, apart, and connected them with optical fiber. When they changed the behavior of a photon at one end, its distant, twin photon changed instantly and to the same degree, without any loss or diminution in the strength of the change. Seven miles is vast compared with subatomic distances. In 2004, Gisin's group replicated this result, this time at more than fifty kilometers, or roughly thirty miles. Most physicists believe these results provide unequivocal evidence that immediate, unmitigated, and unmediated—i.e., nonlocal—quantum connections permeate the entire universe, no matter how great the distance.

Researcher Dean Radin, whose presentiment experiments provide profound evidence for future knowing, believes that the nonlocal events in the subatomic, quantum domain underlie the nonlocal events we experience at the human level. He invokes the concept of entanglement, illustrated by the Aspect and Gisin experiments, as a bridging hypothesis uniting these small- and large-scale happenings. Quantum entanglement and quantum nonlocality are indeed potent possibilities that may eventually explain our nonlocal experiences, but only further research will tell. Meanwhile, there is a gathering tide of opinion favoring these approaches. As physicist Chris Clarke, of the University of Southampton, says, "On one hand, Mind is inherently non-local. On the other, the world is governed by a quantum physics that is inherently non-local. This is no accident, but a precise correspondence. . . . [Mind and the world are] aspects of the same thing. . . . The way ahead, I believe, has to place mind first as *the* key aspect of the universe. . . . We have to start exploring how we can talk about mind in terms of a quantum picture. . . . Only then will we be able to make a genuine bridge between physics and psychology."

Whatever their explanation proves to be, the experiments documenting premonitions are real. They must be reckoned with. And when scientists muster the courage to face this evidence unflinchingly, the greatest superstition of our age—the notion that the brain generates consciousness or is identical with it—will topple. In its place will arise a nonlocal picture of the mind. This view will affirm that consciousness is fundamental, omnipresent, and eternal—a model that is as cordial to premonitions as the materialistic, brain-based view is hostile.

FATE OR FREE WILL?

I've had many conversations with people who are ambivalent toward future knowing. If premonitions are real, they say, then the future is fixed and immutable. Premonitions make a mockery of self-responsibility, render decision making futile, and make automatons of us all. Premonitions, they insist, are utterly incompatible with free will.

My friend Tessa is a novelist whose wide-ranging imagination and literary skills I greatly admire. "I can't accept the possibility that premonitions can be true," she recently told me. Even though Tessa has experienced several precognitive dreams, she discounts them as meaningless coincidences. "If these dreams were really premonitions," she insists, "that means the future is fixed and there is nothing I can do to change it. My experience tells me I have free will, and that the choices and decisions I make now can affect what happens later. If this weren't true, no one would be responsible for anything and civilized life would fall apart."

"But what about the experiments," I asked, "in which people's bodies register future events before they happen? And the precognitive remote-viewing experiments, in which people comprehend future happenings hours, days, or weeks beforehand?" We'd discussed these studies in prior conversations. Tessa frowned in annoyance. "I don't care what they show," she said testily. "I can't give up free will. That's more important to me than your damned experiments!"

I'd hit a nerve and our conversation was over. Tessa had waved her magic wand, and—*poof!*—banished hundreds of experiments, decades of careful scientific work, and the experiences of untold numbers of humans.

This debate is a tempest in a teapot to other individuals. How, they ask, could anyone believe that premonitions nullify free will? Everyone has heard of instances in which people glimpsed the future and acted to change it, as when Amanda removed her infant from its crib before the chandelier crashed into it. These instances are not persuasive to skeptics, however. If you act to change the future, they say it wasn't really the future because it never happened.

Many scholars line up with Tessa, such as my friend David Ray Griffin, professor of philosophy of religion and theology, School of Theology at Claremont and Claremont Graduate School in California. Griffin is a vigorous opponent of precognition. One reason precognition should be rejected, he says, is because it violates our presuppositions about human freedom. If we can know the future, this suggests that it is already in place, in which case the future is predetermined. This would demolish personal freedom of the will, one of our "hardcore commonsense notions" that Griffin believes must be heartily defended.

One way around the problem is to regard precognition not as the knowledge of a *fixed* future, but as a vision of a *probable* future. Viewing the future as an array of possibilities avoids determinism, and preserves our freedom to influence and change potential outcomes.

Another way of skirting the free-will problem in premonitions is through psychokinesis, commonly called mind over matter. When a dream is followed by an event that closely resembles the dream, Griffin says, we don't have to assume that the event caused the dream, which is the most common interpretation of a premonition. It is "more natural," he says, to assume that the dream caused the event. This would mean that in the Aberfan disaster all those dreams of the avalanche provided the critical nudge that sent the unstable, critically poised mountainside tumbling down onto the schoolhouse, and that the precognitive dreams of September 11 caused the chain of events that led to those tragic disasters. It goes without saying that many individuals find this interpretation unspeakably offensive. In his defense, Griffin is not alone in this view; philosopher Stephen Braude has staked out a similar position. And although Griffin finds this line of reasoning rational, he prefers other explanations for premonitions.

An individual who dreams of a plane crash and cancels his reservation prior to the disaster will never be convinced that he cannot change his or her future. Amanda will be forever resolute that her choice to remove her baby from its crib before the chandelier fell expressed her freedom of will. These individuals, and thousands of others like them, look on the arguments about free will and premonitions with bemused boredom. Their experiences tell them that premonitions are not the enemy of free will, but its friend.

LOVING MYSTERY

Growing up on a farm in central Texas, I developed a love of weather. Although there were always weather forecasts on the radio, I paid little attention to them. It was the uncertainty I found exciting, especially during the summer when frightful thunderstorms and, on one occasion a tornado, appeared out of nowhere. Nighttime thunderstorms were especially magical. I remember as a small child lying safe and warm in bed as rain and hail, punctuated with ear-splitting thunder and lightning, pounded the tin roof of our farmhouse with a din that is indescribable to someone who has never experienced it.

Things have changed. I have become an informavore, consuming information as if there's no tomorrow, including knowledge about the weather. I haunt the Weather Channel on my computer countless times every day. I want to know, must know, what lies ahead weatherwise. This has erased most of the uncertainty of the weather—and with it, surprise.

I could retreat from these sources of information, but I'm hooked. I rationalize my weather needs in a million ways. I travel a lot; I need to anticipate airport delays, what clothing to take on a trip, and so on. But this habit goes deeper than practicality. I've become wedded to weather—so bonded I can't tell if I'm consuming information about weather or if weather is consuming me.

There is one exception, one period each year when I go on a weather-information fast. For years, my wife, Barbara, and I have retreated into the high country of Wyoming or Idaho, where we camp for two or three weeks along the Continental Divide. This has become a restorative pilgrimage that energizes and sustains us for the rest of the year. We live in a tent and hike, fly fish, read, and write. Chapters get composed and future book projects outlined. But mostly we just are happy to exist in an environment that is predictable only in its unpredictability. In a couple of weeks during midsummer, we can count on a breathtaking weather display ranging from balmy conditions to violent storms, sleet and snow, with everything in between. We have awakened to two-foot snowdrifts against our tent; had a tent blown right off us; endured nearby lightning strikes; made snowmen in August; thawed frozen water for morning coffee. One of the things that draws us back, year after year, is the sheer surprise of this climactic chaos.

A mystery is a situation whose outcome we don't know, a plunge into the unknown. There is compelling evidence that participation in mystery is important for our mental and physical health. Mice who eagerly run mazes they've never before encountered live significantly longer than mice who hold back. Women who regularly engage in mini-mysteries—reading books, doing crossword and jigsaw puzzles, taking on novel experiences that get them out of familiar routines, preserve their mental faculties later in life to a greater degree than women who stick to familiar habits and eschew novelty.

Software is now available to challenge older individuals to leap into the unknown via a sea of puzzles designed to enhance mental abilities and to improve one's "brain age," through what's being called "neurobics" and "pumping neurons."

All of which suggests that we are meant to be surprised. Nature, it seems, loves a good mystery.

Premonitions represent anti-mystery. They convert the unknown into the known, sometimes saving our skin by alerting us to impending disasters or health problems.

So we encounter a paradox: surprise, mystery, and not-knowing are important for our health, but the eradication of surprise via premonitions can also work to our benefit. We need to make a place in our life for both the known and the unknown, for certainty and uncertainty.

"Either-or" doesn't fit us well as humans. We are complex creatures, able to participate in multiple meanings and disparate interpretations simultaneously. It's when we relax into ambiguity that we are most human.

Future knowing is a valuable quality, but we should hope that it never eradicates *all* the mysteries of life—including, I am learning, the weather.

APPENDIX

"Each person enfolds something of the spirit of the other in his consciousness."

—David Bohm, physicist

INFINITE, ETERNAL, AND ONE: SCIENTISTS ON CONSCIOUSNESS

In premonitions, consciousness expresses itself outside the here and now, behaving as if it is unrestricted by space and time. The implications are majestic, for if our mind is unrestricted by space it is omnipresent, and if unrestricted by time it is immortal or eternal. And if there are no boundaries to individual minds, in some dimension they come together to form a single, unitary mind. In the parlance of modern physics, such a mind is *nonlocal*.

We do not have to wait for scientists to endorse unbounded, infinite, nonlocal mind. They have already done so.

The following quotations are from some of the most prestigious and respected scientists of the twentieth century. They are cordial to the view that consciousness is infinite, eternal, and one, and therefore are hospitable to the possibility of premonitions.

Erwin Schrödinger

Shrödinger is one of the patriarchs of modern physics. He was awarded the Nobel Prize for his wave equation, which lies at the heart of quantum mechanics. One of his deepest interests was the role of consciousness in establishing physical reality.

> "To divide or multiply consciousness is something meaningless. There is obviously only one alternative, namely the unification of minds or consciousness. . . . [I]n truth there is only one mind."

"I venture to call it [the mind] indestructible since it has a peculiar time-table, namely mind is always *now*. There is really no before and after for the mind."

Albert Einstein

Einstein is perhaps the most famous scientist who ever lived. His publication of the special theory of relativity in 1905 forever changed the classical, mechanical, Newtonian worldview.

"A human being is part of the whole, called by us 'universe,' a part limited in time and space. He experiences his thoughts and feelings as something separate from the rest—a kind of optical delusion of his consciousness. This delusion is a kind of prison for us, restricting us to our personal decisions and to affection for a few persons nearest us. Our task must be to free ourselves from this prison by widening our circle of compassion to embrace all living creatures and the whole of nature in its beauty."

"I feel such a sense of solidarity with all living things that it does not matter to me where the individual begins and ends."

Freeman Dyson

Renowned physicist Freeman Dyson, known for his work in deep space propulsion, has been outspoken on his views of the centrality of consciousness in the universe.

"There is evidence . . . that the universe as a whole is hospitable to the growth of mind. . . . Therefore it is reasonable to believe in the existence of . . . a mental component of the universe. If we believe in this mental component of the universe, then we can say that we are small pieces of God's mental apparatus."

Henry Margenau

Henry Margenau was professor of Physics and Natural Philosophy at Yale University for nearly a half century.

> "[There is a physical reality that is] in essence the same for all. . . . [This] oneness of the all implies the universality of mind. . . . If my conclusions are correct, each individual is part of God or part of the Universal Mind."

> "The Universal Mind has no need for memory, since all things and processes—past, present, and future—are open to its grasp."

David Bohm

Bohm is one of the godfathers of modern physics. He was deeply interested in the nature of the mind and its relationship to matter.

> "Ultimately, the entire universe . . . has to be understood as a single undivided whole, in which analysis into separately and independently existent parts has no fundamental status."

> "Deep down the consciousness of mankind is one. This is a virtual certainty . . . and if we don't see this it's because we are blinding ourselves to it."

> "Ultimately all the moments are really one, . . . therefore now is eternity. . . . everything, including me, is dying every moment into eternity and being born again."

> "Everything is alive. What we call dead is an abstraction."

George Wald

Nobelist George Wald is among a growing number of scientists working in biology and medicine who believe that consciousness is fundamental in the universe.

> "Mind, rather than emerging as a late outgrowth in the evolution of life, has existed always . . . the source and condition of physical reality."

Niels Bohr

Bohr originated the principle of complementarity in modern physics. His name is virtually synonymous with the field.

> "We can admittedly find nothing in physics or chemistry that has even a remote bearing on consciousness. Yet all of us know that there is such a thing as consciousness, simply because we have it ourselves. Hence consciousness must be part of nature, or, more generally, of reality."

Sir James Jeans

Sir James Jeans made fundamental contributions to quantum mechanics and was deeply concerned about the role of consciousness in the physical world.

> "[The] universe begins to look more like a great thought than like a great machine."

Sir Arthur Eddington

One of the most famous astronomer-physicist-mathematicians of the twentieth century, Eddington was one of the most passionate writers about how consciousness is involved in constructing reality.

> "The idea of a universal Mind or Logos would be, I think, a fairly plausible inference from the present state of scientific theory; at least it is in harmony with it."

> "[T]he stuff of the world is mind-stuff."

Gregory Bateson

Gregory Bateson, with roots in anthropology and biology, was concerned with the concept of information flow in nature and how consciousness interacted with the physical world. He originated the "double bind" theory in modern psychology.

> "The individual mind is immanent but not only in the body. It is immanent also in the pathways and messages outside the body; and there is a larger Mind of which the individual mind is only a subsystem. This larger Mind is comparable to God and is perhaps what some people mean by 'God,' but it is still immanent in the total interconnected social system and planetary ecology."

NOTES

FOREWORD

xiii. "That grenade, *How to Meditate*": LeShan, L. *How to Meditate: A Guide to Self-Discovery*. Boston: Little, Brown, 1974.

xiv. "bumper sticker says, GRAVITY": Mooney, G. The History of the Gravity poster. http://www.mooneyart.com/gravity/historyof_01.html. Accessed September 16, 2008.

AUTHOR'S NOTE

xv. "is commonly called *mind over matter*: Braud, W. G. *Psi Notes: Answers to Frequently Asked Questions about Parapsychology and Psychic Phenomena*. 2nd ed. San Antonio, TX: The Mind Science Foundation, 1984: 3.

xv. "I wouldn't have much use for a field called *parabiology*": Mayer, E. L. *Extraordinary Knowing: Science, Skepticism, and the Inexplicable Powers of the Human Mind*. New York: Bantam/Random House, 2007: 119.

INTRODUCTION

xvii. "It all began innocently enough": Abridged from Dossey, L. *Reinventing Medicine*. San Francisco: HarperSanFrancisco, 1999: 1–3.

xxii. "Last year alone, literally billions were spent": Schwartz, S. A. "An Arrow Through Time." *Explore: The Journal of Science and Healing*. 2008; 4(2): 95–100.

xxiii. "Past presidents have included several Nobelists": Those interested in the early research in precognition may consult the SPR's Web site at http://www.spr.ac.uk/expcms/.

xxiii. "Rhine's initial laboratory has morphed into the Rhine Research Center": The Web site of the Rhine Research Center is http://www.rhine.org.

xxiii. "The archives of the PA are a rewarding entry point": The Web site of the Para-psychological Association is http://parapsych.org/.

xxiii. "the recent scholarly books *Irreducible Mind*": Kelly, E. F., et al. *Irreducible Mind: Toward a Psychology for the 21st Century*. Lanham, M. D.: Rowman and Littlefield; 2007.

xxiii. "and *Varieties of Anomalous Experience*": Cardeña, E., Lynn, S. J., Krippner, S. (eds.). *Varieties of Anomalous Experience: Examining the Scientific Evidence*. Washington, DC: American Psychological Association; 2000.

xxiii. "A 1987 survey by the University of Chicago's": Greeley, A. M. "Mysticism Goes Mainstream." *American Health*. 1987; 6(1): 47–49.

xxiv. "who helped guide the spiritual and political leader of Tibet": Targ, E., Schlitz, M., Irwin, H. J. "Psi-related experiences." In: *Varieties of Anomalous Experience: Examining the Scientific Evidence*. Cardeña, E., Lynn, S. J., Krippner, S. (eds.) Washington, DC: American Psychological Association; 2000: 219–52.

xxv. "is not to say that I rely solely on the oracle's advice": Gyatso, T. *Freedom in Exile: The Autobiography of the Dalai Lama*. New York: HarperCollins; 1991. Quotation available at Nechung—The State Oracle of Tibet, Web site of the government of Tibet in exile. http://www.tibet.com/Buddhism/nechung_hh.html. Accessed March 2, 2008.

xxv. "in managing President Ronald Reagan's schedule": Carroll, R. T. The Skeptic's Dictionary Online. Astrology. http://skepdic.com/astrolgy.html. Accessed March 3, 2008.

xxv. "that satellites could not see": Puthoff, H. E. "CIA-Initiated Remote Viewing Program at Stanford Research Institute." *Journal of Scientific Exploration*. 1996; 110(1): 75.

xxv. "in the highly classified Star Gate program": May, E. C. "The American Institutes for Research Review of the Department of Defense's STAR GATE program: A commentary." *Journal of Scientific Exploration*. 1996; 10(1): 89–107.

EPIGRAPH

xxix. "I'm sure [my memory] only works one way": Carroll, L. *Alice's Adventures in Wonderland* and *Through the Looking-Glass*. New York: New American Library; 2000: 174.

ONE: THE CASES

3. "and a change in the weather": Feather, S. R., Schmicker, M. *The Gift: ESP, the Extraordinary Experiences of Ordinary People*. New York: St. Martin's Press; 2005: 2.

4. "in a dramatic enough way to make us consider the possibility": Feather, S. R., Schmicker, M. *The Gift*. Op. cit., 185.

4. "before any damage was done.": Targ, R. *Limitless Mind.* Op. cit., 85–86.

5. "for the sorrow that I knew she would feel": Feather, S. R., Schmicker, M. *The Gift.* Op. cit., 189.

5. "the same dog I dreamed of that bit him": Feather, S. R., Schmicker, M. *The Gift.* Op. cit., 196.

5. "failed intervention attempts are greatly outnumbered by successful interventions": Feather, S. R., Schmicker, M. *The Gift.* 198.

6. "the near accident that he had to be relieved from work": Feather, S. R., Schmicker, M. *The Gift.* Op. cit., 198–99.

6. "Dale E. Graff is a physicist": Graff's book *Tracks in the Psychic Wilderness* is a fascinating description of his experiences. See: Graff, D. E. *Tracks in the Psychic Wilderness: An Exploration of ESP, Remote Viewing, Precognitive Dreaming and Synchronicity.* New ed. London: Vega; 2003.

6. "beginning in the 1970s during the Cold War": Puthoff, H. E. "CIA-Initiated Remote Viewing at Stanford Research Institute." http://www.biomindsuperpowers.com/Pages/CIA-InitiatedRV.html. Accessed February 6, 2008. Also: Utts, J. "An Assessment of the Evidence for Psychic Functioning." *Journal of Scientific Exploration.* 1996; 10(1): 3–30. http://anson.ucdavis.edu/~utts/air2.html. Accessed February 6, 2008. Also: Targ, R. "Remote Viewing at Stanford Research Institute in the 1970s: A Memoir." *Journal of Scientific Exploration.* 1996; 10(1): 77–88. Also: May, E. C. "The American Institutes for Research Review of the Department of Defense's STAR GATE Program: A Commentary." *Journal of Scientific Exploration.* 1996; 10(1): 89–107. Also: Nelson, R. D., et al. "Precognitive Remote Perception: Replication of Remote Viewing." *Journal of Scientific Exploration.* 1996; 10(1): 109–10.

6. "he promptly intervened upon waking, possibly saving a life": Feather, S. R., Schmicker, M. *The Gift.* Op. cit., 202–203.

7. "Future events are always casting their shadows": Graff, D. E. "Explorations in Precognitive Dreaming." *Journal of Scientific Exploration.* 2007; 21(4): 707–22.

7. "they will flicker in and out of our experience": Graff, D. E. "Explorations in Precognitive Dreaming." *Journal of Scientific Exploration.* 2007; 21(4): 707–22.

8. "a true precognitive warning we need to act on": Feather, S. R., Schmicker, M. *The Gift.* Op. cit., 201.

8. "after spending eleven days in intensive care": Kroft, S. "Dennis Quaid Recounts Twins' Drug Ordeal." *60 Minutes.* CBS online; http://www.cbsnews.com/stories/2008/03/13/60minutes/main3936412.shtml. Accessed March 26, 2008. Also: Kimberly Quaid said she had premonition at nine P.M. that something was wrong. Celebrity Blend. http://www.celebrityblend.com/kimberly-quaid-said-she-had-premonition-at-9pm-that-something-was-wrong/. Accessed March 26, 2008. Also: Ornstein, C. "Quaids Recall Twins' Drug Overdosage." *Los Angeles Times.* January 15, 2008. Available at ZAP2it. http://www.zap2it.com/movies/news/zap-story-quaidsrecalltwinsdrugoverdose,0,2286448.

story. Accessed March 26, 2008. Also: Ornstein, C. "State Cites Safety Drug Lapses at Cedars-Sinai." *Los Angeles Times.* January 10, 2008. Available at: *Portland Tribune* online. http://portlandscw.trb.com/news/la-me-cedars10jan 10,0,4490595.story?coll=kwbp-news-1. Accessed March 26, 2008.

9. "informing him that his dad had died": Cohn, S. Personal communication to the author. March 26, 2008. Used with permission.

10. "They're ovarian cysts, completely benign": Dossey, L. "Distant Nonlocal Awareness: A Different Kind of DNA." *Alternative Therapies in Health and Medicine.* 2000; 6(6): 10–14, 102–10.

11. "at the site the nurse was illuminating": Mitchell, E. "The Physiological Diagnostic Dream." *New York Medical Journal.* 1923; 188, 416.

11. "which had not metastasized, and was surgically resected": Schneider, D. *Revolution in the Body-Mind. I. Forewarning Cancer Dreams and the Bioplasma Concept.* Easthampton, NY: Alexa Press; 1976: 7.

11. "with cavities in the lungs and shortness of breath": Van de Castle, R. *Our Dreaming Mind.* New York: Ballantine; 1994: 367.

13. "he 'stepped off into the air' ": Jung, C. G. "Symbols and interpretations of dreams 3." *The Collected Works of C. G. Jung. Volume 18.* Read, H., Fordham, M., and Adler, G. (eds.). Hull, R. F. C. (trans.). London: Routledge and Kegan Paul; 1961: 207–208.

13. "we may not have a second chance": Bernstein, J. S. *Living in the Borderland: The Evolution of Consciousness and the Challenge of Healing Trauma.* New York: Routledge; 2005: 185.

13. "coined the term *telesomatic*": Schwarz, B. E. "Possible Telesomatic Reactions." *The Journal of the Medical Society of New Jersey.* 1967; 64(11): 600–603. Also: Bernstein, J. S. *Living in the Borderland: The Evolution of Consciousness and the Challenge of Healing Trauma.* New York: Routledge; 2005: 185.

13. "at the estimated time his wife felt the blow": Gurney, E., Myers, F. W. H., Podmore, F. *Phantasms of the Living. Volume 1.* London: Trübner; 1886: 188–89.

14. "reported that James had indeed drowned": Gurney, E., Myers, F. W. H., Podmore, F. *Phantasms of the Living. Volume 2.* London: Trübner; 1886: 132.

14. "children, spouses, siblings, twins, lovers, and very close friends": Stevenson, I. *Telepathic Impressions: A Review of 35 New Cases.* Charlottesville: University Press of Virginia; 1970.

14. "at the same time that she, the mother, had felt the burning pain": Rush, J. H. "New Directions in Parapsychological Research." *Parapsychological Monographs No. 4.* New York: Parapsychological Foundation; 1964: 18–19.

14. "a piece of the steering wheel had penetrated her chest": Rhine, L. E. "Psychological Processes in ESP Experiences. Part I. Waking Experiences." *Journal of Parapsychology.* 1962; 29: 88–111.

15. "his twin brother had died at the time he had stated": Blaksley, T. "Impression." *Journal of the Society for Psychical Research.* 1892; 5: 241.

15. "We got it going again and he's going to be fine": Pearsall, P. "The Heart Re-members." *Natural Health*. March–April, 1998. http://findarticles.com/p/arti cles/mi_m0NAH/is_n2_v27/ai_20353562/pg_4. Accessed January 29, 2007.

15. "how premonitions and bodily sensations can combine to influence patient care": Kincheloe, L. Personal communication to Larry Dossey. November 2003. Used with permission. Also available at: Kincheloe, L. "Intuitive Obstetrics." *Alternative Therapies in Health & Medicine*. 2003; 9(6): 16–17.

17. "Then the healing professions will be transformed": I have described what this future "Era III" or "nonlocal medicine" might look like in my book *Reinventing Medicine*. San Francisco: HarperSanFrancisco; 1999.

17. "continue to be promoted by SIDS organizations": Reducing the Risk. California SIDS Program. http://www.californiasids.com. Accessed January 8, 2007; Amer-ican Academy of Pediatrics Task Force on Sudden Infant Death Syndrome. "The Changing Concept of Sudden Infant Death Syndrome: Diagnostic Coding Shifts, Controversies Regarding the Sleeping Environment, and New Variables in Con-sider in Reducing Risk." *Pediatrics*. 2005; 116(5): 1245–55. Abstract available at: http://www.ncbi.nlm.nih.gov/entrez/query.fcgi?db=pubmed&cmd=Retrieve& dopt=AbstractPlus&list_uids=16216901&query_hl=3&itool=pubmed_docsum. Accessed January 8, 2007.

Recent evidence suggests that the use of a circulating fan around a sleeping baby may reduce the incidence of SIDS by up to 72 percent. It is hypothesized that the rebreathing of exhaled carbon dioxide trapped near an infant's mouth is a risk factor for SIDS. See: Coleman-Phox, K., et al. "Use of a Fan During Sleep and the Risk of Sudden Infant Death Syndrome." *Archives of Pediatric and Adolescent Medicine*. 2008; 162: 963–68.

18. "This is the last time you will see him": Horchler, J. N., Morris, R. R. "Dreams and Premonitions (Chapter 17)." In: *SIDS & Infant Death Survival Guide: Infor-mation and Comfort for Grieving Family & Friends & Professionals Who Seek to Help Them*. 3rd ed. Hyattsville, MD: SIDS Educational Services; 2003: 276–85.

18. "I think people have the ability to perceive things and give it a purposeful meaning": Horchler, J. N., Morris, R. R. "Dreams and Premonitions (Chapter 17)." In: *SIDS & Infant Death Survival Guide: Information and Comfort for Grieving Family & Friends & Professionals Who Seek to Help Them*. 3rd ed. Hyattsville, MD: SIDS Educational Services; 2003: 276–85.

18. "Don was one of many SIDS parents who participated in the largest study ever done": Henslee, J. A., et al. "The Impact of Premonitions of SIDS on Grieving and Healing." *Pediatric Pulmonology*. 1993; 16: 393. Details of the study are available online at: The SIDS & Infant Death Survival Guide. http://sidssurviv alguide.org/chapter17.htm. Accessed January 8, 2007. Southwest SIDS Re-search Institute, Inc., Brazosport Memorial Hospital,100 Medical Drive, Lake Jackson, TX 77566. 800-245-7437; 979-299-2814. http://www.swsids.com/.

19. "They did not renounce their premonitions": Horchler, J. N., Morris, R. R. Op. cit.

21. "Europe's worst mining accident": Courrières Mine Disaster. Wikipedia. http://en.wikipedia.org/wiki/Courrières_mine_disaster. Accessed January 2, 2007.

21. "America's worst mining tragedy": Monongah Mining Disaster. http://www.bois-estate.edu/history/ncasner/hy210/mining.htm. Accessed July 1, 2007.

21. "The 2006 Sago Mine disaster in Sago, West Virginia": Sago Mine Disaster. Wikipedia. http://en.wikipedia.org/wiki/2006_Sago_Mine_disaster. Accessed January 2, 2007.

21. "2007 collapse of the Crandall Canyon Mine in Crandall Canyon, Utah": Torres, K. Legislators Seek Investigation in Utah Mine Disaster. Occupational Hazards.com. August 28, 2007. http://www.occupationalhazards.com/News/Article/70536/Legislators_Seek_Investigation_into_Utah_Mine_Disaster.aspx. Accessed October 15, 2007.

21. "the villagers of Aberfan, Wales, discovered": The Aberfan Disaster. http://www.nuffield.ox.ac.uk/politics/aberfan/home2.htm. Accessed January 2, 2007.

22. "In that silence you couldn't hear a bird or a child": The Aberfan Disaster. Brief Description. http://www.nuffield.ox.ac.uk/politics/aberfan/desc.htm. Accessed January 2, 2007.

22. "a horrible nightmare had just begun in front of my eyes": The Aberfan Disaster. Brief Description. http://www.nuffield.ox.ac.uk/politics/aberfan/desc.htm. Accessed January 2, 2007.

22. "threw a shovel in the car, and drove to Aberfan to help": The description is from Iain McLean, "On Moles and the Habits of Birds: The Unpolitics of Aberfan," *Twentieth Century British History, Vol. 8*. Oxford: Oxford University Press; 1997. Quotes are from: Gaynor Madgewick, *Aberfan: Struggling Out of the Darkness*. Blaengarw, UK: Valley & Vale; 1996: 23; and from Report of the Tribunal Appointed to Inquire into the Disaster at Aberfan on October 21, 1966, Chairman Lord Justice Edmund Davies, HMSO, 1967, HL 316 & HC 553: 27. Photographs of the disaster taken in November and December of 1966 can be found in Rapoport IC. *Aberfan—The Days After*. Cardigan, UK; 2005, many of which are available at http://www.rapo.com/lcgallery/Aberfan.htm. Accessed January 2, 2007.

23. "Not villains but decent men": The Tribunal of Inquiry into the Aberfan Disaster. http://www.nuff.ox.ac.uk/politics/aberfan/tri.htm. Accessed January 2, 2007. Also: Corporatism and Regulatory Failure: Government Response to the Aberfan Disaster. Professor Iain McLean, project director. 1999. Available at http://www.nuffield.ox.ac.uk/politics/aberfan.esrc.html. Accessesd January 2, 2007.

23. "we are still one nation": McLean, I., Johnes, M. Remembering Aberfan. http://www.nuffield.ox.ac.uk/politics/aberfan/remem.htm. Accessed January 2, 2007. See also: McLean, I., Johnes, M. *Aberfan: Disasters and Government*. Cardiff: Welsh Academic Press; 2000.

23. "Fourteen months after the tragedy": Barker, J. C. "Premonitions of the Aberfan Disaster." *Journal of the Society for Psychical Research.* 1967; 44: 169–81.

24. "In another dream, a telephone operator from Brighton": Van de Castle, R. L. "Dreams of Natural Disasters." In: *Our Dreaming Mind.* New York: Ballantine; 1994: 408–409.

25. "A year later a kindred organization": Guiley, R. E. *Harper's Encyclopedia of Mystical and Paranormal Experience.* New York; HarperCollins; 1991: 465–66; Deem, J. M., Costantino V. *How to Travel Through Time.* New York: Avon Books; 1993.

25. "The institute's premise": The Arlington Institute. http://www.arlingtoninstitute.org/. See: TAI Alert 15—Impending Event Alert, at http://www.arlingtoninstitute.org/tai-alert-15-impending-event-alert. Accessed September 15, 2008.

26. "A Gallup Poll in 2005": Moore, D. W. "Three in Four Americans Believe in Paranormal." Gallup News Service. June 16, 2005. Available at: http://home.sandiego.edu/%7Ebaber/logic/gallup.html. Accessed October 13, 2007.

27. "There is also evidence that precognitive dreams are the most common psychic events": Targ, R. Preface to: Dunne, J. W. *An Experiment with Time.* Reprint ed. Charlottesville, VA: Hampton Roads; 2001: viii.

27. "dreams of future events make up more than half of the ESP experiences": Feather, S. R., Schmicker, M. *The Gift: ESP, the Extraordinary Experiences of Ordinary People.* New York: St. Martin's Press; 2005: 3.

27. "a great deal madder than [he] could bring [himself] to believe": Dunne, J. W. *An Experiment with Time.* Reprint ed. Charlottesville, VA: Hampton Roads; 2001: 23.

29. "He expanded his views of immortality": Dunne, J. W. *Nothing Dies.* London: Faber and Faber; 1946.

29. "as shown by scholar of world religions Mircea Eliade in his landmark book": Eliade, M. *The Myth of the Eternal Return.* Willard R. Trask (trans.) Bollingen Foundation edition. Princeton, NJ: Princeton University Press; 1954.

29. "such as physicists David Bohm": Bohm, D. *Wholeness and the Implicate Order.* Reprint ed. New York: Routledge; 2002. Also: Krishnamurti, J., Bohm, D. *The Ending of Time.* New York: HarperOne; 1985.

29. "and Julian Barbour": Barbour, J. *The End of Time.* New York: Oxford University Press; 2001.

30. "we can hope to advance to a broader understanding": Dunne, J. W. *An Experiment with Time.* Reprint ed. Charlottesville, VA: Hampton Roads; 2001: 111.

30. "trains involved in accidents between 1950 and 1955": Cox, W. E. "Precognition: An Analysis II." *Journal of the American Society for Psychical Research.* 1956; 50 (1): 99–109.

30. "that it had carried five days earlier": Cox, W. E. "Precognition: An Analysis II." *Journal of the American Society for Psychical Research.* 1956; 50 (1): 466.

30. "something bad is going to happen": Guiley, R. E. *Harper's Encyclopedia of Mystical & Paranormal Experience.* New York: HarperCollins; 1991: 456–65.

31. "cancel their travel plans without a clue about why": Watson, L. "The Importance of Pattern." In: *The Dreams of Dragons.* Rochester, VT: Destiny Books; 1992: 28–29.

31. "related to a public, national catastrophe": Feather, S. R., Schmicker, M. *The Gift: ESP, the Extraordinary Experiences of Ordinary People.* New York: St. Martin's Press; 2005: 165.

31. "help in dealing with a disturbing series of events": Feather, S. R., Schmicker, M. *The Gift: ESP, the Extraordinary Experiences of Ordinary People.* New York: St. Martin's Press; 2005: 172–81.

32. "approximately 2,830 deaths have been confirmed' in the World Trade Center disaster": Rubin, C. B., Renda-Tanali, I. Effects of the Terrorist Attacks of September 11, 2001, on Federal Emergency Management in the United States. Institute for Crisis, Disaster and Risk Management, The George Washington University, Washington, DC. http://www.gwu.edu/~icdrm/publications/sept11book_ch22_rubin.pdf. Accessed August 18, 2008.

32. "her husband stopped behaving disapprovingly when she spoke about them": Feather, S. R., Schmicker, M. *The Gift.* Op. cit., 172–81.

33. "billows of thick, black smoke": Feather, S. R., Schmicker, M. *The Gift: ESP, the Extraordinary Experiences of Ordinary People.* New York: St. Martin's Press; 2005: 24–25.

    The Rhine Research Center was not alone in being swamped with reports following 9/11. So too was the Boundary Institute of Saratoga, California. The Boundary Institute is a research organization where scientists explore the foundations of physics, mathematics, and computer science, and how consciousness manifests in the world. Some of the 9/11 premonitions they received can be viewed online at http://www.boundaryinstitute.org/premon911.htm.

34. "before the planes crashed into the WTC or the Pentagon": Bernstein, J. S. *Living in the Borderland: The Evolution of Consciousness and the Challenge of Healing Trauma.* New York: Routledge; 2005: 174.

34. "The grandparents of several of the children": Boisseau, L. F. Chez Diva. http://chezdiva.com/lawrence-francis-boisseau/. Accessed January 7, 2007.

35. "difficult for them to consider their premonitions as literally prophetic": Bernstein, J. S. Op. cit., 174–75.

35. "Otto defined the numinous": Otto, R. *The Idea of the Holy.* John W. Harvey (trans.). 2nd ed. New York: Oxford University Press; 1958: 5–14.

36. "She was certain at the time that it was a precognitive dream": Fitzgerald, R. *Lucky You: Proven Strategies for Finding Good Fortune.* New York: Citadel Free Press/Kensington; 2004: 128.

36. "a vague, gnawing feeling that something was not quite right": Feather, S. R., Schmicker, M. *The Gift.* New York: St. Martin's Press; 2005: 165–81.

36. "but missed her flight and lived to tell the story": Is this really proof that man can see into the future? *Daily Mail* (London). May 4, 2007. http://www.daily mail.co.uk/pages/live/articles/technology/technology.html?in_article_id= 452833&in_page_id=1965. Accessed October 6, 2007.

36. "with only 45 of 289 seats filled": September 11, 2001. Pennsylvania Council for Exceptional Children. http://www.pfcec.org/pf8708.htm. Accessed October 8, 2007.

37. "who were investigating in minute detail every booking, cancellation and no-show": Sheldrake, R. *The Sense of Being Stared At, and Other Aspects of the Extended Mind.* London: Arrow Books/Random House; 2003: 242.

38. "a Lower Manhattan dweller posted on YouTube": 9/11 Psychic Premonition and Dream. YouTube. http://www.youtube.com/watch?v=uxBPWCaP6fM. Accessed September 15, 2008.

38. "by highly acclaimed visionary artist Alex Grey": Grey, A. *Gaia.* http://gaia.tribe .net/photos/23eb69f2-5b73-40d2-80fa-6fb850fc15b4. Accessed September 15, 2008.

38. "the release of the CD was delayed to allow new cover art to be developed": Party Music. Wikipedia. http://en.wikipedia.org/wiki/Party_Music. Accessed April 17, 2008. Also: Glasner, J. Eerie image pulled from CD. Wired online.

38. "The Pentagon wanted to know what could happen next": "Hollywood: The Pentagon's New Advisor." BBC online. October 8, 2001. http://news.bbc.co.uk/ 2/hi/programmes/panorama/1891196.stm. Accessed April 18, 2008.

38. "The Pentagon's film liaison officer officially maintained": "September 11: A Warning from Hollywood." BBC online. http://news.bbc.co.uk/2/hi/programmes/pan- orama/1875186.stm. Accessed April 18, 2008.

38. "a relationship between creativity or artistic ability and psi performance": Schmeidler, G. R. *Parapsycholoogy and Psychology: Matches and Mismatches.* Jef- ferson, NC: McFarland; 1988.

39. "the highest scores ever recorded in a so-called ganzfeld experiment": Schlitz, M. J., Honorton, C. "Ganzfeld Psi Performance Within an Artistically Gifted Population." *Journal of the American Society for Psychical Research.* 1992; 86: 83–98. Also: Bem, D. J., Honorton, C. "Does Psi Exist? Replicable Evidence for an Anomalous Process of Information Transfer." *Psychological Bulletin.* 1994; 5(1): 1, 4–18. http://homepage.psy.utexas.edu/homepage/Class/Psy391P/Bem &Honorton.1984.pdf. Accessed at April 18, 2008.

39. "Insiders in the intelligence community have suggested": Clarke, R. A. *Against All Enemies.* New York: Free Press; 2004. Also: American Civil Liberties On- line. Sibel Edmonds. http://www.aclu.org/safefree/general/18828res20050126 .html. Accessed March 5, 2008.

40. "But they don't tell us when": CNN.com. Transcript of Rice's 9/11 commission statement. May 19, 2004. http://www.cnn.com/2004/ALLPOLITICS/04/08/ rice.transcript/. Accessed March 5, 2008.

40. "we are actively working to gain that knowledge": "Officials: Bin Laden Guiding Plots Against U.S." CNN.com. July 8, 2004. http://www.cnn.com/2004/US/07/08/ridge.alqaeda/index.html. Accessed March 5, 2008.

40. "how carefully the secret was guarded": Jung, C. G. *The Structure and Dynamics of the Psyche. Collected Works, Volume VIII.* 2nd ed. Adler, G. and Hull, R. F. C. (trans.). Princeton, NJ: Princeton University Press; 1970: 420.

41. "the only British prime minister to have been assassinated": Van de Castle, R. L. *Our Dreaming Mind.* New York: Ballantine; 1994: 29–30. Also: Spencer Perceval. Wikipedia. http://en.wikipedia.org/wiki/Spencer_Perceval. Accessed March 6, 2008. Also: British History. Prime Ministers and Politics Timeline. BBC Online. http://www.bbc.co.uk/history/british/pm_and_pol_tl.shtml. Accessed March 6, 2008. Also: Hill, B. *Gates of Horn and Ivory: An Anthology of Dreams.* New York: Taplinger; 1967: 21–22.

41. "fundamental questions about the nature of consciousness": Edeal, G. "Why the Choir Was Late." *Life.* March 27, 1950: 19–23. The Beatrice account is drawn from the following sources: Watson, L. *Dreams of Dragons.* Rochester, VT: Destiny Books; 1992: 26. Edeal, G. "Why the Choir Was Late." *Life.* March 27, 1950: 19–23. Jordan, P. A. The Mystery of Chance. http://www.strangemag.com/mysteryofchance.html. Accessed November 23, 2004. Fritts, R. Is the Universe Random, or Is There Something Out There Controlling Things? http://www.cedarlane.org/96serms/s960505.html. Accessed November 23, 2004. Unsolved Mysteries. http://www.unsolved.com/moreinfo3.html. Accessed November 23, 2004. Choir Non-quorum. Snopes.com. http://www.snopes.com/luck/choir.htmSnn-Quorum. Accessed November 23, 2004. Beatrice history. http://www.beatricene.com/gagecountymuseum/beatricehistory.html. Accessed November 23, 2004. Frontier trails across Gage County. http://www.beatricene.com/gagecountymuseum/trails.html#deroin. Accessed November 23, 2004. Beatrice, NE. http://www.epodunk.com/cgi-bin/genInfo.php?locIndex=27259. Accessed November 23, 2004. Beatrice, Nebraska. Wikipedia. http://en.wikipedia.org/wiki/Beatrice%2C_Nebraska. Accessed December 10, 2006. Clara Bewick Colby. SDPB/South Dakota Public Broadcasting. http://www.sdpb.org/tv/oto/lostbird/clara.asp. Accessed December 12, 2006. Choir Non-quorum. Snopes.com. http://www.snopes.com/luck/choir.htm. Accessed December 10, 2006. Lee Enterprises/*The Beatrice Daily Sun.* http://www.lee.net/walk/visit/beatrice.htm. Accessed December 10, 2006. Homestead National Monument of America. National Park Service. http://www.nps.gov/home/. Accessed December 10, 2006. The Struggle for Suffrage. Nebraska Studies.org. http://www.nebraskastudies.org/0700/frameset_reset.html?http://www.nebraskastudies.org/0700/stories/0701_0111.html. Accessed December 10, 2006.

42. "served as the Otoe-Missouri Indian Reservation": Gage County Museum. http://www.byjake.com/gagecountymuseum/. Accessed September 29, 2007.

43. "When a reporter from *Life* magazine": Edeal, G. "Why the Choir Was Late." *Life*. March 27, 1950: 19–23.

43. "In his book *Lady Luck*": Weaver, W. *Lady Luck: The Theory of Probability*. New York: Dover; 1982.

43. "He placed the odds even higher, at one in a billion": Watson, L. "The Importance of Pattern." In: *The Dreams of Dragons*. Op. cit., 26.

43. "But past performance indicated": Choir Non-quorum. Snopes.com. http://www.snopes.com/luck/choir.htm. Accessed December 10, 2006.

44. "Einstein postulated": This version of Einstein's comment is a variant of his more complex statement, "It can scarcely be denied that the supreme goal of all theory is to make the irreducible basic elements as simple and as few as possible without having to surrender the adequate representation of a single datum of experience." The source of his observation is "On the Method of Theoretical Physics," The Herbert Spencer Lecture, delivered at Oxford (June 10, 1933); also published in *Philosophy of Science*, April 1934; 1(2): 163–69.

45. "the 1815 eruption of Mount Tambora in Indonesia": The Year Fall Fell. Opinion. *The New York Times*. December 13, 1989. http://query.nytimes.com/gst/full page.html?res=950DE0DC133CF930A25751C1A96F948260. Accessed March 29, 2008.

45. "the annual distribution of the *Almanac*": Old Farmer's Almanac, http://www.almanac.com/advertising/pdf/OFA_10_Distribution.pdf. Accessed January 4, 2009.

46. "showing him the way and guiding him to safety": Nasht, S. *The Last Explorer*. New York: Arcade Publishing; 2006: 71–72.

46. "miles beyond their range of sight and hearing": Wilkins, H, Sherman, H. M. *Thoughts Through Space: A Remarkable Adventure in the Realm of the Mind*. 2nd ed. New York: C & R Anthony; 1951: 34. Cited also in: Nasht, S. *The Last Explorer*. New York: Arcade Publishing; 2006: 267.

47. "could be transferred between two people at a distance": Nasht, S. *The Last Explorer*. New York: Arcade Publishing; 2006: 269.

47. "ten days in advance of the actual happenings": Wilkins, H., Sherman, H. M. *Thoughts Through Space: A Remarkable Adventure in the Realm of the Mind*. Reprint ed. Charlottesville, VA: Hampton Roads; 2004: xxii–xxiii.

47. "Wilkins was seldom given to hyperbole": Stefansson, V. Quoted in: Nasht, S. *The Last Explorer*. New York: Arcade Publishing; 2006: 313.

47. "He considered the results": Wilkins, H. In: Wilkins, H., Sherman, H. M. *Thoughts Through Space: A Remarkable Adventure in the Realm of the Mind*. Reprint ed. Charlottesville, VA: Hampton Roads; 2004: xvi–xvii.

47. "with equal facility, when so moved to function": Sherman, H. M. In: Wilkins, H, Sherman, H. M. *Thoughts Through Space: A Remarkable Adventure in the Realm of the Mind*. Reprint ed. Charlottesville, VA: Hampton Roads; 2004: xvi–xvii.

48. "Mitchell generated four tables of twenty-five random numbers": Random numbers tables, first developed in the 1920s, have been replaced by electronic random number generators.

48. "The receivers . . . wrote down their impressions": In an interview with *The New York Times* on June 22, 1971, Mitchell reported that two of the four earthbound receivers whose score was highest got fifty-one correct answers of two hundred guesses, while only forty would have been expected by chance. These experiments, Mitchell said, "far exceeding anything expected," were judged by him to be "moderately significant." See: "Astronaut tells of E.S.P. Tests." *The New York Times.* June 22, 1971.

48– "Mitchell described how many of these scientists came to his office": Back-
49. ström, F. "Private Lunar ESP: An Interview with Edgar Mitchell." Cabinet Magazine. http://www.cabinetmagazine.org/issues/5/esp.php. Accessed October 11, 2007.

49. "von Braun speaking at a fund-raising dinner": Backström, F. "Private Lunar ESP: An Interview with Edgar Mitchell." CabinetMagazine. http://www.cabi netmagazine.org/issues/5/esp.php. Accessed October 11, 2007.

50. "cool intellectuals guided solely by reason": Agor, W. H. "Intuition: A Brain Skill Top Executives Use to Increase Productivity." *Public Productivity Review.* 1985; 9(4): 357–72.

50. "experiments that shed light on this area": Dean, D., Mihalasky, J. *Executive ESP.* Englewood Cliffs, NJ: Prentice-Hall; 1974.

51. "Dean was able to examine financial reports and predict": Schwartz, S. A. "An Arrow Through Time." *Explore: The Journal of Science and Healing.* 2008; 4(2): 95–100.

51. "did slightly worse than those making lower grades": Does Precognition Exist? UltraMind. http://www.ultramind.ws/id358.htm. Accessed January 26, 2008.

51. "When questioned, they admitted their belief": Does Precognition Exist? Ultra-Mind. http://www.ultramind.ws/id358.htm. Accessed January 26, 2008.

51. "smacking a little of the occult": Delphi method. Wikipedia. http://en.wikipedia .org/wiki/Delphi_method. Accessed January 26, 2008.

51. "what ESP researchers would call precognition": Does Precognition Exist? Ul-traMind. http://www.ultramind.ws/id358.htm. Accessed January 26, 2008.

52. "it becomes necessary to rely on intuition": Harteis, C., Gruber, H. "Intuition and Professional Competence: Intuitive versus Rational Forecasting of the Stock Market." *Vocations and Learning* (online version). December 28, 2007. http://www .springerlink.com/content/wt804572x37883x8/. Accessed January 26, 2008.

52. "advises business executives to write down their dreams": Goman, C. K. "Business Intuition." Link&Learn eNewsletter. April 2005. http://www.linkageinc. com/company/news_events/link_learn_enewsletter/archive/2005/04_05_ business_intuition_goman.aspx. Accessed January 25, 2008.

52. "Only one stockbroker did better": Russell, S. "Second Sight." *St. Louis Maga-*

zine. July 2007. http://www.stlmag.com/media/St-Louis-Magazine/July-2007/
Second-Sight/. Accessed July 26, 2008.

53. "He made millions and made good on his promise": Russell, S. "Second Sight."
St. Louis Magazine. July 2007. http://www.stlmag.com/media/St-Louis-Maga
zine/July-2007/Second-Sight/. Accessed July 26, 2008.

53. "the information could turn out to have been subtly misleading": Inglis, B. Op.
cit., 127–32.

54. "I cried for a week": Barasch, M. I. *Healing Dreams.* New York: Riverhead; 2000:
241–42.

54. "featured on the front page of *The Wall Street Journal*": Larson, E. "Did Psychic
Powers Give Firm a Killing in the Silver Market?" *The Wall Street Journal.* October 22, 1984.

54. "became a NOVA film": NOVA TV Programs. *A Case of ESP.* Broadcast date
January 17, 1984. http://www.pbs.org/wgbh/nova/listseason/11.html. Accessed
March 12, 2008.

54. "make money in the marketplace by using psychic functioning": Targ, R. *Limitless
Mind: A Guide to Remote Viewing and Transformation of Consciousness.* Novato,
CA: New World Library; 2004: 89–92.

55. "the group lost its 'spiritual focus'": Schwartz, S. A. *Opening to the Infinite.* Op.
cit., 172.

56. "Serious greed had entered": Targ, R. *Limitless Mind: A Guide to Remote Viewing
and Transformation of Consciousness.* Novato, CA: New World Library; 2004:
91.

56. "removed the investment factor from the study": Targ, R., Katra, J., Brown, D.,
Wiegand, W. Viewing the future: A pilot study with an error-detecting protocol.
Journal of Scientific Exploration. 1995; 9(3): 367–380.

56. "and promptly withdrew from the market": Puthoff, H. Associative Remote
Viewing Experiment. Proceedings of the 1984 Parapsychological Association
Conference, Dallas, Texas.

56. "a tripling of their investment": Schwartz, S. A. *Opening to the Infinite.* Op. cit., 166.

56. "other than the satisfaction of doing it": Schwartz, S. A. *Opening to the Infinite.*
Op. cit., 166–70.

57. "Senator Barack Obama": Obama, B. Quoted in: Scott A. Barack in Elko: "We
need a President who will lead us out of this mess." Obama/Biden Web site.
September 17, 2008.

57. "Senator John McCain": McCain, J. Quoted in: Shovelan, J. McCain roasts "reckless, greedy" Wall Street. ABC News online. September 17, 2008. http://www.
abc.net.au/news/stories/2008/09/17/2366611.htm. Accessed October 3, 2008.

57. "loans they could not afford": Hanson, V. D. "Public Shares the Blame in Creating Dr. Frankenstein's Wall Street." *The Salt Lake Tribune.* September 25, 2008.
http://www.sltrib.com/opinion/ci_10550559. Accessed October 3, 2008.

57. "Buffett supports a variety of causes": "Warren Buffett's Charity Work." Look to

the Stars: The World of Celebrity Giving. http://www.looktothestars.org/celeb
rity/183-warren-buffett. Accessed October 3, 2008.

57. "Newman donated more than $200 million": Saunders, T. "Paul Newman—A Life
Spent Giving." Look to the Stars: The World of Celebrity Giving. September 29,
2008. http://www.looktothestars.org/news/1287-paul-newman-a-life-spent-giv-
ing. Accessed October 3, 2008.

57. "*The Wisdom of Crowds* by James Surowiecki": Surowiecki, J. *The Wisdom of
Crowds*. New York: Anchor/Random House; 2005.

58. "it just happens to be the way the world works": Surowiecki, J. *The Wisdom of
Crowds*. New York: Anchor/Random House; 2005: 278–79.

TWO: EVIDENCE

63. "Radin has found that our central nervous system": Radin, D. I. "Unconscious
Perception of Future Emotions." *Journal of Consciousness Studies Abstracts*. Tucson II conference, University of Arizona, Tucson, April 8–13, 1996; Abstract
No. 430: 163. Also: Radin, D. I. "Electroderman Presentiments of Future Emotions." *Journal of Scientific Exploration*. 2004; 18 (2): 253–74.

63. "this is currently the most important experiment in psi research": Kierulff, S.,
Krippner, S. *Becoming Psychic: Spiritual Lessons for Focusing Your Hidden Abilities*. Franklin Lakes, NJ: New Page Books; 2004: 137.

63. "To this day, he keeps the bullet": Precognition, Presentiment & Remote Viewing.
A conference at Esalen Center for Theory & Research: Subtle Energies and the
Uncharted Realms of Mind. June 6–11, 1999. Big Sur, California. http://www.es
alenctr.org/display/confpage.cfm?confid=2&pageid=5&pgtype=1. Accessed September 20, 2007.

65. "The studies are a profound challenge to common sense": Radin, D. I. *Entangled Minds*. New York: Paraview/Simon & Schuster; 2006: 168. Also: Radin, D.
I. "Unconscious Perception of Future Emotions." *Journal of Scientific Exploration*. 1997; 11(2): 163–80.

65. "with odds against chance of 125 to 1": Radin, D. I. *Entangled Minds*. New York:
Paraview/Simon & Schuster; 2006: 168.

65. "when compared to peaceful, serene pictures": Radin, D. I. Gazing at the Mind's
Eye and Other Experiments Exploring the Capacities of Consciousness. Presentation at Mind Before Matter Conference, San Francisco, California, February 23, 2008.

65. "with a silent shutter and no flash": Radin, D. I. Dean Radin's Blog. Entry for
June 13, 2007. http://deanradin.blogspot.com/2007/06/presentiment-in-brain.
html. Accessed February 29, 2008.

66. "To date, nineteen presentiment studies have been done": Radin, D. I. Gazing at
the Mind's Eye and Other Experiments Exploring the Capacities of Con-

sciousness. Presentation at Mind Before Matter Conference, San Francisco, California, February 23, 2008.

66. "Bierman employed essentially the same protocol as Radin": Bierman, D. J., Radin, D. I. "Anomalous Anticipatory Response on Randomized Future Conditions." *Perceptual and Motor Skills.* 1997; 84: 689–90.

66. "Experiments in 2004 at the HeartMath Research Center": McCraty, R., Atkinson, M., Bradley, R. T. "Electrophysiological Evidence of Intuition: Part 1. The Surprising Role of the Heart." *Journal of Alternative and Complementary Medicine.* 2004; 10(1): 133–43. Also: McCraty, R., Atkinson, M., Bradley, R. T. "Electrophysiological Evidence of Intuition: Part 2. A System-wide Process?" *Journal of Alternative and Complementary Medicine.* 2004; 10: 325–36.

67. "Hungarian physicist Zoltán Vassy used electric shocks": Radin, D. *Entangled Minds.* New York: Paraview/Simon & Schuster; 2006: 164. Also: Vassy, Z. "A Study of Telepathy by Classical Conditioning." *Journal of Parapsychology.* Fall 2004. http://findarticles.com/p/articles/mi_m2320/is_2_68/ai_n16107401/pg_1. Accessed February 8, 2008. Also: Vassy, Z. "Method for Measuring the Probability of One-Bit Extrasensory Information Transfer Between Living Organisms." *Journal of Parapsychology.* 1978; 42: 158–60.

67. "One of the most offensive, stress-producing experiences in modern life": Dossey, L. "Quiet Please: Observations on Noise." *Explore* (NY). 2008; 4(3): 157–63.

67– "death toll from exposure to noise at 210,000 deaths": Coghlan, A. "News
68. Review 2007: Hidden Harm from Noise Pollution." *New Scientist.* December 22, 2007; 2635: 25. http://www.newscientist.com/channel/health/mg19626355 .700-news-review-2007-hidden-harm-from-noise-pollution.html. Accessed January 23, 2008.

68. "This compares with an estimated four million people": The Scoop on Smoking. American Council on Smoking and Health. http://thescooponsmoking.org/ xhtml/quizzes/deathAndDiseaseData.php#top. Accessed January 23, 2008.

68. "The presentiment effect was quite strong": Spottiswoode, S. J. P., May, E. C. "Skin Conductance Prestimulus Response: Analyses, Artifacts and a Pilot Study." *Journal of Scientific Exploration.* 2003; 17(4): 617–41.

68. "Physicist Vassy in Budapest": Vassy, Z. Personal communication to Dean Radin, December 14, 2004.

68. "In his studies, a person was shown a patch of color": Klintman, H. "Is There a Paranormal (Precognitive) Influence in Certain Types of Perceptual Sequences? Part I." *European Journal of Parapsychology.* 1983; 5: 19–49. Also: Klintman, H. "Is There a Paranormal (Precognitive) Influence in Certain Types of Perceptual Sequences? Part II." *European Journal of Parapsychology.* 1984; 5: 125–40.

69. "In summarizing these various experiments, Radin states": Radin, D. *The Conscious Universe.* San Francisco: HarperSanFrancdisco; 1997: 125.

69. "I could see about three seconds into the future": "Is This Really Proof That

Man Can See into the Future?" *Daily Mail* (London). May 4, 2007. http://www
.dailymail.co.uk/pages/live/articles/technology/technology.html?in_article_id
=452833&in_page_id=1965. Accessed October 6, 2007.

69. "There's something funny about time": Mullis, K. Quoted in: Radin, D. I. *Entangled Minds.* New York: Paraview/Simon & Schuster; 2006: 170.

69. "We'd now like to move on": Bierman, D. Quoted in: "Is This Really Proof That Man Can See into the Future?" *Daily Mail* (London). May 4, 2007. http://www
.dailymail.co.uk/pages/live/articles/technology/technology.html?in_article_id
=452833&in_page_id=1965. Accessed October 6, 2007.

70. " 'I was alone,' Sheldrake said,": Sheldrake, R. *The Sense of Being Stared At, and Other Aspects of the Extended Mind.* London: Arrow Books/Random House; 2003: 251.

70. "The presentiment window was narrower in his earthworms": Radin, D. I. *Entangled Minds.* New York: Paraview/Simon & Schuster; 2006: 170–71. Chester R. Wildey's master's thesis, "Biological Response to Stimulus," is available at http://lkm.fri.uni-lj.si/xaigor/slo/znanclanki/Wildey1.pdf and http://lkm.fri.uni
-lj.si/xaigor/slo/znanclanki/Wildey2.pdf. Accessed February 29, 2008.

71. "As psychologist and psi researcher James C. Carpenter says": Carpenter, J. C. "First Sight: Part One, A Model of Psi and the Mind." *Journal of Parapsychology.* 2004; 68(2): 217–54.

72. "Neither does time seem to matter": Jahn, R. G., Dunne, B. J. *Margins of Reality: The Role of Consciousness in the Physical World.* New York: Harcourt Brace Jovanovich; 1987: 149–91. Also: Radin, D. *The Conscious Universe.* San Francisco: HarperSanFrancisco; 1997: 103–105.

74. "The odds against chance in the SRI data are a billion billion to one": Radin, D. I. *The Conscious Universe.* San Francisco: HarperSanFrancisco; 1997: 100–103.

74. "These results have been published in prestigious scientific journals such as *Nature*": *Proceedings of the IEEE* and the *Journal of Scientific Exploration*: Targ, R., Puthoff, H. E. "Information Transmission Under Conditions of Sensory Shielding." *Nature.* 1974; 251: 602–607. Also: Puthoff, H. E, Targ, R. A Perceptual Channel for Information Transfer over Kilometer Distances: Historical Perspective and Recent Research. *Proceedings of the IEEE.* 1976; 64: 329–54. Also: Puthoff, H. E. "CIA-Initiated Remote Viewing Program at Stanford Research Institute." *Journal of Scientific Exploration.* 1996; 10(1): 63–76. Also: Targ, R. "Remote Viewing at Stanford Research Institute in the 1970s: A Memoir." *Journal of Scientific Exploration.* 1996; 10(1): 77–88.

74. "Following his evaluation of the SAIC tests, Ray Hyman": Hyman, R. "Evaluation of Program on Anomalous Mental Phenomena." *Journal of Scientific Exploration.* 1996; 10(1): 31–58. Unyielding positions such as Hyman's are not uncommon. Research Dean Radin, echoing philosopher Arthur Schopenhauer, suggests there are four stages through which controversial ideas in science pass. First,

the skeptics say there is no effect. Second, they say that there could be an effect, but it is trivial and insignificant. Third, they concede that there is an effect and it is larger than previously thought. The fourth and final stage is when skeptics say, "We thought of it first."

74. "researchers Charles Honorton and Diane C. Ferrari analyzed the published studies in foreknowledge": Honorton, C., Ferrari, D. "Future-Telling: A Meta-Analysis of Forced-Choice Precognition Experiments." *Journal of Parapsychology.* 1989; 53: 281–309.

74. "that cannot be ascribed to somebody's lucky day": Targ, R. Preface to: Dunne, J. W. *An Experiment with Time.* Reprint ed. Charlottesville, VA: Hampton Roads; 2001: viii–ix.

74. "Further evidence for premonitions is an online experiment": Got Psi? Boundary Institute. http://www.gotpsi.org/bi/gotpsi.htm. Accessed June 6, 2007.

74. "The Got Psi? Web site has several tests for psi ability": Radin, D. *The Conscious Universe.* San Francisco: HarperSanFrancisco; 1997. Also: Radin, D. *Entangled Minds.* New York: Paraview/Simon & Schuster; 2006.

75. "the famous parapsychology research project led by the legendary J. B. Rhine": Radin, D. I. "Preliminary Analysis of a Suite of Informal Web-Based Psi Experiments." http://www.boundary.org/articles/GotPsi-public.pdf. Accessed June 5, 2007.

75. "Although it is conceivable these deviations could have happened by chance alone": Shoup, R. Physics Without Causality—Theory and Evidence. Paper presented to the Society for Scientific Exploration, 26th Annual Meeting, East Lansing, Michigan, May 30–June 2, 2007: 16.

76. "subliminal awareness interfered with their psi performance": Shoup, R. Physics Without Causality—Theory and Evidence. Paper presented to the Society for Scientific Exploration, 26th Annual Meeting, East Lansing, Michigan, May 30–June 2, 2007: 17.

77. "it is equally foolish to refuse to be convinced by real evidence": Hansel, C.E.M. *ESP: A Scientific Explanation.* New York: Charles Scribner's Sons; 1966: 124–27.

77. "pass over this book heedlessly": Einstein, A. Preface to *Mental Radio.* Charlottesville, VA: Hampton Roads; 2001: xi.

77. "Einstein wrote, 'I read your book'": Ehrenwald, J. *Telepathy and Medical Psychology.* New York: Norton; 1948.

78. "You may show this letter": Pilkington, R. *Men and Women of Parapsychology: Personal Reflections.* Jefferson, NC: McFarland; 1987: 40.

78. "One of Sinclair's friends": Sinclair, U. *Mental Radio.* Charlottesville, VA: Hampton Roads; 2001: 124.

78. "the most famous feline on Earth": Dosa, D. M. "A Day in the Life of Oscar the Cat." *New England Journal of Medicine.* 2007; 357(4): 328–29.

78– "Steere House, founded in 1874": Steere House Nursing and Rehabilitation
79. Center. Providence, Rhode Island. http://www.steerehouse.org/matriarch/One PiecePage.asp?PageID=65&PageName=AboutUs. Accessed October 2, 2007.

80. "trying to help these people walk over into the other world": Moore, V. "Grim Rea-purr: The Cat That Can Predict Death." *Daily Mail* (London) online. http://www.dailymail.co.uk/pages/live/articles/news/news.html?in_article_id=470906&in_page_id=1770. Accessed October 2, 2007.

80. "geriatrician David M. Dosa": Dosa, D. M. Quoted in: Oscar (cat). Wikipedia. http://en.wikipedia.org/wiki/Oscar_(cat). Accessed October 2, 2007.

80. "Dr. Joan Teno": Teno, J. Quoted in: "Nursing Home Cat Can Sense Death." RevolutionHealth.com. July 26, 2007. http://www.revolutionhealth.com/news/?id=article.2007-07-26.2739737210. Accessed October 3, 2007.

80. "They will hold a vigil": Teno, J. Quoted in: Doheny, K. "Cat's 'Sixth Sense' Predicting Death?" CBSNews.com. July 25, 2007. http://www.cbsnews.com/stories/2007/07/25/health/webmd/main3097899.shtml. Accessed October 3, 2007.

80. "But I can't": Teno, J. Quoted in: Nickerson, C. "Feline Intuition." *Boston Globe* online. July 25, 2007. http://www.boston.com/yourlife/health/aging/articles/2007/07/25/feline_intuition/. Accessed October 2, 2007.

81. "cats can definitely detect illness": Scherk, M. Quoted in: Doheny, K. "Cat's 'Sixth Sense' Predicting Death?" CBSNews.com. July 25, 2007. http://www.cbsnews.com/stories/2007/07/25/health/webmd/main3097899.shtml. Accessed October 3, 2007.

81. "Jill Goldman, Ph.D.": Goldman, J. Quoted in: Doheny, K. "Cat's 'Sixth Sense' Predicting Death?" CBSNews.com. July 25, 2007. http://www.cbsnews.com/stories/2007/07/25/health/webmd/main3097899.shtml. Accessed October 3, 2007.

81. "just the lack of movement": Estep, D. Quoted in: Doheny, K. "Cat's 'Sixth Sense' Predicting Death?" CBSNews.com. July 25, 2007. http://www.cbsnews.com/stories/2007/07/25/health/webmd/main3097899.shtml. Accessed October 3, 2007.

81. "Dr. Nicholas H. Dodman": Dodman, N. H. Quoted in: Nickerson, C. "Feline Intuition." *Boston Globe* online. July 25, 2007. http://www.boston.com/yourlife/health/aging/articles/2007/07/25/feline_intuition/. Accessed October 2, 2007.

81. "sensitive to premonitions of earthquakes": Graves, T. Quoted in: "U.S. Cat 'Predicts Patient Deaths.'" BBC News online. July 26, 2007. http://news.bbc.co.uk/1/hi/world/americas/6917113.stm. Accessed October 3, 2007.

81. "a televised Oscar story on *CBS News*": Doheny, K. "Cat's 'Sixth Sense' Predicting Death?" CBSNews.com. July 25, 2007. http://www.cbsnews.com/stories/2007/07/25/health/webmd/main3097899.shtml. Accessed October 3, 2007.

81. "cats suck out your soul while you sleep": Oscar the Cat, posted by torydrroy. blogspot.com. Tailrank.com. http://tailrank.com/2323872/A-Day-in-the-Life-of-Oscar-the-Cat. Accessed October 3, 2007.

81. "Dosa emphatically rejected": *Glenn Beck Show*. Transcript of July 26, 2007. http://transcripts.cnn.com/TRANSCRIPTS/0707/26/gb.01.html.   Accessed October 3, 2007.

82. "The man's conscience was pricked": Bardens, D. *Psychic Animals*. New York: Barnes & Noble; 1996: 61.

82. "Minosch, a German cat": Scheib, R. Timeline. *Utne Reader*. January–February 1996: 52–61.

82. "Bobbie, a pedigreed Collie": Rhine, J. B., Feather, S. R. "The Study of Cases of 'Psi-Trailing' in Animals." *The Journal of Parapsychology*. 1962; 26(1): 1–21. Also: Schul, B. *The Psychic Power of Animals*. New York: Fawcett; 1977: 52.

83. "many of them charged with tear-gas": Trapman, A. H. *The Dog, Man's Best Friend*. London: Hutchinson; 1929.

83. "British biologist Rupert Sheldrake": Sheldrake, R. *Dogs That Know When Their Owners Are Coming Home*. New York: Crown; 1999.

83. "roused servants from all over the White House": Martin, J., Birnes, W. J. *The Haunting of the Presidents*. New York: Signet/New American Library; 2003: 261.

83. "Just before the tsunami struck": "Acoustic Senses May Have Saved Animals in Tsunami." Australian Broadcasting Company News online. January 4, 2005. http://www.abc.net.au/news/newsitems/200501/s1276513.htm. Accessed October 5, 2007. Also: Mott, M. "Did Animals Sense Tsunami Was Coming?" *National Geographic* News Online. January 4, 2005. http://news.nationalgeographic .com/news/2005/01/0104_050104_tsunami_animals.html. Accessed October 5, 2007.

83. "On India's southern coast": Oldenburg, D. "A Sense of Doom: Animal Instinct for Disaster." *The Washington Post*. January 8, 2005: C1. http://www. washingtonpost.com/wp-dyn/articles/A57653-2005Jan7.html. Accessed January 5, 2009.

84. "dogs were seen running inland": Oldenburg, D. "A Sense of Doom: Animal Instinct for Disaster." *The Washington Post*. January 8, 2005: C1. http://www.wash ingtonpost.com/wp-dyn/articles/A57653-2005Jan7.html. Accessed January 5, 2009. Also: Mott, M. "Did Animals Sense Tsunami Was Coming?" *National Geographic* News online. January 4, 2007. http://news.nationalgeographic.com/news/ 2005/01/0104_050104_tsunami_animals.html. Accessed October 5, 2007.

84. "It remains unclear": Oldenburg, D. "A Sense of Doom: Animal Instinct for Disaster." *The Washington Post*. January 8, 2005: C1. http://www.washingtonpost .com/wp-dyn/articles/A57653-2005Jan7.html. Accessed January 5, 2009.

84. "the USGS did a few studies on animal prediction": Mott, M. "Did Animals Sense Tsunami Was Coming?" *National Geographic* News online. January 4, 2007. http://news.nationalgeographic.com/news/2005/01/0104_050104_tsu nami_animals.html. Accessed October 5, 2007.

84. "The indigenous tribes of the Andaman and Nicobar Islands": Oldenburg, D. "A Sense of Doom: Animal Instinct for Disaster." *The Washington Post*. January 8,

2005: C1. http://www.washingtonpost.com/wp-dyn/articles/A57653-2005Jan7 .html. Accessed January 5, 2009.

85. "Chinese researchers are now focusing on": Oldenburg, D. "A Sense of Doom: Animal Instinct for Disaster." *The Washington Post*. January 8, 2005: C1. http://www.washingtonpost.com/wp-dyn/articles/A57653-2005Jan7.html. Accessed January 5, 2009.

86. "their poodle had saved their lives": Sheldrake, R. *Dogs That Know When Their Owners Are Coming Home*. New York: Crown; 1999: 261–62.

86. "Carpenter proposed calling the human ability for distant and future knowing *first sight*": Carpenter, J. C. "First Sight: Part One. A Model of Psi and the Mind." *Journal of Parapsychology*. 2004; 68(2): 217–54. Also: Carpenter, J. C. "First Sight: Part Two. Elaboration of Model of Psi and the Mind." *Journal of Parapsychology*. 2004; 69(1): 63–112.

87. "First sight is not limited to short distances": Carpenter, J. C. "First Sight: Part Two. Elaboration of Model of Psi and the Mind." *Journal of Parapsychology*. 2004; 69(1): 90.

88. "a distinctive state of transcendental awareness he calls *mindsight*": Ring, K., Valarino, E. E. *Lessons from the Light: What We Can Learn from the Near-Death Experience*. New York: Insight/Plenum Press; 1998: 93.

88. "On one occasion he watched a Comanche": Lavender, D. *Bent's Fort*. Lincoln: University of Nebraska Press; 1954: 125.

88. "The intensity of the sensation": Ball, E. *In the Days of Victorio*. Tucson: University of Arizona Press; 1992: 11.

89. "the function of the smoke signal": Inglis, B. *Natural and Supernatural: A History of the Paranormal*. Bridport, Dorset, UK: Prism Press; 1992: 34.

89. "DNA extracted from his preserved eye": Hunt, D. M., et al. "The Chemistry of John Dalton's Color Blindness." *Science*. 1995; 267(5200): 984–88.

89. "After he published his famous paper": Dalton, J. "Extraordinary Facts Relating to the Vision of Colours: With Observations." *Memoirs of the Literary and Philosophical Society of Manchester*; 1798; 5: 28–45.

89. "After they pointed out the images": Blair, L. *Rhythms of Vision*. New York: Schoken; 1976.

90. "Their belief system had a place for small craft": Polanyi, M. "The Stability of Scientific Theories Against Experience." In: *Witchcraft and Sorcery*, Max Marwick (ed.). New York: Penguin; 1982: 452–59.

90. "Everything else will slip through the net": Darling, D. *Soul Search*. New York: Villard; 198: 158.

91. "The sky in the daytime": Carpenter, J. C. "First Sight: Part One. A Model of Psi and the Mind." *Journal of Parapsychology*. 2004; 68(2): 224.

91. "Some persons are able to exercise control": Carpenter, J. C. "First Sight: Part Two. Elaboration of Model of Psi and the Mind." *Journal of Parapsychology*. 2004; 69(1): 89. Carpenter's first-sight hypothesis builds on a similar idea of psi re-

searcher Rex G. Stanford. In a seminal paper in 1990, Stanford suggested that living organisms constantly scan the environment through the normal senses and ESP, looking for information that can help fulfill their needs. Stanford gave this proposed function a tongue-twisting name, "psi-mediated instrumental response" or PMIR. When important information is detected in the environment, either through the senses or nonlocally, this leads to an "instrumental response" in the organism to satisfy the need indicated by the information that is acquired. Stanford suggested that this process can be so subtle it is seldom noticed. It might result in inexplicable happenings usually attributed to chance, luck, and coincidence, such as being in the right place at the right moment—a phenomena that psychologist Carl G. Jung called a synchronicity. See: Stanford, R. G. "An Experimentally Testable Model for Spontaneous Psi Events." In: *Advances in Parapsychological Research, Vol. 6*, S. Krippner (ed.). Jefferson, NC: McFarland; 1990: 54–167.

93. "amnesia is really worse than we thought": Hassabis, D., et al. "Patients with Hippocampal Amnesia Cannot Imagine New Experiences." *Proceedings of the National Academy of Sciences USA*. 2007; 104(5): 1726–31. Also: Khamsi, R. "Amnesiacs Struggle to Imagine Future Events." New Scientist.com. January 15, 2007. http://www.newscientist.com/channel/being-human/dn10950-amnesiacs-struggle-to-imagine-future-events.html. Accessed May 18, 2007.

93. "Kathleen McDermott and her colleagues at Washington University": Szpunar, K. K., Watson, J. M., McDermott, K. B. Neural Substrates of Envisioning the Future. *Proceedings of the National Academy of Sciences USA*. 2007; 104(2): 642–47.

94. "The longer they were on job, the larger the region became": Maguire, E. A., et al. Navigation-Related Structural Change in the Hippocampi of Taxi Drivers. *Proceedings of the National Academy of Sciences USA*. 2000; 97(8): 4398–4403. Also: "Taxi Drivers' Brains 'Grow' on the Job." BBC Online. March 14, 2000. http://news.bbc.co.uk/2/hi/science/nature/677048.stm. Accessed May 18, 2007.

95. "The young man credits the discourteous taxi driver": "Cabbies' Brain Power— Your Reaction." BBC News online. March 15, 2000. http://news.bbc.co.uk/2/hi/science/nature/677202.stm. Accessed October 3, 2008.

95. "If they all start using GPS": Dobson, R. "Taxi Drivers' Knowledge Helps Their Brains Grow." *The Independent* (UK). December 17, 2006. http://news.independent.co.uk/uk/health_medical/article2081652.ece. Accessed May 18, 2007. Also: Maguire, E. A., et al. "Navigation Expertise and the Human Hippocampus: A Structural Brain Imaging Analysis." *Hippocampus*. 2003; 12(2): 250–59.

95. "preservation of their cognitive function as they aged": Hurdle, J. Lose Weight, Stay Active, Prevent Alzheimer's—Studies. VirtualMedicalCentre.com. July 20, 2004. http://www.virtualcancercentre.com/news.asp?artid=2358. Accessed September 18, 2008.

96. "Psychotherapist Sandra Ingerman has been 'shaken up'": Ingerman, S. *Soul*

Retrieval: Mending the Fragmented Self. Rev. ed. New York: HarperOne; 2006. Also: Ingerman, S. *Shamanic Journeying.* Boulder, CO: Sounds True (Har/Com edition); 2004.

97. "Although these experiences occurred following her near-lethal injury": Moss, R. *The Secret History of Dreaming.* Novato, CA: New World Library; 2009: 177–91.

98. "one of the greatest dreamers of all time": Moss, R. *Dreaming True.* New York: Pocket Books; 2000.

98. "statistically significant in both normal individuals and in those seeking care for neuropsychiatric problems": Palmer, J., Neppe, V. M. "Exploratory Analyses of Refined Predictors of Subjective ESP Experiences and Temporal Lobe Dysfunction in a Neuropsychiatric Population." *European Journal of Parapsychology.* 2004; 19: 33–65. Also: Neppe, V. M. "Temporal Lobe Symptomatology in Subjective Paranormal Eexperients." *Journal of the American Society for Psychical Research.* 1983; 77(1): 1–29.

THREE: PREMONITIONS: WHY, WHAT, HOW?

101. "There is really no before and after for the mind": Schrödinger, E. *What Is Life? and Mind and Matter.* London: Cambridge University Press; 1969: 145.

103. "As Carpenter describes the process": Carpenter, J. C. "First Sight: Part One. A Model of Psi and the Mind." *Journal of Parapsychology.* 2004; 68(2): 224.

103. "Symbolism erupted in the experiences of Susan Faludi": Faludi, S. *The Terror Dream: Fear and Fantasy in Post-9/11 America.* New York: Metropolitan; 2007.

104. "There was this whole message to women": Interview of Susan Faludi by Amy Goodman. Democracy Now radio. October 4, 2007. Transcript available at: http://www.democracynow.org/print.pl?sid=07/10/04/1355237. Accessed October 5, 2007.

104. "the way our culture silenced any kind of questioning": Faludi, S. *The Terror Dream: Fear and Fantasy in Post-9/11 America.* New York: Metropolitan Books; 2007.

104. "she got a real workout in translating the language of premonitions": Hall, K. The Vultures. http://www.stressinstitute.com/AboutDrKathleenHall/Blog.aspx?pageId=274. March 12, 2007. Accessed May 11, 2007. Also: Hall, K. http://www.stressinstitute.com/AboutDrKathleenHall/Blog.aspx?pageId=275. March 12, 2007. Accessed May 11, 2007.

108. "If it's so great to be smart, why have most animals remained dumb?": Kawecki, T. Quoted in: Soundbites. *New Scientist.* May 10, 2008: 198(2655): 8. Also: Zimmer, C. "Lots of Animals Learn, but Smarter Isn't Better." *The New York Times* online. May 6, 2008. Accessed May 21, 2008.

108. "it would carry 1,523 souls to their deaths?": Veacock, C. *Titanic*: Anatomy of a Disaster Shrouded in Mystery. Merseyside Anomalies Research Association. http://www.mara.org.uk/titanic.htm. Accessed July 23, 2007.

108. "that occurred within two weeks prior to the tragedy": Stevenson, I. "Seven More Paranormal Experiences Associated with the Sinking of the *Titanic*." *Journal of the American Society for Psychical Research.* 1965; 59: 211–24. Also: Stevenson, I. "Precognition of Disasters." *Journal of the American Society for Psychical Research.* 1970; 1864: 187–210.

108. "because of a change of business plans": Van de Castle, R. L. *Our Dreaming Mind.* New York: Ballantine; 1994: 408.

109. "who cancelled at the last minute was financier John Pierpont Morgan": J. P. Morgan. Wikipedia. http://en.wikipedia.org/wiki/Jp_morgan. Accessed January 27, 2007.

109. "the famous Vanderbilt family": George Washington Vanderbilt II. Wikipedia. http://en.wikipedia.org/wiki/George_Washington_Vanderbilt_II. Accessed January 26, 2007.

109. "he ignored her and perished with the ship": Dennett, P. E. "Premonitions of Disaster." *Atlantis Rising.* http://www.atlantisrising.com/issue18/18premonitions.html. Accessed January 26, 2007.

109. "saved them from a watery grave": Hefner, A. G. Premonition. http://www.themystica.com/mystica/articles/p/premonition.html. Accessed January 26, 2007.

109. "He designed a suite of Web-based games": Radin, D. Got Psi? http://www.GotPsi.org. Accessed September 19, 2008.

111. "This may be why verified premonitions of major disasters": Radin, D. *Entangled Minds.* New York: Paraview/Simon & Schuster; 2006: 31–33.

111. "Radin calculated that the odds against chance": Radin, D. *Entangled Minds.* New York: Paraview/Simon & Schuster; 2006: 33.

112. "They confessed under torture": Stroud, A. *Stuart England.* London: Routledge; 1999: 27.

113. "Her family was assessed the cost of her trial": Of the Apprehension of Sundrye Witches Lately Taken in Scotland. Internet Sacred Text Archive. http://www.sacred-texts.com/pag/kjd/kjd11.htm. Accessed September 20, 2008. Also: Goodare, J., et al. *The Survey of Scottish Witchcraft: 1563–1736.* University of Edinburgh. School of History, Classics and Archaeology. January 2003. http://www.shc.ed.ac.uk/Research/witches/. Accessed September 20, 2008.

113. "Scotland was second only to Germany": Smout, T. C. *A History of the Scottish People, 1560–1830.* 2nd ed. New York: Collins; 1970.

113. "the last person to be burned as a witch": "News from Scotland, or, a True Discourse of the Damnable Life of Doctor Fian, and Sundry Other Witches Taken in Scotland." In: A Collection of Rare and Curious Tracts on Witchcraft and the Second Sight: With an Original Essay on Witchcraft." Edinburgh: Printed for D. Webster; 1820. University of Sydney Library. http://www.library.usyd.edu.au/libraries/rare/witchcraft/w-scottish/newes-desc.html. Accessed September 20, 2008. Scottish Witchcraft. http://www.library.usyd.edu.au/libraries/rare/witchcraft/w-scottish/w-scottish.html. Accessed September 20, 2008. Also:

Smout, T. C. *A History of the Scottish People, 1560–1830.* New ed. Waukegan, IL: Fontana Press; 1998.

114. "Broughton suggested that if psi in general": Broughton, R. *Parapsychology: The Controversial Science.* New York: Ballantine; 1991: 341–47.

115. "Many of the targets were aesthetically more compelling": Schwartz, S. A. *Opening to the Infinite.* Buda, TX: Nemoseen; 2007: 105.

116. "This resulted in a spatial gradient": Schwartz, S. A. *Opening to the Infinite.* Buda, TX: Nemoseen; 2007: 111–12.

116. "depending on the entropy gradient involved": May, E. C., Spottiswoode, S. J. P., and James, C. L. "Shannon Entropy: A Possible Intrinsic Target Property." *Journal of Parapsychology.* 1994; 58, 384–401. Also: May, E. C., et al. "Advances in Remote-Viewing Analysis." *Journal of Parapsychology.* 1990; 54, 193–228. Also: May, E. C., Vilenskaya, L. "Overview of Current Parapsychology Research in the Former Soviet Union." *Subtle Energies.* 1992; 3(3): 45–67. Also: May, E. C., Spottiswoode, S. J. P., James, C. L. "Managing the Target-Pool Bandwidth: Possible Noise Reduction for Anomalous Cognition Experiments." *Journal of Parapsychology.* 1994; 58, 303–13.

117. "He wrote, 'One wants to destroy the Semitic element'": Kirsch, J. *The Reluctant Prophet.* Los Angeles: Sherbourne Press; 1973: 30.

117. "Rabbi Wechsler's dreams came true a half century": Van de Castle, R. L. *Our Dreaming Mind.* New York: Ballantine; 1994: 31.

117. "They have been reprinted in The Reluctant Prophet": Kirsch, J. *The Reluctant Prophet.* Los Angeles: Sherbourne Press; 1973.

117. "At last I also waxed old": Macnish, R. *The Philosophy of Sleep.* 3rd ed. Glasgow: MM'Phun; 1836: 96. Reprint ed. by Kitla, MT: Kessinger Publishing; 2006: 87.

117. "Months later Macnish contracted typhus": Significant Scots. Robert Macnish. ElectricScotland.com. http://www.electricscotland.com/history/other/macnish_robert.htm. Accessed October 30, 2008.

118. "In the middle of the bouquet": Blum, D. *Ghost Hunters: William James and the Search for Scientific Proof of Life After Death.* New York: Penguin; 2006: 73–74.

FOUR: WHY SHOULD WE WANT TO CULTIVATE PREMONITIONS, AND HOW DO WE DO IT?

121. "consciousness may choose to sample the 'there and then'": Jahn, R. G. and Dunne, B. J. *Margins of Reality: The Role of Consciousness in the Physical World.* New York: Harcourt Brace; 1987: 280–81.

123– "by which things distant or future are perceived, and seen as if they were
24.   present": Johnson, S. *Journey to the Western Isles of Scotland.* Kitla, MT: Kessinger Publishing; 2004: 85 ff. Original publication: London; 1775. Available at: eBook.com. http://www.ebookmall.com/ebook/6751-ebook.htm. Accessed May 25, 2007.

124. "Visions, voices, and premonitions were in the air": Inglis, B. *Natural and Supernatural: A History of the Paranormal*. Bridport, Dorset, UK: Prism Press; 1992: 127–32. Original publication: Sevenoaks, Kent, UK: Hodder and Stoughton; 1977.

124. "The physician Martin Martin": Martin, M. "An Account of the Second-Sight." In *A Description of the Western Islands of Scotland*. Original publication 1703. "An Account of the Second-Sight" is available at Undiscovered Scotland e-books. http://www.undiscoveredscotland.co.uk/usebooks/martin-westernislands/section15.html. Accessed May 26, 2007.

124. "Martin was diligent in his reportage": Inglis, B. *Natural and Supernatural: A History of the Paranormal*. Bridport, Dorset, UK: Prism Press; 1992: 127–32. Original publication: Sevenoaks, Kent, UK: Hodder and Stoughton; 1977.

124. "holding something in his hand that looked like flesh": Inglis, B. *Natural and Supernatural: A History of the Paranormal*. Bridport, Dorset, UK: Prism Press; 1992: 127–32. Original publication: Sevenoaks, Kent, UK: Hodder and Stoughton; 1977.

124. "accepted the existence of second sight": Inglis, B. *Natural and Supernatural: A History of the Paranormal*. Bridport, Dorset, UK: Prism Press; 1992: 127–32. Original publication: Sevenoaks, Kent, UK: Hodder and Stoughton; 1977.

124. "Johnson summarized his views": Johnson, S. *Journey to the Western Isles of Scotland*. Kitla, MT: Kessinger Publishing; 2004: 85 ff. Original publication: London; 1775. Available at: eBook.com. http://www.ebookmall.com/ebook/6751-ebook.htm. Accessed May 25, 2007.

125. "They have no temptation to feign": Johnson, S. *Journey to the Western Isles of Scotland*. Kitla, MT: Kessinger Publishing; 2004: 86–87. Original publication: London; 1775. Available at: eBook.com. http://www.ebookmall.com/ebook/6751-ebook.htm. Accessed May 25, 2007.

125. "stabbed the king to death while he rode in his coach": Inglis, B. *Natural and Supernatural: A History of the Paranormal*. Bridport, Dorset, UK: Prism Press; 1992: 127–32. Original publication: Sevenoaks, Kent, UK: Hodder and Stoughton; 1977. Also: Henri IV of France. Wikipedia. http://en.wikipedia.org/wiki/Henry_IV_of_France. Accessed May 26, 2007.

125. "to the mean and the ignorant": Johnson, S. *Journey to the Western Isles of Scotland*. Kitla, MT: Kessinger Publishing; 2004: 88. Original publication: London; 1775. Available at: eBook.com. http://www.ebookmall.com/ebook/6751-ebook.htm. Accessed May 25, 2007.

125–26. "a country in which the great majority believes in 'psychic dreams'": The distance of 517 miles is reported by BlurtIt.com. http://www.blurtit.com/q570105.html. Accessed September 23, 2008.

126. "Icelanders always were and still are great dreamers!": Moss, R. *The Secret History of Dreaming*. Novato, CA: New World Library; 2009: 128. The 2003 Gallup Poll posed forty questions. It was designed by Dr. Björg Bjarnadóttir and her

colleagues at the Skuggsjá Dream Center in Akureyri, Iceland. See: http://skuggsja.is. Accessed September 23, 2008.

126. "only three percent considered them unlikely or impossible": Haraldsson, E. "Representative National Surveys of Psychic Phenomena: Iceland, Great Britain, Sweden, USA and Gallup's Multinational Survey." *Journal of the Society for Psychical Research.* 1985; 53(801): 145–58.

126. "have remained consistent over the years": Haraldsson, E., Houtkooper, J. M. "Psychic Experiences in the Multi-National Human Values Survey." *Journal of the American Society for Psychical Research.* 1991; 85(2), 145–65.

126. "lost or stolen property and ships at sea": Gissurarson, L. R., Haraldsson, E. "History of Parapsychology in Iceland." *International Journal of Parapsychology.* 2001; 12(1): 31–52.

127. "His crew landed a huge catch": *I Am Nothing but a Sailor.* Keflavik, Iceland: Faxi; 1976; 5: 9.

127. "A terrible storm arose": I'm grateful to dream researcher Robert Moss for information on Iceland and its dream lore. See: Moss, R. *The Secret History of Dreaming.* Novato, CA: New World Library; 2009: 128–31.

127. "Italy and the United States": Haraldsson, E., Houtkooper, J. M. "Psychic Experiences in the Multi-National Human Values Survey." *Journal of the American Society for Psychical Research.* 1991; 85(2), 145–65.

128. "Fortunately, her husband survived": Feather, S. R., Schmicker, M. *The Gift.* New York: St. Martin's Press; 2005: 153.

129. "When pressed, the nurse volunteered": Feather, S. R, Schmicker, M. *The Gift.* New York: St. Martin's Press; 2005: 152–53.

129. "The MBTI is based on the theories of psychologist Carl G. Jung": Jung, C. G. *Psychological Types (Collected Works of C. G. Jung, Volume 6).* Princeton, NJ: Princeton University Press; 1971. You can take the Myers-Briggs Type Indicator test and score it for free online at HumanMetrics, http://www.humanmetrics.com/cgi-win/JTypes2.asp. Accessed October 5, 2008.

129. "Indeed, the originators of the test": Myers, I. B., with Myers, P. *Gifts Differing: Understanding Personality Type.* Mountain View, CA: Davies-Black; 1995.

129. "intuition and extraversion correlate with psi abilities in general": Honorton, C. The Ganzfeld Novice: Four Predictors of Initial ESP Performance. Paper presented at the Parapsychological Association's 35th Annual Convention, Las Vegas, Nevada; 1992.

131. "Comfort with chaos and disorder": A tolerance for chaos and disorder is also a characteristic of highly creative individuals, many of whom are also premonition-prone. Psychologist Frank Barron was an authority of the value of disorder and complexity in creative individuals. In the following passage from Barron's classic paper "The Psychology of Imagination," one may safely substitute *premonition-prone* for *creative*: "[C]reative individuals are more at home with complexity and apparent disorder than other people are. . . . The creative individual, in his gener-

alized preference for apparent disorder, turns to the dimly realized life of the unconscious, and is likely to have more than the usual amount of respect for the
forces of the irrational in himself and in others. . . . [T]he creative individual not
only respects the irrational in himself, but courts it as the most promising source
of novelty in his own thought. . . . The truly creative individual stands ready to
abandon old classifications and to acknowledge that life, particularly his own
unique life, is rich in new possibilities. To him, disorder offers the potentiality of
order." From: Barron, F. "The Psychology of Imagination." *Scientific American,*
September 1958; 199: 150–70.

131. "depend overwhelmingly on factors inside themselves": Irwin, H. J. "Belief in
the paranormal: A review of the empirical literature." *Journal of the American
Society for Psychical Research.* 1993; 87: 1–39.

132. "As psychologist David Keirsey puts it": Keirsey, D., Bates, M. *Please Understand
Me II.* Del Mar, CA: Prometheus Nemesis; 1998; 145. Neuroscientists have
recently teamed up with psychologists to explore the areas of the brain that are
involved in what many psychologists consider to be the "big five" personality
traits—extroversion, neuroticism, conscientiousness, openness, and agreeable-
ness. In highly extroverted persons, increased activity is seen in the dopamine
reward system in the midbrain. In conscientiousness, the prefrontal cortex of
the brain appears to be involved. In neuroticism, the serotonin system in the
amygdala, deep in the brain, appears highly active. In openness and agreeable-
ness, it isn't yet clear which brain areas are involved. See: Nettle, D. "It Takes All
Sorts." *New Scientist.* February 9, 2008; 197(2642): 36–39.

133. "related by the sinologist Richard Wilhelm": Story told in Hannah, B. *Jung: His
Life and Work.* Boston: Shambhala; 1991: 128.

134. "The trailblazer in this research was Dr. Gertrude Schmeidler": Schmeidler,
G. R., McConnell RA. *ESP and Personality Patterns.* Westport, CT: Greenwood
Press; 1958.

135. "There was only one chance in a trillion": Lawrence, T. Gathering in the Sheep
and Goats. A Meta-Analysis of Forced-Choice Sheep-Goat ESP Studies, 1947–
1993. Proceedings of Presented Papers: The Parapsychological Association
36th Annual Convention, Toronto, Canada; 1993: 75–86.

135. "Belief in psi is also highly important": Walsh, K., Moddel, G. "Effect of Belief
on Psi Performance in a Card Guessing Task." *Journal of Scientific Exploration.*
2007; 21(3): 501–10.

135. "after 'conversion' attempts were made to change the skeptics' minds": Storm,
L., Thalbourne, M. A. "The Effect of a Change in Pro Attitude on Paranormal
Performance: A Pilot Study Using Naïve and Sophisticated Skeptics." *Journal of
Scientific Exploration.* 2005; 19: 11–29.

137. "Respecting chaos and disorder involves a tolerance for ambiguity": Lewis
Thomas, MD, was one of the most graceful essayists in the profession of medicine during the twentieth century. In the following comment, he describes the

value of ambiguity in language, and his point of view can be extended to life it-self: "Ambiguity seems to be an essential, indispensable element for the transfer of information from one place to another by words, where matters of real impor-tance are concerned. It is often necessary, for meaning to come through, that there be an almost vague sense of strangeness and askewness. Speechless animals and cells cannot do this. . . . Only the human mind is designed to work in this way, programmed to drift away in the presence of locked-on information, stray-ing from each point in a hunt for a better, different point." See: Thomas, L. *Lives of a Cell.* New York: Bantam: 1974: 111. Ambiguity can be thought of as differ-ence. The importance of difference has arisen in modern biology, and has been linked to our ability to know anything at all. As developmental biologist Richard Davenport says, "If we examine the experiences from which our knowledge of the world arises, we can see that they consist of various types of differences. Without difference, there can be no experience. The experience of difference is basic to our notion of existence, the latter being derived from the Latin *ex sistere*, which means "to stand apart," i.e., to be different. . . . [S]ince all properties must be experienced as difference, the physical world exists for us only in terms of relationships. . . . [P]hysical reality does not exist before us as an object of study but *emerges from our consciousness during our changing experience within nature.*"[Emphasis in original] See: Davenport, R. *An Outline of Animal Devel-opment.* Reading, MA: Addison-Wesley; 1979: 353.

138. "They often don't ask for anything specific to happen, only that the best out-come prevail in any situation": Psychologist Lawrence LeShan calls this ap-proach Type I healing. Type I healers, who constitute the majority of those doing healing work, conceive of themselves as a conveyer or conduit for healing that originates outside themselves. In contrast, Type II healers try to actively "send energy" or some type of healing force that originates within themselves. See: LeShan, L. *The Medium, the Mystic, and the Physicist.* New York: Viking Press; 1974: 106.

138. "When we put them under the microscope, we hinder their appearance.": Von Lucadou, W. Quoted in: Broderick, D. *Outside the Gates of Science: Why It's Time for the Paranormal to Come In from the Cold.* New York: Thunder's Mouth Press/Avalon; 2007: 270.

138. "This is precisely what most psi researchers have found": Broderick, D. *Outside the Gates of Science: Why It's Time for the Paranormal to Come In from the Cold.* New York: Thunder's Mouth Press/Avalon; 2007: 269.

139. "there's evidence that the phenomenon may recover and reappear": Broderick, D. *Outside the Gates of Science: Why It's Time for the Paranormal to Come In from the Cold.* New York: Thunder's Mouth Press/Avalon; 2007: 68.

140. "Freud only stared aghast at me": Jung, C. G. *Memories, Dreams, Reflections.* Aniela Jaffé (ed.). Richard and Clara Winston (trans.). New York: Random House/Vintage; 1965: 155.

140. "He could not swim and almost drowned": Jung, C. G. *Memories, Dreams, Reflections.* Aniela Jaffé (ed.). Richard and Clara Winston (trans.). New York: Random House/Vintage; 1965: 302–303.

140. "He knew at once it was the woman in the dream": Jung, C. G. *Memories, Dreams, Reflections.* Aniela Jaffé (ed.). Richard and Clara Winston (trans.). New York: Random House/Vintage; 1965: 300–303.

141. "for we may not have a second chance": Bernstein, J. S. *Borderland: The Evolution of Consciousness and the Challenge of Healing Trauma.* New York: Routledge; 2005: 185.

141. "a compendium of cases from the files of the Rhine Research Center": Feather, S. R., Schmicker, M. *The Gift.* New York: St. Martin's Press; 2005.

141. "the International Association for the Study of Dreams": Public Discussion Board for Dreams and Dreaming. International Association for the Study of Dreams. http://dreamtalk.hypermart.net/bb2005/index.php. Accessed September 24, 2008.

141. "three books on the role of prayer, healing intentions, and spirituality": Dossey, L. *Healing Words: The Power of Prayer in the Practice of Medicine.* San Francisco: HarperSanFrancisco; 1993. Also: Dossey, L. *Prayer Is Good Medicine.* San Francisco: HarperSanFrancisco; 1996. Also: Dossey, L. *Be Careful What You Pray For.* San Francisco: HarperSanFrancisco; 1997.

141. "5 percent of Americans have prayed for harm": Gallup Poll reported in *Life* magazine, March 1994.

142. "One building still standing had smoke billowing": The preceding two precognitive dreams are from: Wilkerson, R. C. Dreams About the Terrorist Attacks on NY and DC. Electric Dreams.com. http://improverse.com/ed-articles/richard_wilkerson_2001_oct_dreams_of_terrorism.htm#1.%20Precognitive%20dreams%20about%20the%20Attack. Accessed September 27, 2008.

142. "Three months after the carnage": Transcript of Osama bin Laden videotape. CNN.com. December 13, 2001. http://archives.cnn.com/2001/US/12/13/tape.transcript/. Accessed January 22, 2007.

144. "but as an inspiration of divine origin": Freud, S. *The Interpretation of Dreams.* Oxford World's Classics. Joyce Crick (trans.). Reprint ed. New York: Oxford University Press; 1999: 8.

144. "there is no God but Allah": Boxer, S. "The Banality of Terror: Dreams of Holy War over a Quiet Evening." *The New York Times.* December 16, 2001. Ideas & Trends section. http://query.nytimes.com/gst/fullpage.html?res=9C0CE6D61E3FF935A25751C1A9679C8B63. Accessed September 26, 2008. Also: Do Violent Dreams Bother You? Terrorists Get Inspired by Them. ScientificBlogging.com. June 7, 2008. http://www.scientificblogging.com/news_releases/do_violent_dreams_bother_you_terrorists_get_inspired_by_them. Accessed September 26, 2008.

144. "Minutes later a bomb struck the house": Historical Premonitions. Waupaca

Naturals. http://www.waupacanaturals.com/articles/premonitions.htm. Accessed July 2, 2007.

144. "a voice told a young Adolf Hitler": Alschuler, A. S. "Recognizing Inner Teachers— Inner Voices Throughout History." *Gnosis Magazine.* Fall 1987; 5: 8–12. Also: Alschuler, A. S. "Inner Teachers and Transcendent Education. In Rao, K. R. (ed.). *Cultivating Consciousness: Enhancing Human Potential, Wellness, and Healing.* Westport, CT: Praeger; 1993: 181–93. Also: Alschuler, A. S. "Inner Voices and Inspired Lives Through the Ages." In Thayer, S. J., Nathanson, L. S. (eds.). *Interview with an Angel: Our World, Our Selves, Our Destiny.* Gillette, NJ: Edin Books; 1996: 1–62.

145. "Little attention has been devoted to the ethical issues surrounding the intentional uses of future knowing": In many cultures where future knowing and other forms of psi are taken for granted, methods of protection from psychic intrusion and malevolence abound. Consider the widespread belief in the evil eye, which is particularly prevalent in the Mediterranean world, the Middle East, and in Latin America. A dizzying variety of protective strategies has arisen in the cultures, ranging from prayers and incantations, to visualizations, the use of aromas, talismans and amulets, and exorcism. See: Dossey, L. "Protection." In: *Be Careful What You Pray For.* San Francisco: HarperSanFrancisco; 1997: 195–217.

145. "the most common cause being offered is greed": Klein, N. "Crisis called 'Katrina Without the water.'" *Seattle Real Estate News.* September 16, 2008. http:// blog.seattlepi.nwsource.com/realestatenews/archives/148904.asp. Accessed September 27, 2008.

146. "Nothing ever happened to me which I did not foresee": Napoleon: Quotations and Commentary. Hammond, L. J. (ed.). http://www.ljhammond.com/notebook/nap.htm. Accessed September 26, 2008.

147. "the largest mass suicide in the history of the United States": Applewhite, M. Planet About to Be Recycled. Heaven's Gate Web site. http://www.heavensgate.com/misc/vt100596.htm. Accessed March 1, 2008. Also: Ramsland, K. "Death Mansion." TrueTV Crime Library. http://www.crimelibrary.com/notorious_murders/mass/heavens_gate/5.html. Accessed March 1, 2008. Also: Heaven's Gate. Wikipedia. http://en.wikipedia.org/wiki/Heaven's_Gate_(cult). Accessed March 1, 2008.

147. "The videotapes of his final statements were shown": Ross, R. Heaven's Gate Suicides. Cult Education and Recovery. October 1999. http://www.culteducation.com/hgate.html. Accessed March 1, 2008. Also: Fisher, M., Pressley, S. A. "Founder Sought to Purge Sexuality via Cult." *The Washington Post.* March 29, 1997. Available at: Cult Education and Recovery. http://www.rickross.com/reference/heavensgate/gate13.html. Accessed March 1, 2008.

148. "In one survey of fifteen thousand people living in Baltimore": Romme, M., Escher, S. *Making Sense of Voices.* London: Mind Publications; 2000.

148. "no more than one percent of the population": Goldner, E. M., et al. "Prevalence

and Incidence Studies of Schizophrenic Disorders: A Systematic Review of the Literature." *Canadian Journal of Psychiatry.* 2002; 47(9): 833–43.

148. "Not one of these nursing leaders mentioned fear": Barnum, B. "Expanded Consciousness: Nurses' Experiences." *Nursing Outlook.* 1989; 37(6): 260–66.

148. "anomalous experiences in general appear to be good for people's mental health": Berenbaum, H., Kerns, J., Raghavan, C. "Anomalous Experiences, Peculiarity, and Psychopathology." In: *Varieties of Anomalous Experience: Examining the Scientific Evidence.* Cardeña, E., Lynn, S. J., Krippner, S. (eds.). Washington, DC: American Psychological Association; 2000: 32.

149. "no other factor had ever been found to correlate so highly": Greeley, A. "The Impossible: It's Happening." *Noetic Sciences Review.* Spring 1987: 7–9.

150. "Psychoanalyst Elizabeth Lloyd Mayer describes": Mayer, E. L. *Extraordinary Knowing.* New York: Bantam/Random House; 2007: 11–12.

151. "The neurosurgeon with his headaches": Mayer, E. L. *Extraordinary Knowing.* New York: Bantam/Random House; 2007: 13.

153. "they are psychosexual biographies": Moss, R. *The Secret History of Dreaming.* Novato, CA: New World Library; 2009: 44–49.

153. "In 1895 Freud had a dream": Freud, S. *The Interpretation of Dreams.* John Strachey (trans.) Reprint ed. New York: Avon; 1965: 138–51.

153. "Dr. José Schavelzon, an Argentinian cancer surgeon and psychoanalyst": Resnik, S. "The Theatre of the Dream." *New Library of Psychoanalysis, Vol. 6.* Tuckett, D. (general ed.). Sheridan, A. (trans.) New York: Routledge; 1987: 119–20. Schavelzon's original report is his monograph: Schavelzon, J. *Freud, Un Paciente con Cancer.* Buenos Aires: Editorial Paidos; 1983.

155. "unlike Jung, who gave up smoking because of a dream": Moss, R. *The Secret History of Dreaming.* Novato, CA: New World Library; 2009: 49.

155. "He considered the dream a validation": Sprengnether, M. "Mouth to Mouth: Freud, Irma, and the Dream of Psychoanalysis." *American Imago.* 2003; 60(3): 259–84. Abstract available at: http://muse.jhu.edu/login?uri=/journals/american_imago/v060/60.3sprengnether.html. Accessed September 21, 2008.

155. "IN THIS HOUSE, ON JULY 24, 1895, THE SECRET OF DREAMS WAS REVEALED TO DR. SIGM. FREUD": Freud, S. Letter to Wilhelm Fliess. See: Breger, L. *Freud: Darkness in the Midst of Vision.* New York: John Wiley & Sons; 2000: 143.

155. "I would devote myself to psychical research": Freud, S. Quoted in: McLynn, F. *Carl Gustav Jung.* New York: St. Martin's Press; 1996: 128.

155. "endorsing the paranormal would provide his enemies a weapon": McLynn, F. *Carl Gustav Jung.* New York: St. Martin's Press; 1996: 127.

156. "Joe Farman, an obscure British geophysicist": Farman, J. C., Gardiner, B. G., Shanklin, J. D. "Large Losses of Total Ozone in Antarctica Reveal Seasonal Clox/NOx Interaction." *Nature.* 1985; 315: 207–10.

157. "One expert said the data was misread": Opinions vary about why NASA was late in recognizing the ozone hole over Antarctica. The account given here is

that of science journalist Fred Pearce. See his article: "Ozone Hole? What Ozone Hole?" *New Scientist.* September 20, 2008; 199 (2674): 46–47. http://www.tmcnet.com/usubmit/-joe-farmans-old-tech-triumph-/2008/09/19/3660472.htm. Accessed October 1, 2008. NASA's current version of the story is available at: Ozone Depletion, History, and Politics. http://www.nas.nasa.gov/About/Education/Ozone/history.html. Accessed October 1, 2008. Farman's views on the issue are revealed in an interview broadcast on BBC World Service, July 6, 1999: http://www.bbc.co.uk/worldservice/people/features/mycentury/transcript/wk27d2.shtml. Accessed October 1, 2008.

157. "The ozone layer isn't vanishing after all": Pearce, F. "Ozone Hole? What Ozone Hole?" *New Scientist.* September 20, 2008; 199 (2674): 46–47. http://www.tmcnet.com/usubmit/-joe-farmans-old-tech-triumph-/2008/09/19/3660472.htm. Accessed October 1, 2008.

158. "St. Thomas Aquinas, in *Summa Theologica*, affirmed that dreams": Hearne, K. Lucid Dreams—An Electrophysiological and Psychological Study. Chapters III and IV. Ph.D. thesis. Department of Psychology, University of Liverpool, England. May 1978. http://www.european-college.co.uk/thesis.htm. Accessed March 15, 2008. Also: De Becker, R. *The Understanding of Dreaming, or The Machinations of the Night.* London: George Allen & Unwin; 1968.

158. "It seems that this ghostly assassin tried his hand on some one else": Ward Hill Lamon. Wikipedia. http://en.wikipedia.org/wiki/Ward_Hill_Lamon. Accessed January 28, 2007.

159. "If the premonitions of Bishop Joseph Lanyi": Van de Castle, R. L. *Our Dreaming Mind.* New York: Ballantine; 1994: 28–29.

160. "the priest confirmed receiving the letter and the sketch": Boss, M. *The Analysis of Dreams.* New York: Philosophical Library; 1958: 186–87.

160. "Hinckley had been a member of a neo-Nazi group": Van de Castle, R. *Our Dreaming Mind.* New York: Ballantine; 1994: 30.

161. "President Anwar Sadat of Egypt was shot dead": Van de Castle, R. *Our Dreaming Mind.* New York: Ballantine; 1994: 41.

161. "it could provide authorities time to act": Melbourne, D. F., Hearne, K. Premonitions.Ourworld.com. http://ourworld.compuserve.com/homepages/dreamthemes/. Accessed March 15, 2008. Those wishing to aid Dr. Keith Hearne in his research can report their premonitions to dreamthemes@compuserve.com.

161. "before his father was shot by Arthur Bremer": Van de Castle, R. *Our Dreaming Mind.* New York: Ballantine; 1994: 30.

162. "Joseph, thus, in one version of the story": Josephus. *Jewish Antiquities.* H. St. J. Thackeray (trans.) Cambridge, MA: Harvard University Press; 1967: 205. Cited in: Moss, R. *The Secret History of Dreaming.* Novato, CA: New World Library; 2009: 60.

163. "Second, the dreamer must tell his dream to the goddess Isis": Szpakowska, K. M. The Perception of Dreams and Nightmares in Ancient Egypt: Old Kingdom to

Third Intermediate Period. Ph.D. dissertation; University of California, Los Angeles; 2000: 273. Also: Moss, R. *The Secret History of Dreaming.* Novato, CA: New World Library; 2009: 31. Also: Kenyon, F. G. *The Chester Beatty Biblical Papyri: Descriptions and Texts of Twenty Manuscripts on Papyrus of the Greek Bible.* London: Emery Walker; 1933, 1937.

163. "A Mesopotamian practice": Oppenheim, A. L. *The Interpretation of Dreams in the Ancient Near East.* Philadelphia, PA: American Philosophical Society; 1956: 302–303. See also: Moss, R. *The Secret History of Dreaming.* Novato, CA: New World Library; 2009: 31.

163. "Similar practices date to the eighth century B.C.E. in central Asia": Crescenzi, A., Torricelli, F. "A Tun-Huang Text on Dreams: Ms Pelliot Tibetan 55-IX." *Tibet Journal.* 1995; 20(2): 3–17. See also: Moss, R. *The Secret History of Dreaming.* Novato, CA: New World Library; 2009: 31.

163. "He had his fellow villagers bind him and burn him": Thwaites, R. G. (ed.). *Jesuit Relations and Allied Documents: Travels and Explorations of the Jesuit Missionairies in New France, 1610–1791.* Cleveland, OH: Burrows Brothers; 1896–1901: 12, 121–23.

163. "He describes how the Ashanti": Rattray, R. S. *Religion and Art in Ashanti.* Oxford: Clarendon Press; 1927: 192–96. See also: Moss, R. *The Secret History of Dreaming.* Novato, CA: New World Library; 2009: 181.

163. "And if . . . we do act to change the future that we've glimpsed, was it really the future . . . ?": This twist on free will is called the Bierman paradox: You can't prove you changed the future, because if you successfully acted to change it, it really wasn't the future because it never really happened.

163. "in the one-third of cases in which the individual did try to intervene": Feather, S. R., Schmicker, M. *The Gift: ESP, the Extraordinary Experiences of Ordinary People.* New York: St. Martin's Press; 2005: 184, 198.

164. "The woman was a wreck for weeks": L. E. Rhine Collection of Spontaneous Psi Experiences, Rhine Research Center, Durham, NC. See: Broughton, R. *Parapsychology: The Controversial Science.* New York: Ballantine; 1991: 19–20.

164. "people try to intervene, only to make matters worse": Rhine, L. E. *Hidden Channels of the Mind.* New York: William Morrow; 1961. Also: Rhine, L. E. "Precognition and Intervention." *Journal of Parapsychology.* 1955; 19: 1–34.

165. "The little boy had somehow left the house": Archives of the Rhine Research Center. See: Feather, S. R., Schmicker, M. *The Gift: ESP, the Extraordinary Experiences of Ordinary People.* New York: St. Martin's Press; 2005: 197.

165. "a tornado blew the sign into the window": Archives of the Rhine Research Center. See: Feather, S. R., Schmicker, M. *The Gift: ESP, the Extraordinary Experiences of Ordinary People.* New York: St. Martin's Press; 2005: 204.

165. "Rhine suggested that the paucity of details": Feather, S. R., Schmicker, M. *The Gift: ESP, the Extraordinary Experiences of Ordinary People.* New York: St. Martin's Press; 2005: 183.

165. "Nobody can convince anybody of the actuality of precognition": Kierulff, S., Krippner, S. *Becoming Psychic: Spiritual Lessons for Focusing Your Hidden Abilities*. Franklin Lakes, NJ: New Page Books; 2004: 119.

166. "An example was the CIA-sponsored remote-viewing research": Puthoff, H. E. CIA-Initiated Remote Viewing at Stanford Research Institute. Available at http://www.biomindsuperpowers.com/Pages/CIA-InitiatedRV.html. Accessed December 17, 2007. Also: Targ, R. "Remote Viewing at Stanford Research Institute in the 1970s: A Memoir." *Journal of Scientific Exploration*. 1996; 10(1): 77–88. Also: May, E. C. "The American Institutes for Research Review of the Department of Defense's STAR GATE Program: A commentary." *Journal of Scientific Exploration*. 1996; 10(1): 89–108.

166. "Targ was asked by Soviet psi researchers": Broderick, D. *Outside the Gates of Science: Why It's Time for the Paranormal to Come In from the Cold*. New York: Thunder's Mouth Press/Avalon; 2007: 70.

166. "So I don't do it in general": Edwin C. May to Damien Broderick, July 5, 2006. In: Broderick, D. *Outside the Gates of Science: Why It's Time for the Paranormal to Come In from the Cold*. New York: Thunder's Mouth Press/Avalon; 2007: 70.

166. "Alison Holman, a professor in nursing science": Holman, E. A., et al. "Terrorism, Acute Stress, and Cardiovascular Health: A 3-Year National Study Following the September 11th Attacks." *Archives of General Psychiatry*. 2008; 65(1): 73–80. Abstract available at: http://archpsyc.ama-assn.org/cgi/content/abstract/65/1/73. Accessed January 25, 2008.

167. "The statistical risk of dying from a terrorist attack in America": Harris, A. W. Harris on Terrorism and Asteroid Risk. Undated. http://psweb.sbs.ohio-state.edu/faculty/jmueller/HARRIS.PDF. Accessed January 25, 2008.

167. "In spite of this, the apprehension lingers": Tierney, J. "Living in Fear and Paying a High Cost in Heart Risk." *The New York Times* Online. January 15, 2008. http://www.nytimes.com/2008/01/15/science/15tier.html. Accessed January 25, 2007. Also: Tierney, J. "The Endless Fear of Terrorism." *The New York Times* Online. January 16, 2008. http://tierneylab.blogs.nytimes.com/2008/01/16/the-endless-fear-of-terrorism/. Accessed January 25, 2008.

167. "the number of terrorists arrested . . . was zero": Tierney, J. "Living in Fear and Paying a High Cost in Heart Risk." *The New York Times* Online. January 15, 2008. http://www.nytimes.com/2008/01/15/science/15tier.html. Accessed January 25, 2007.

167. "These findings prompted science journalist John Tierney": Tierney, J. "Living in Fear and Paying a High Cost in Heart Risk." *The New York Times* Online. January 15, 2008. http://www.nytimes.com/2008/01/15/science/15tier.html. Accessed January 25, 2007.

168 "Psychological tests of people who have had profound mystical experiences": Greeley, A. "The Impossible: It's Happening." *Noetic Sciences Review*. Spring 1987: 7–9.

168. "I simply want to hide away somewhere!": Lanier, J. "From Having a Mystical Experience to Becoming a Mystic." *ReVision.* 1989; 12(1): 41–44. Reprint and epilogue.

168. "The master soberly responded": Lanier, J. "From Having a Mystical Experience to Becoming a Mystic." *ReVision.* 1989; 12(1): 41–44.

168. "As miserable as ever . . .": Source unknown. Quoted in: Syfransky, S. (ed.). *Sunbeams: A Book of Quotations.* Berkeley, CA: North Atlantic; 1990: 45.

169. "Individuals experiencing any of these problems should think twice": Berenbaum, H., Kerns, J., Raghavan, C. "Anomalous Experiences, Peculiarity, and Psychopathology." In: *Varieties of Anomalous Experience: Examining the Scientific Evidence.* Cardeña, E., Lynn, S. J., Krippner, S. (eds.). Washington, DC: American Psychological Association; 2000: 38–39.

169. "Psi researcher Ian Stevenson found": Stevenson, I. *Telepathic Impressions: A Review and Report of Thirty-five New Cases.* Charlottesville: University Press of Virginia; 1970.

169. "But in larger surveys of extrasensory experiences": Irwin, H. J. *An Introduction to Parapsychology.* 3rd ed. Jefferson, NC: McFarland; 1999. Also: Milton, J. "Effects of 'Paranormal' Experiences on People's Lives. An Unusual Survey of Spontaneous Cases." *Journal of the Society for Psychical Research.* 1992; 58: 314–23.

170. "[M]y career prospects might have been seriously damaged": Milton, J. "Effects of 'Paranormal' Experiences on People's Lives. An Unusual Survey of Spontaneous Cases." *Journal of the Society for Psychical Research.* 1992; 58: 314–23.

170. "In Brazil, for instance": Zangari, W., Machado, F. R. Incidence and Social Relevance of Brazilian University Students' Psychic Experiences. Paper presented at the 37th Annual Convention of the Parapsychological Association, Amsterdam, August 1994.

170. "Concerns center on what one's peers will think": Targ, E., Schlitz, M., Irwin, H. J. "Psi-Related Experiences." In: *Varieties of Anomalous Experience: Examining the Scientific Evidence.* Cardeña, E., Lynn, S. J., Krippner, S. (eds.). Washington, DC: American Psychological Association; 2000: 226.

170. "Consider what happened to Anna Martínez": Targ, E., Schlitz, M., Irwin, H. J. "Psi-Related Experiences." In: *Varieties of Anomalous Experience: Examining the Scientific Evidence.* Cardeña, E., Lynn, S. J., Krippner, S. (eds.). Washington, DC: American Psychological Association; 2000: 219–20.

171. "knowing that her thoughts might have killed him?": Targ, E., Schlitz, M., Irwin, H. J. "Psi-Related Experiences." In: *Varieties of Anomalous Experience: Examining the Scientific Evidence.* Cardeña, E., Lynn, S. J, Krippner, S. (eds.). Washington, DC: American Psychological Association; 2000: 219–20.

171. "There are monumental differences in their attitudes toward psi": *Psi and Clinical Practice.* Coly, L., McMahon, J. (eds.). New York: Parapsychology Foundation; 1993.

171. "if I were distressed following a premonition": Neppe, V. M. "Clinical Psychiatry, Psychopharmacology, and Anomalous Experience." In: *Psi and Clinical Practice*. Coly, L., McMahon, J. (eds.). New York: Parapsychology Foundation; 1993. Available at: http://www.pni.org/research/anomalous/classif_art/clinical _psychiatry.html. Accessed September 26, 2008.

172. "if your doctor consistently makes you feel worse, find another one": One way of locating an understanding therapist is to contact the Spiritual Emergence Network (SEN) at http://www.cpsh.org/. SEN provides support services and referrals to a therapist for individuals who are experiencing difficulties with psychospiritual growth and anomalous experiences. The SEN referral office is staffed by trained graduate students. The referrals are to licensed mental health professionals, often in the caller's area, who specialize in or have been trained to deal with psychospiritual issues.

FIVE: PREMONITIONS AND OUR WORLDVIEW

173. "[C]onsciousness must be part of nature": Bohr, N. Quoted in Heisenberg, W. *Physics and Beyond*. Pomerans, A. J. (trans.). New York: Harper and Row; 1971: 88–91.

175. "there's no reason why you can't have causes from the future": Barry, P. Science Hopes to Change Events That Have Already Occurred. SFGate.com. January 21, 2007. http://www.sfgate.com/cgi-bin/article.cgi?f=/c/a/2007/01/21/ING5L NJSBF1.DTL. Accessed October 31, 2008.

176. "If there were ever an occasion in science": Rhine, J. B. *The Reach of the Mind*. New York: William Sloane; 1947: 66.

177. "The greatest tragedy of science": Huxley, T. H. Presidential address, 1870, to the British Association for the Advancement of Science. In: Huxley, T. H. *Collected Essays. Discourses: Biological and Geological. Volume 8*. Reprint ed. Kitla, MT: Kessinger Publishing; 2005: 244. Original ed: London: Macmillan; 1894.

178. "for those who love, time is eternity": Van Dyke, H. ThinkExist.com http:// thinkexist.com/quotation/time_is_too_slow_for_those_who_wait-too_swift_ for/8953.html. Accessed September 28, 2008.

178. " 'Time,' says physicist Paul Davies": Davies, P. *About Time: Einstein's Unfinished Revolution*. New York: Simon & Schuster; 1996.

178. "St. Augustine expressed his frustration": St. Augustine. *The Confessions of St. Augustine, Bishop of Hippo*. Chapter XIV. CyberLibrary. http://www.leaderu.com/cyber/books/augconfessions/bk11.html. Accessed September 28, 2008.

178. "It's just too difficult to think about": Feynman, R. Quoted in: Boslough, J. "The Enigma of Time." *National Geographic*. March 1990; 177(3): 109–32.

179. "says Princeton astrophysicist J. Richard Gott": Gott, J. R. J. Richard Gott on

Life, the Universe, and Everything. Interview with Jill Neimark. Science&Spirit.com. 2007. http://www.science-spirit.org/article_detail.php?article_id=270. Accessed October 31, 2008.

179. "Summing up these views, Gefter suggests": Gefter, A. "Time's Up." *New Scientist*. January 19, 2008; 197(2639): 26–29.

179. "As physicist Davies describes this trick": Davies, P. *Space and Time in the Modern Universe*. New York: Cambridge University Press; 1977: 221.

179. "In a letter of condolence": Einstein, A. Quoted in: Jammer, M. *Einstein and Religion: Physics and Theology*. Princeton, NJ: Princeton University Press; 2002: 161. See also: Einstein Archive, reel 7–245, reprinted in Albert Einstein—Michele Besso Correspondence 1903–1955. Paris: Hermann; 1972: 537–38.

180. "Opinions varied so wildly": Glanz, J. "Physics' Big Puzzle Has Big Question: What Is Time?" *The New York Times* online. June 19, 2001. http://query.nytimes.com/gst/fullpage.html?res=9D06E0DE1031F93AA25755C0A9679C8B63&sec=&spon=&pagewanted=print. Accessed October 21, 2007.

180. "The LHC is a $6 billion particle accelerator": Harrell, E. "Collider Triggers End-of-World Fears." *Time*. September 4, 2008. http://www.time.com/time/health/article/0,8599,1838947,00.html?imw=Y. Accessed October 31, 2008.

180. "One British newspaper, *The Sun*, trumpeted": Sutherland, P. "End of the World Due in Nine Days." *The Sun* online. September 1, 2008. http://www.thesun.co.uk/sol/homepage/features/article1630897.ece Accessed October 31, 2008.

180. "A few days after startup": Higgins, A. G. Broken Atom Smasher Inaugurated Anyway. MSNBC.com. October 21, 2008. http://www.msnbc.msn.com/id/27296827/. Accessed October 31, 2008.

181. "you certainly cannot completely rule out this effect": Josephson, B. Quoted in: "Is This Really Proof That Man Can See into the Future?" *Daily Mail* (London). May 4, 2007. http://www.dailymail.co.uk/pages/live/articles/technology/technology.html?in_article_id=452833&in_page_id=1965. Accessed October 6, 2007.

181. "Physicist Richard Shoup": Shoup, R. Physics Without Causality—Theory and Evidence. Paper presented to the Society for Scientific Exploration, 26th Annual Meeting, East Lansing, Michigan, May 30–June 2, 2007: 1.

181. "It may demand a re-interpretation or reformulation of quantum theory": Shoup, R. Physics Without Causality—Theory and Evidence. Paper presented to the Society for Scientific Exploration, 26th Annual Meeting, East Lansing, Michigan, May 30–June 2, 2007: 12.

181. "the eminent physicist Gerald Feinberg": Feinberg, G. "Precognition—A Memory of Things Future." In: Oteri, L. (ed.). *Quantum Physics and Parapsychology*. New York: Parapsychology Foundation; 1975.

182. "The same can be said of Schödinger's famous equation": Haynie, D. T. *Biological Thermodynamics*. New York: Cambridge University Press; 2008: 66.

182. "The whole concept of 'non-locality' in contemporary physics": De Beauregard, O. C. "The Paranormal Is Not Excluded from Physics." *Journal of Scientific Exploration.* 1998; 12: 315–20.

182. "Physicist Henry Margenau concurred": Margenau, H. Quoted in: LeShan, L. *The Science of the Paranormal.* Northamptonshire, UK: Aquarian Press; 1987: 118.

182. "William Braud . . . reviewed twenty-four published experiments": Braud, W. "Wellness Implications of Retroactive Intentional Influence: Exploring an Outrageous Hypothesis." *Alternative Therapies in Health and Medicine.* 2000; 6(1): 37–48.

183. "There was less than one chance in ten thousand": Schmidt, H., Morris, R., Rudolph, L. "Channeling Evidence for a Psychokinetic Effect to Independent Observers." *Journal of Parapsychology.* 1986; 50: 1–15. Also: Schmidt, H., Schlitz, M. *A Large Scale Pilot PK Experiment with Prerecorded Random Events: Mind Science Foundation Research Report.* San Antonio, TX: Mind Science Foundation; 1988. Also: Schmidt, H., Morris, R. L., Hardin, C. L. *Channeling Evidence for a Psychokinetic Effect to Independent Observers: An Attempted Replication: Mind Science Foundation Research Report.* San Antonio, TX: Mind Science Foundation; 1990. Also: Schmidt, H., Braud, W. "New PK Tests with an Independent Observer." *Journal of Parapsychology.* 1993; 57: 227–40. Also: Schmidt, H., Stapp, H. "PK with Prerecorded Random Events and the Effects of Preobservation." *Journal of Parapsychology.*1993; 57: 331–49.

183. "It's as if the individual's intentions reached back in time": Nelson, R. D., et al. Analysis of Variance of REG Experiments: Operator Intention, Secondary Parameters, Database Structure: Technical Note PEAR 91004. Princeton, NJ: Princeton Engineering Anomalies Research Laboratory, Princeton University School of Engineering/Applied Science; 1991. Also: Nelson, R. D., Dunne, B. J., Jahn, R. G. An REG Experiment with Large Database Capability: HP Operator Related Anomalies: Technical Note PEAR 84003 (September). Princeton, NJ: Princeton Engineering Anomalies Research Laboratory Princeton University School of Engineering/Applied Science; 1984. Also: Jahn, R. G., Dobyns, Y. H., Dunne, B. J. "Count Population Profiles in Engineering Anomalies Experiments." *Journal of Scientific Exploration.* 1991; 5: 205–32. Also: Dunne, B., Jahn, R. "Experiments in Remote Human/Machine Interaction. *Journal of Scientific Exploration.* 1992; 6: 311–32.

184. "only 1.6 chances in a hundred that the results could be explained by chance": Radin, D. I., Machado, E. R., Zangari, W. Effects of Distant Healing Intention Through Time and Space: Two Exploratory Studies. Proceedings of Presented Papers: The 41st Annual Convention of the Parapsychological Association. Halifax, Nova Scotia, Canada: Parapsychological Association; 1998: 143–61.

184. "In two of three experiments, they were successful in doing so": Gruber, E. R.

"PK Effects on Prerecorded Group Behavior of Living Systems." *European Journal of Parapsychology*. 1980; 3(2): 167–75.

184. "Braud found that the average effect size was ten times as great": Kolata, G. "Drug Found to Help Heart Attack Survivors." *Science*. 1981; 214: 774–75. Also: Steering Committee of Physicians' Health Study Research Group. "Preliminary Report: Findings from the Aspirin Component of the Ongoing Physicians' Health Study." *New England Journal of Medicine*. 1988; 318: 262–64.

184. "Leonard Leibovici . . . tested this possibility": Leibovici, L. "Effects of Remote, Retroactive Intercessory Prayer on Outcomes in Patients with Bloodstream Infection: A Randomized Controlled Trial." *British Medical Journal*. 2001(323): 1450–51. For a discussion of this experiment, see: Olshansky, B., Dossey, L. "Retroactive Prayer: A Preposterous Hypothesis?" *British Medical Journal*. December 20, 2003; 327: 1465–68.

186. "Psi researcher and theorist Dean Radin": Radin, D. *Entangled Minds*. New York: Paraview/Simon & Schuster; 2006: 217.

187. "you will get 'down the drain' into a blind alley": Feynman, R. P. *The Character of Physical Law*. Cambridge, MA: MIT Press; 1967: 129.

187. "as historian-philosopher Willis Harman believed": Harman, W. Personal communication to Larry Dossey. June 1990.

187. "Chalmers proposes that consciousness may be fundamental in the world": Chalmers, D. J. "The Puzzle of Conscious Experience." *Scientific American*. 1995: 273(6): 80–86.

188. "a third level of mind, a mental component of the universe": Dyson, F. *Infinite in All Directions*. New York: Harper and Row; 1988: 297.

188. "So much for the philosophy of consciousness": Fodor, J. A. "The Big Idea." *Times* Literary Supplement. July 3, 1992: 20.

188. "As astronomer Carl Sagan expressed this position": Sagan, C. *The Dragons of Eden*. New York: Random House; 1977: 7.

189. "Nobelist Francis Crick agreed": Crick, F. *The Astonishing Hypothesis*. New York: Simon & Schuster; 1994: 271.

189. "cognitive scientist Daniel Dennett says": Dennett, D. *Consciousness Explained*. Boston: Back Bay Books; 1992: 406. In fairness to Dennett, here is the context in which this remarkable claim is made: "Are zombies possible? They're not just possible, they're actual. We're all zombies. Nobody is conscious—not in the systematically mysterious way that supports such doctrines as epiphenomenalism! I can't prove that no such sort of consciousness exists. I also cannot prove that gremlins don't exist. The best I can do is show that there is no respectable motivation for believing it."

189. "This led Nobel neurophysiologist Sir John Eccles to remark": Eccles, J., Robinson, D. N. *The Wonder of Being Human*. Boston: Shambhala; 1985: 53.

189. "It has all the features of a messianic prophecy": Eccles, J., Robinson, D. N. *The Wonder of Being Human*. Boston: Shambhala; 1985: 36.

190. "The odds that these results were not due to chance was greater than 10^{20} to 1": Honorton, C., Ferrari, D. "Future-Telling: A Meta-Analysis of Forced-Choice Precognition Experiments." *Journal of Parapsychology.* 1989; 53: 281–308.

190. "a flood of scholarly work has appeared": Kelly, E. F., et al. *Irreducible Mind: Toward a Psychology for the 21st Century.* Lanham, MD: Rowman and Litlefield; 2007.

190. "such as Cambridge philosopher Chris Carter's admirable [book]": Carter, C. *Parapsychology and the Skeptics: A Scientific Argument for ESP.* Pittsburgh, PA: Paja Books/SterlingHouse Publishers; 2007.

191. "I do not believe anyone has any good ideas about how to solve it": McGinn, C. "Can We Ever Understand Consciousness?" *The New York Review.* June 10, 1999; 46(10). http://www.nybooks.com/articles/article-preview?article_id=458. Accessed October 4, 2008.

191. "British neuropsychiatrist Peter Fenwick, a leading authority on near-death experiences": Fenwick, P., Fenwick, E. *The Truth in the Light.* New York: Berkley; 1997: 259–62. As American inventor Thomas Alva Edison expressed the "transmission" point of view: "People say I have created things. I have never created anything. I get impressions from the Universe at large and work them out, but I am only a plate on a record or a receiving apparatus—what you will. Thoughts are really impressions that we get from outside." (Quoted in: Baldwin, N. *Edison: Inventing the Century.* New York: Hyperion; 1995: 376.) Fenwick, writing in 1999, suggests that there is not much actual evidence favoring transmission theories. The pendulum is shifting, evidenced by experiments demonstrating that consciousness can do things brains cannot do: function remotely, nonlocally, in space and time. In view of this evidence, hypotheses suggesting that the brain is a receiver of consciousness make increasingly good sense, for they entail the premise that conscious is fundamental in the world, not derivative of local entities such as the human brain. For two seminal papers supporting the view of conscious as fundamental, see: Chalmers, D. "The Puzzle of Conscious Experience." *Scientific American.* 1995; 273(6): 80–86, available at: http://jamaica.u.arizona.edu/~chalmers/papers/puzzle.html; accessed October 4, 2008; and Clarke, C.J.S. "The Nonlocality of Mind." *Journal of Consciousness Studies.* 1995; 2(3): 231–40.

191. "physicist David Darling suggests that we are conscious not because of the brain": Darling, D. *Soul Search.* New York: Villard; 1995: 154–66.

192. "James took a courageous stand": James, W. Human Immortality: Two Supposed Objections to the Doctrine. Ingersoll Lecture. 1898. Available at: Wikisource. http://en.wikisource.org/wiki/Human_Immortality:_Two_Supposed_Objections_to_the_Doctrine. Accessed March 1, 2008.

192. "British philosopher Chris Carter endorses this analogy.": Carter, C. *Parapsychology and the Skeptics: A Scientific Argument for ESP.* Pittsburgh, PA: Paja Books/SterlingHouse Publishers; 2007.

192. "thereby concluding that the radio was *producing* the music.": Carter, C. Does Consciousness Depend on the Brain? Survival After Death Web site. http://www.survivalafterdeath.org/articles/carter/consciousness.htm. Accessed March 10, 2008.

192. "Thoughts are really impressions that we get from the outside": Edison, T. A. Quoted in: Baldwin, N. *Edison: Inventing the Century.* New York: Hyperion; 1995: 376.

193. "If our stomach is diseased our digestion suffers": Darling, D. *Soul Search.* New York: Villard; 1995: 154–66.

193. "sea water is known to block EM signals completely": Schwartz, S. A. *Opening to the Infinite: The Art and Science of Nonlocal Awareness.* Buda, TX: Nemoseen; 2007: 42.

193. "In precognitive remote-viewing experiments": Jahn, R. G., Dunne, B. J. *Margins of Reality: The Role of Consciousness in the Physical World.* New York: Harcourt Brace Jovanovich; 1987: 182–91.

193. "Furthermore, consciousness can operate into the past": Braud, W. "Wellness Implications of Retroactive Intentional Influence: Exploring an Outrageous Hypothesis." *Alternative Therapies in Health & Medicine.* 2000; 6(1): 37–48. Available at: http://www.integral-inquiry.com/cybrary.html#wellness.\

193. "we can conclude that consciousness is not an energetic signal": Dossey, L. *Reinventing Medicine.* San Francisco: HarperSanFrancisco; 1999: 13–84.

193. "consciousness is not a thing or substance, but is a *nonlocal* phenomenon": Dossey, L. *Recovering the Soul.* New York: Bantam; 1989: 1–11.

193. "They are *unmitigated*": Herbert, N. *Quantum Reality.* Garden City, NY: Anchor/Doubleday; 1987: 214.

194. "meaning they are *eternal*": Dossey, L. *Reinventing Medicine.* San Francisco: HarperSanFrancisco: 26–31.

194. "As the great physicist Niels Bohr said": Bohr, N. Wikiquote. http://en.wikiquote.org/wiki/Niels_Bohr. Accessed October 6, 2008.

194. "nonlocal events are no longer a matter of debate": Nadeau, R., Kafatos, M. *The Non-Local Universe: The New Physics and Matters of the Mind.* New York: Oxford University Press; 1999.

194. "The best-known studies": Nadeau, R., Kafatos, M. "Over Any Distance in 'no time'": Bell's Theorem and the Aspect and Gisin Experiments." *The Non-local Universe.* New York: Oxford University Press; 1999: 65–82. Also: Aspect, A., Dalibard, J., Roger, G. "Experimental Tests of Realistic Local Theories via Bell's Theorem. *Physical Review Letters.* 1981; 47: 460. Also: Aspect, A., Dalibard, J., Roger, G. "Experimental Realization of Einstein-Podolsky-Rosen-Bohm Gedankenexperiment: A New Violation of Bell's Inequalities." *Physical Review Letters.* 1982; 49, 91. Also: Aspect, A., Dalibard, J., Roger, G. "Experimental Test of Bell's Inequalities Using Time-Varying Analyzers." *Physical Review Letters.* 1982; 49: 1804.

194. "In 1998, Nicholas Gisen and his team": Tittell, W., et al. "Experimental Demonstration of Quantum Correlations over More Than 10 km." *Physical Review.* 1998; 57: 3229–232.

194. "In 2004, Gisen's group replicated this result": Marcikic, I., et al. "Distribution of Time-Bin Entangled Qubits over 30km of Optical Fiber. *Physical Review Letters.* 2004; 93.

195. "He invokes the concept of entanglement": Radin, D. *Entangled Minds.* New York: Paraview/Simon & Schuster; 2006.

195. "but only further research will tell": Thaheld, F. H. "An Interdisciplinary Approach to Certain Fundamental Issues in the Fields of Physics and Biology: Toward a Unified Theory." *BioSystems.* 2005; 80: 41–56.

195. "Only then will we be able to make a genuine bridge": Clarke, C. "The Nonlocality of Mind." *Journal of Consciousness Studies.* 1995; 2(3): 231–40. Available at: http://www.scispirit.com/tex/. Accessed November 2, 2008.

196. "This would demolish personal freedom of the will": Griffin, D. R. *Parapsychology, Philosophy, and Spirituality: A Postmodern Exploration.* Albany, NY: SUNY Press; 1997: 92.

197. "although Griffin finds this line of reasoning rational": Griffin, D. R. *Parapsychology, Philosophy, and Spirituality: A Postmodern Exploration.* Albany, NY: SUNY Press; 1997: 94. Griffin's goal is to preserve the cause-and-effect sequence, which he regards as sacrosanct. If premonitions are real, he believes this would permit the outrageous possibility that effects could precede causes. Griffin's reasoning is nuanced and sophisticated. I cannot do it justice here.

198. "Mice who eagerly run mazes they've never before encountered": Cohen, P. "Fear of New Things Shortens Life." *New Scientist.* December 8, 2003. http://www.newscientist.com/article.ns?id=dn4458. Accessed May 6, 2007.

198. "Women who regularly engage in mini-mysteries": Peck, P. "Diet, Activity May Help Prevent Alzheimer's." WebMD Medical News. July 19, 2004. http://www.webmd.com/alzheimers/news/20040719/diet-activity-may-help-prevent-alzheimers. Accessed May 7, 2007.

198. "Software is now available": Kam, K. "Keeping Your Brain Fit for Life." WebMD Medical News. November 6, 2006. http://www.webmd.com/brain/features/keeping-your-brain-fit-for-life. Accessed May 7, 2007.

APPENDIX

201. "Each person enfolds something of the spirit": Bohm, D. Quoted in: *About Time.* Christopher Rawlence (ed.). London: Jonathan Cape; 1985: 147.

203. "To divide or multiply consciousness": Schrödinger, E. *My View of the World.* Woodbridge, CT: Ox Bow Press; 1983: 31–34. Original English publication: Cambridge: Cambridge University Press; 1964.

203. "There is obviously only one alternative": Schrödinger, E. *What Is Life? and Mind and Matter.* London: Cambridge University Press; 1969: 139.

204. "I venture to call it [the mind] indestructible": Schrödinger, E. *What Is Life? and Mind and Matter.* London: Cambridge University Press; 1969: 145.

204. "A human being is part of the whole": Einstein, A. Quoted in: Bloomfield, H. "Transcendental Meditation as an Adjunct to Therapy," *Transpersonal Psychotherapy,* Seymour Boorstein (ed.). Palo Alto, CA: Science and Behavior Books, 1980; 136.

204. "I feel such a sense of solidarity with all living things": Einstein, A. Quoted in: Born, M. *The Born-Einstein Letters.* New York: Walker; 1971: 151.

204. "There is evidence . . . that the universe as a whole is hospitable to the growth of mind": Dyson, F. *Infinite in All Directions.* New York: Harper and Row; 1988: 297.

205. "[There is a physical reality that is] in essence the same for all": Margenau, H. *The Miracle of Existence.* Woodbridge, CT: Ox Bow Press; 1984: 111. Reprinted by Boston: Shambhala/New Science Library, 1987. The references that follow refer to the Ox Bow Press edition.

205. "each individual is part of God or part of the Universal Mind": Margenau, H. *The Miracle of Existence.* Woodbridge, CT: Ox Bow Press; 1984: 120.

205. "The Universal Mind has no need for memory": Margenau, H. *The Miracle of Existence.* Woodbridge, CT: Ox Bow Press; 1984: 126.

205. "Ultimately, the entire universe . . . has to be understood as a single undivided whole": Bohm, D. *Wholeness and the Implicate Order.* London: Routledge and Kegan Paul; 1980: 175.

205. "Deep down the consciousness of mankind is one": Bohm, D. Quoted in: Weber, R. *Dialogues with Scientists and Sages.* New York: Routledge and Kegan Paul; 1986: 41.

205. "Ultimately all the moments are really one": Bohm, D. Interview by John Briggs and F. David Peat. *OMNI.* January 1987: 68ff.

205. "Everything is alive": Bohm, D. In: Weber, R. "The Physicist and the Mystic—Is the Dialogue Between them Possible? A Conversation with David Bohm." *ReVision.* 4(1): 26. Also: Weber, R. "Conversations with David Bohm." *Dialogues with Scientists and Sages.* New York: Routledge and Kegan Paul; 1986: 23–52, 91–104, 139–56, 231–42.

206. "Mind, rather than emerging as a late outgrowth . . . has existed always": Wald, G. Quoted in *Bulletin of the Foundation for Mind-Being Research.* Los Altos, CA; September 1988: 3. Also: Wald, G. "Life and Mind in the Universe." *The Evolution of Consciousness.* Gandhi, K. (ed.). New York: Paragon House; 1986: 1–27.

206. "We can admittedly find nothing in physics or chemistry": Bohr, N. Quoted in: Heisenberg, W. *Physics and Beyond.* Pomerans, A. J. (trans.). New York: Harper and Row; 1971: 88–91.

206. "[The] universe begins to look more like a great thought": Jeans, J. *The Mysterious Universe.* New York: Macmillan; 1948: 186–87.

206. "The idea of a universal Mind or Logos": Eddington, A. "Defense of Mysticism." Quoted in: Wilber, K. *Quantum Questions: Mystical Writings of the World's Great Physicists.* Boston: Shambhala/New Science Library, 1984: 206.

206. "[T]he stuff of the world": Eddington, A. *The Nature of the Physical World.* Ann Arbor: University of Michigan Press, 1978: 276.

207. "The individual mind is immanent": Bateson, G. *Steps to an Ecology of Mind.* San Francisco: Chandler Press, 1972: 467.

REFERENCES

Aberfan Disaster. http://www.nuffield.ox.ac.uk/politics/aberfan/home2.htm. Accessed November 22, 2008.

Agor, W. H. "Intuition: A Brain Skill Top Executives Use to Increase Productivity." *Public Productivity Review*. 1985; 9(4): 357–72.

Alschuler, A. S. "Recognizing Inner Teachers—Inner Voices Throughout History." *Gnosis Magazine*. Fall 1987; 5: 8–12.

Applewhite, M. "Planet About to Be Recycled." Heaven's Gate Web site. http://www.heavensgate.com/misc/vt100596.htm. Accessed November 18, 2008.

Aspect, A., Dalibard, J., Roger, G. "Experimental Tests of Realistic Local Theories Via Bell's Theorem." *Physical Review* Letters. 1981; 47: 460.

———. "Experimental Realization of Einstein-Podolsky-Rosen-Bohm Gedankenexperiment: A New Violation of Bell's inequalities." *Physical Review* Letters. 1982; 49, 91.

———. "Experimental Test of Bell's Inequalities Using Time-Varying Analyzers." *Physical Review* Letters. 1982; 49: 1804.

Backström, F. "Private Lunar ESP: An Interview with Edgar Mitchell." CabinetMagazine.org. http://www.cabinetmagazine.org/issues/5/esp.php. Accessed October 11, 2008.

Ball, E. *In the Days of Victorio*. Tucson: University of Arizona Press; 1992: 11.

Barasch, M. I. *Healing Dreams*. New York: Riverhead; 2000: 241–42.

Barbour, J. *The End of Time*. New York: Oxford University Press; 2001.

Bardens, D. *Psychic Animals*. New York: Barnes & Noble; 1996: 61.

Barnum, B. "Expanded Consciousness: Nurses' Experiences." *Nursing Outlook*. 1989; 37(6): 260–66.

Barry, P. "Science Hopes to Change Events That Have Already Occurred." SFGate.com. January 21, 2007. http://www.sfgate.com/cgi-bin/article.cgi?f=/c/a/2007/01/21/ING5LNJSBF1.DTL. Accessed October 31, 2008.

Bem, D. J., Honorton, C. "Does Psi Exist? Replicable Evidence for an Anomalous Process of Information Transfer." *Psychological Bulletin*. 1994; 5(1): 1, 4–18. Available at: http://homepage.psy.utexas.edu/homepage/Class/Psy391P/Bem&Honorton.1984 .pdf. Accessed April 18, 2008.

Berenbaum, H., Kerns, J., Raghavan, C. "Anomalous Experiences, Peculiarity, and Psychopathology." In *Varieties of Anomalous Experience: Examining the Scientific Evidence.* Cardeña, E., Lynn, S. J., Krippner, S. (eds.). Washington, DC: American Psychological Association, 2000: 32.

Bernstein, J. S. *Living in the Borderland: The Evolution of Consciousness and the Challenge of Healing Trauma.* New York: Routledge; 2005: 185.

Bierman, D. J., Radin, D. I. "Anomalous Anticipatory Response on Randomized Future Conditions." *Perceptual and Motor Skills.* 1997; 84: 689–90.

Blair, L. *Rhythms of Vision.* New York: Schoken, 1976.

Blaksley, T. "Impression." *Journal of the Society for Psychical Research.* 1892; 5: 241.

Blum, D. *Ghost Hunters: William James and the Search for Scientific Proof of Life After Death.* New York: Penguin; 2006: 73–74.

Bohm, D. *Wholeness and the Implicate Order.* New York: Routledge; 2002.

Bohr, N. Quoted in Werner Heisenberg, *Physics and Beyond.* A. J. Pomerans, trans. New York: Harper and Row; 1971: 88–91.

Boss, M. *The Analysis of Dreams.* New York: Philosophical Library; 1958: 186–87.

Boxer, S. "The Banality of Terror; Dreams of Holy War over a Quiet Evening." *The New York Times.* December 16, 2001. Ideas & Trends section. http://query.ny times.com/gst/fullpage.html?res=9C0CE6D61E3FF935A25751C1A9679 C8B63. Accessed September 26, 2008.

Braud, W. G. *Psi Notes: Answers to Frequently Asked Questions about Parapsychology and Psychic Phenomena.* 2nd ed. San Antonio, TX: The Mind Science Foundation; 1984: 3.

———. "Wellness Implications of Retroactive Intentional Influence: Exploring an Outrageous Hypothesis." *Alternative Therapies in Health and Medicine.* 2000; 6(1): 37–48.

Broderick, D. *Outside the Gates of Science: Why It's Time for the Paranormal to Come in from the Cold.* New York: Thunder's Mouth Press/Avalon; 2007: 68.

Broughton, R. *Parapsychology: The Controversial Science.* New York: Ballantine; 1991: 341–47.

Cardeña, E., Lynn, S. J., Krippner, S. (eds.). *Varieties of Anomalous Experience: Examining the Scientific Evidence.* Washington, DC: American Psychological Association; 2000.

Carpenter, J. C. "First Sight: Part One. A Model of Psi and the Mind." *Journal of Parapsychology.* 2004; 68(2): 217–54.

——— "First sight: Part Two. Elaboration of Model of Psi and the Mind." *Journal of Parapsychology.* 2004; 69(1): 63–112.

Carroll, L. *Alice's Adventures in Wonderland* and *Through the Looking-Glass.* New York: New American Library; 2000: 174.

Carroll, R. T. Astrology. The Skeptic's Dictionary Online. http://skepdic.com/astrolgy .html. Accessed March 3, 2008.

Carter, C. *Parapsychology and the Skeptics: A Scientific Argument for ESP*. Pittsburgh, PA: Paja Books/SterlingHouse; 2007.

Carter, C. "Does Consciousness Depend on the Brain?" Survival After Death Web site. http://www.survivalafterdeath.org/articles/carter/consciousness.htm. Accessed March 10, 2008.

Chalmers, D. J. "The Puzzle of Conscious Experience." *Scientific American*. 1995: 273(6): 80–86.

Clarke, C. "The Nonlocality of Mind." *Journal of Consciousness Studies*. 1995; 2(3): 231–40. Available at: http://www.scispirit.com/tex/. Accessed November 2, 2008.

Clarke, R. A. *Against All Enemies*. New York: Free Press, 2004; American Civil Liberties Online. Sibel Edmonds. http://www.aclu.org/safefree/general/18828res20050126 .html. Accessed March 5, 2008.

Coghlan, A. "News review 2007: Hidden Harm from Noise Pollution." *New Scientist*. December 22, 2007; 2635: 25. http://www.newscientist.com/channel/health/ mg19626355.700-news-review-2007-hidden-harm-from-noise-pollution.html. Accessed January 23, 2008.

Cohen, P. "Fear of New Things Shortens Life." *New Scientist*. December 8, 2003. http://www.newscientist.com/article.ns?id=dn4458. Accessed May 6, 2008.

Cohn, S. Personal communication to the author. March 26, 2008. Used with permission.

Coly, L., McMahon, J. (eds.) *Psi and Clinical Practice*. New York: Parapsychology Foundation; 1993.

Cox, W. E. "Precognition: An Analysis II." *Journal of the American Society for Psychical Research*. 1956; 50(1): 99–109.

Crescenzi, A., Torricelli, F. "A Tun-Huang Text on Dreams: Ms Pelliot Tibetan 55-IX." *Tibet Journal*. 1995; 20(2): 3–17.

Crick, F. *The Astonishing Hypothesis*. New York: Simon & Schuster; 1994: 271.

Dalai Lama (Gyatsu, T). *Freedom in Exile: The Autobiography of the Dalai Lama*. New York: HarperCollins; 1991. Quotation available at: Nechung—The State Oracle of Tibet. Web site of the government of Tibet in exile. http://www.tibet.com/Bud dhism/nechung_hh.html. Accessed March 2, 2008.

Dalton, J. "Extraordinary Facts Relating to the Vision of Colours: With Observations." *Memoirs of the Literary and Philosophical Society of Manchester*. 1798; 5: 28–45.

Darling, D. *Soul Search*. New York: Villard; 1995: 158.

Davies, E. Report of the Tribunal Appointed to Inquire into the Disaster at Aberfan on October 21, 1966. HMSO. 1967; HL 316 & HC 553: 27.

Davies, P. *Space and Time in the Modern Universe*. New York: Cambridge University Press; 1977: 221.

————. *About Time: Einstein's Unfinished Revolution.* New York: Simon & Schuster; 1996.

Dean, D., Mihalasky, J. *Executive ESP.* Englewood Cliffs, NJ: Prentice-Hall; 1974.

De Beauregard, O. C. "The Paranormal Is Not Excluded from Physics." *Journal of Scientific Exploration.* 1998; 12: 315–20.

De Becker, R. *The Understanding of Dreaming, or The Machinations of the Night.* London: George Allen & Unwin; 1968.

Dennett, D. *Consciousness Explained.* Boston: Back Bay Books; 1992: 406.

Dennett, P. E. "Premonitions of Disaster." http://www.atlantisrising.com/issue18/18premonitions.html. Accessed January 26, 2008.

Dobson, R. "Taxi Drivers' Knowledge Helps Their Brains Grow." *The Independent* (UK). December 17, 2006. http://news.independent.co.uk/uk/health_medical/article2081652.ece. Accessed May 18, 2008.

Doheny, K. "Cat's 'Sixth Sense' Predicting Death?" CBSNews.com. http://www.cbsnews.com/stories/2007/07/25/health/webmd/main3097899.shtml. July 25, 2007. Accessed October 3, 2008.

Dosa, D. M. "A Day in the Life of Oscar the Cat." *New England Journal of Medicine.* 2007; 357(4): 328–29.

Dossey, L. *Recovering the Soul.* New York: Bantam; 1989: 1–11.

————. *Healing Words: The Power of Prayer in the Practice of Medicine.* San Francisco: HarperSanFrancisco; 1993.

————. *Prayer Is Good Medicine.* San Francisco: HarperSanFrancisco; 1996.

————. *Be Careful What You Pray For.* San Francisco, CA: HarperSanFrancisco; 1997.

————. *Reinventing Medicine.* SanFrancisco; HarperSanFrancisco; 1999.

————. "Distant Nonlocal Awareness: A Different Kind of DNA." *Alternative Therapies in Health and Medicine.* 2000; 6(6): 10–14, 102–10.

————. "Quiet Please: Observations on Noise." *Explore* (NY). 2008; 4(3): 157–63.

Dunne, B., Jahn, R. "Experiments in Remote Human/Machine Interaction." *Journal of Scientific Exploration.* 1992; 6: 311–32.

Dunne, J. W. *Nothing Dies.* London: Faber and Faber; 1946.

————. *An Experiment with Time.* Reprint. Charlottesville, VA: Hampton Roads; 2001: 23.

Dyson, F. *Infinite in All Directions.* New York: Harper and Row; 1988: 297.

Eccles, J., Robinson, D. N. *The Wonder of Being Human.* Boston: Shambhala; 1985: 53.

Edeal, G. "Why the Choir Was Late." *Life.* March 27, 1950: 19–23.

Edison, T. A. Quoted in: Neil Baldwin, *Edison: Inventing the Century.* New York: Hyperion; 1995: 376.

Ehrenwald, J. *Telepathy and Medical Psychology.* New York: Norton; 1948.

Einstein Archive, reel 7–245. Reprinted in *Albert Einstein—Michele Besso Correspondence, 1903–1955.* Paris: Hermann; 1972: 537–38.

Einstein, A. Preface to Upton Sinclair, *Mental Radio.* Charlottesville, VA: Hampton Roads; 2001: xi.

———. Quoted in Max Jammer, *Einstein and Religion: Physics and Theology.* Princeton, NJ: Princeton University Press; 2002: 161.

Eliade, M. *The Myth of the Eternal Return.* Willard R. Trask, trans. Bollingen Foundation edition. Princeton, NJ: Princeton University Press; 1954.

Faludi, S. *The Terror Dream: Fear and Fantasy in Post-9/11 America.* New York: Metropolitan Books; 2007.

———. Interview by Amy Goodman. Democracy Now radio. October 4, 2007. Transcript available at: http://www.democracynow.org/print.pl?sid=07/10/04/1355237. Accessed October 5, 2008.

Farman, J. C., Gardiner, B. G., Shanklin, J. D. "Large Losses of Total Ozone in Antarctica Reveal Seasonal Clox/NOx Interaction." *Nature.* 1985; 315: 207–10.

Feather, S. R., Schmicker, M. *The Gift: ESP, the Extraordinary Experiences of Ordinary People.* New York: St. Martin's Press; 2005.

Feinberg, G. "Precognition—A Memory of Things Future." In Oteri, L., ed. *Quantum Physics and Parapsychology.* New York: Parapsychology Foundation; 1975.

Fenwick, P., Fenwick, E. *The Truth in the Light.* New York: Berkley; 1997: 259–62.

Feynman, R. Quoted in Boslough, J. "The Enigma of Time." *National Geographic.* March 1990; 177(3): 109–32.

Feynman, R. P. *The Character of Physical Law.* Cambridge, MA: MIT Press; 1967: 129.

Fisher, M., Pressley, S. A. "Founder Sought to Purge Sexuality Via Cult." *Washington Post.* March 29, 1997. Available at Cult Education and Recovery. http://www.rickross.com/reference/heavensgate/gate13.html. Accessed March 1, 2008.

Fitzgerald, R. *Lucky You: Proven Strategies for Finding Good Fortune.* New York: Citadel/Kensington; 2004: 128.

Fodor, J. A. "The Big Idea." *Times Literary Supplement.* July 3, 1992: 20.

Freud, S. *The Interpretation of Dreams.* Joyce Crick, trans. Reprint. New York: Oxford University Press; 1999: 8.

———. Letter to Wilhelm Fliess. See Breger, L. *Freud: Darkness in the Midst of Vision.* New York: John Wiley; 2000: 143.

———. Quoted in McLynn, F. *Carl Gustav Jung.* New York: St. Martin's Press; 1996: 128.

Fritts, R. "Is the Universe Random, or Is There Something Out There Controlling Things?" http://www.cedarlane.org/96serms/s960505.html. Accessed November 23, 2008.

Gallup Poll on prayer habits of Americans, reported in *Life* magazine, March 1994.

Gefter, A. "Time's Up." *New Scientist.* January 19, 2008; 197(2639): 26–29.

Gissurarson, L. R., Haraldsson, E. "History of Parapsychology in Iceland." *International Journal of Parapsychology.* 2001; 12(1): 31–52.

Glanz, J. "Physics' Big Puzzle Has Big Question: What Is Time?" *New York Times* online. June 19, 2001. http://query.nytimes.com/gst/fullpage.html?res=9D06E

0DE1031F93AA25755C0A9679C8B63&sec=&spon=&pagewanted=print. Accessed October 21, 2008.

Goldner, E. M., et al. "Prevalence and Incidence Studies of Schizophrenic Disorders: A Systematic Review of the Literature." *Canadian Journal of Psychiatry.* 2002; 47(9): 833–43.

Goman, C. K. "Business Intuition." *Link&Learn* eNewsletter. April 2005. http://www.linkageinc.com/company/news_events/link_learn_enewsletter/archive/2005/04_05_business_intuition_goman.aspx. Accessed January 25, 2008.

Goodare, J., et al. The Survey of Scottish Witchcraft: 1563–1736. University of Edinburgh. School of History, Classics, and Archaeology. January 2003. http://www.shc.ed.ac.uk/Research/witches/. Accessed September 20, 2008.

Gott, J. R. "J. Richard Gott on Life, the Universe, and Everything." Interview with Jill Neimark. Science&Spirit.com. 2007. http://www.science-spirit.org/article_detail.php?article_id=270. Accessed October 31, 2008.

Graff, D. E. "Explorations in Precognitive Dreaming." *Journal of Scientific Exploration.* 2007; 21(4): 707–22.

Greeley, A. "The Impossible: It's Happening." *Noetic Sciences Review.* Spring 1987: 7–9.

———. "Mysticism Goes Mainstream." *American Health.* 1987; 6(1): 47–49.

Grey, A. *Gaia.* http://gaia.tribe.net/photos/23eb69f2-5b73-40d2-80fa-6fb850fc15b4. Accessed September 15, 2008.

Griffin, D. R. *Parapsychology, Philosophy, and Spirituality: A Postmodern Exploration.* Albany, NY: SUNY Press; 1997: 92.

Gruber, E. R. "PK Effects on Prerecorded Group Behavior of Living Systems." *European Journal of Parapsychology.* 1980; 3(2): 167–75.

Guiley, R. E. *Harper's Encyclopedia of Mystical & Paranormal Experience.* New York: HarperCollins; 1991: 465–66.

Gurney, E., Myers, F. W. H., Podmore, F. *Phantasms of the Living.* Volume 1. London: Trübner; 1886: 188–89.

———. *Phantasms of the Living.* Volume 2. London: Trübner; 1886: 132.

Hall, K. The Vultures. http://www.stressinstitute.com/AboutDrKathleenHall/Blog.aspx?pageId=274. March 12, 2007. Accessed May 11, 2008.

———. http://www.stressinstitute.com/AboutDrKathleenHall/Blog.aspx?pageId=275. March 12, 2007. Accessed May 11, 2008.

Hannah, B. *Jung: His Life and Work.* Boston: Shambhala; 1991: 128.

Hansel, C. E. M. *ESP: A Scientific Explanation.* New York: Charles Scribner's Sons; 1966: 124–27.

Hanson, V. D. "Public Shares the Blame in Creating Dr. Frankenstein's Wall Street." *Salt Lake Tribune* online. September 25, 2008. http://www.sltrib.com/opinion/ci_10550559. Accessed October 3, 2008.

Haraldsson, E., Houtkooper, J. M. "Psychic Experiences in the Multi-National Human Values Survey." *Journal of the American Society for Psychical Research.* 1991; 85(2), 145–65.

Harrell, E. "Collider Triggers End-of-World Fears." Time.com. September 4, 2008. http://www.time.com/time/health/article/0,8599,1838947,00.html?imw=Y. Accessed October 31, 2008.

Harris, A. W. Harris on Terrorism and Asteroid Risk. Undated. http://psweb.sbs.ohio-state.edu/faculty/jmueller/HARRIS.PDF. Accessed November 22, 2008.

Harteis, C., Gruber, H. "Intuition and Professional Competence: Intuitive versus Rational Forecasting of the Stock Market." Vocations and Learning (online version). December 28, 2007. http://www.springerlink.com/content/wt804572x37883x8/. Accessed January 26, 2008.

Hassabis. D., et al. Patients with Hippocampal Amnesia Cannot Imagine New Experiences. *Proceedings of the National Academy of Sciences USA.* 2007; 104(5): 1726–31.

Haynie, D. T. *Biological Thermodynamics.* New York: Cambridge University Press; 2008: 66.

Hearne, K. "Lucid Dreams—An Electrophysiological and Psychological Study." Chapters III and IV. Ph.D. thesis. Department of Psychology, University of Liverpool, England. May 1978. http://www.european-college.co.uk/thesis.htm. Accessed March 15, 2008.

Hefner, A. G. Premonition. http://www.themystica.com/mystica/articles/p/premonition.html. Accessed January 26, 2008.

Henslee, J. A., et al. "The Impact of Premonitions of SIDS on Grieving and Healing." *Pediatric Pulmonology.* 1993; 16: 393.

Herbert, N. *Quantum Reality.* Garden City, NY: Anchor/Doubleday; 1987: 214.

Herbert, N. *Elemental Mind.* New York: Dutton; 1993.

Higgins, A. G. Broken Atom Smasher Inaugurated Anyway. MSNBC.com. October 21, 2008. http://www.msnbc.msn.com/id/27296827/. Accessed November 22, 2008.

Holman, E. A., et al. "Terrorism, Acute Stress, and Cardiovascular Health: A 3-Year National Study Following the September 11th Attacks." *Archives of General Psychiatry.* 2008; 65(1): 73–80. Abstract available at http://archpsyc.ama-assn.org/cgi/content/abstract/65/1/73. Accessed January 25, 2008.

Honorton, C. The Ganzfeld Novice: Four Predictors of Initial ESP Performance. Paper presented at the Parapsychological Association's 35th Annual Convention, Las Vegas, NV; 1992.

Honorton, C., Ferrari, D. "Future-Telling: A Meta-Analysis of Forced-Choice Precognition Experiments." *Journal of Parapsychology.* 1989; 53: 281–309.

Horchler, J. N., Morris, R. R. "Dreams and Premonitions." In *SIDS & Infant Death Survival Guide: Information and Comfort for Grieving Family & Friends & Professionals Who Seek to Help Them.* 3rd ed. Hyattsville, MD: SIDS Educational Services; 2003: 276–85.

Hurdle, J. Lose Weight, Stay Active, Prevent Alzheimer's—Studies. VirtualMedicalCentre.com. July 20, 2004. http://www.virtualcancercentre.com/news.asp?artid=2358. Accessed September 18, 2008.

Huxley, T. H. Presidential address, 1870, to the British Association for the Advancement of Science. In Huxley, T. H. *Collected Essays. Discourses: Biological and Geological*. Volume 8. Reprint. Kitla, MT: Kessinger Publishing; 2005: 244. Original edition: London: Macmillan, 1894.

Hyman, R. "Evaluation of Program on Anomalous Mental Phenomena." *Journal of Scientific Exploration*. 1996; 10(1): 31–58.

Ingerman, S. *Shamanic Journeying*. Boulder, CO: Sounds True (Har/Com edition); 2004.

———. *Soul Retrieval: Mending the Fragmented Self*. Revised ed. New York: HarperOne; 2006.

Inglis, B. *Natural and Supernatural: A History of the Paranormal*. Bridport, Dorset, UK: Prism Press; 1992: 34. Original publication: Sevenoaks, Kent, UK: Hodder and Stoughton; 1977.

Irwin, H. J. *An Introduction to Parapsychology*. 3rd ed. Jefferson, NC: McFarland; 1999.

Jahn, R. G., Dunne, B. J. *Margins of Reality: The Role of Consciousness in the Physical World*. New York: Harcourt Brace Jovanovich; 1987: 149–91.

Jahn, R. G., Dobyns, Y. H., Dunne, B. J. "Count Population Profiles in Engineering Anomalies Experiments." *Journal of Scientific Exploration*. 1991; 5: 205–32.

James, W. Human Immortality: Two Supposed Objections to the Doctrine. Ingersoll Lecture. 1898. Available at Wikisource. http://en.wikisource.org/wiki/Human_Immortality:_Two_Supposed_Objections_to_the_Doctrine. Accessed March 1, 2008.

Johnson, S. *Journey to the Western Isles of Scotland*. Kitla, MT: Kessinger, 2004: 85ff. Original publication: London; 1775. Available at: eBook.com. http://www.ebook mall.com/ebook/6751-ebook.htm. Accessed May 25, 2008.

Jordan, P. A. The Mystery of Chance. http://www.strangemag.com/mysteryofchance .html. Accessed November 23, 2008.

Josephson, B. Quoted in "Is This Really Proof That Man Can See into the Future?" *Daily Mail* (London). May 4, 2007. http://www.dailymail.co.uk/pages/live/articles/technology/technology.html?in_article_id=452833&in_page_id=1965. Accessed October 6, 2008.

Josephus, F. *Jewish Antiquities*. H. St. J. Thackeray, trans. Cambridge, MA: Harvard University Press; 1967: 205.

Jung, C. G. *Symbols and Interpretations of Dreams 3: The Collected Works of C. G. Jung*. Volume 18. H. Read, M. Fordham, and G. Adler, eds. R. F. C. Hull, trans. London: Routledge and Kegan Paul; 1961: 207–208.

———. *Memories, Dreams, Reflections*. Aniela Jaffé, ed. Richard and Clara Winston, trans. New York: Vintage/Random House; 1965: 155.

———. *The Structure and Dynamics of the Psyche. Collected Works*, Volume VIII. 2nd ed. Gerhard Adler and R. F. C. Hull, trans. Princeton, NJ: Princeton University Press; 1970: 420.

————. *Psychological Types. Collected Works of C. G. Jung*, Volume 6. Princeton, NJ: Princeton University Press; 1971.

Kam, K. Keeping Your Brain Fit for Life. WebMD. http://www.webmd.com/brain/features/keeping-your-brain-fit-for-life. November 6, 2006. Accessed May 7, 2008.

Kawecki, T. Quoted in "Soundbites." *New Scientist*. May 10, 2008; 198(2655): 8.

Kelly, E. F., et al. *Irreducible Mind: Toward a Psychology for the 21st Century*. Lanham, MD: Rowman and Littlefield; 2007.

Kenyon, F. G. *The Chester Beatty Biblical Papyri: Descriptions and Texts of Twenty Manuscripts on Papyrus of the Greek Bible*. London: Emery Walker; 1933, 1937.

Khamsi, R. "Amnesiacs Struggle to Imagine Future Events." New Scientist.com. January 15, 2007. http://www.newscientist.com/channel/being-human/dn10950-amnesiacs-struggle-to-imagine-future-events.html. Accessed May 18, 2008.

Kiersey, D., Bates, M. *Please Understand Me II*. Del Mar, CA: Prometheus Nemesis; 1998: 145.

Kierulff, S., Krippner, S. *Becoming Psychic: Spiritual Lessons for Focusing Your Hidden Abilities*. Franklin Lakes, NJ: New Page Books; 2004: 137.

Kincheloe, L. Personal communication to Larry Dossey. November 2003. Used with permission. Also available at Kincheloe, L. "Intuitive Obstetrics." *Alternative Therapies in Health & Medicine*. 2003; 9(6): 16–17.

Kirsch, J. *The Reluctant Prophet*. Los Angeles: Sherbourne Press; 1973: 30.

Klein, N. "Crisis called 'Katrina without the water.'" *Seattle Post-Intelligencer*. http://blog.seattlepi.nwsource.com/realestatenews/archives/148904.asp. September 16, 2008. Accessed September 27, 2008.

Klintman, H. "Is There a Paranormal (Precognitive) Influence in Certain Types of Perceptual Sequences? Part I." *European Journal of Parapsychology*. 1983; 5: 19–49.

————. "Is There a Paranormal (Precognitive) Influence in Certain Types of Perceptual Sequences? Part II." *European Journal of Parapsychology*. 1984; 5: 125–40.

Kolata, G. "Drug Found to Help Heart Attack Survivors." *Science*. 1981; 214: 774–75.

Krishnamurti, J., Bohm, D. *The Ending of Time*. New York: HarperOne; 1985.

Kroft, S. "Dennis Quaid Recounts Twins' Drug Ordeal." *60 Minutes*. CBS online; http://www.cbsnews.com/stories/2008/03/13/60minutes/main3936412.shtml. Accessed March 26, 2008.

Lamon, Ward Hill. Wikipedia. http://en.wikipedia.org/wiki/Ward_Hill_Lamon. Accessed January 28, 2007.

Lanier, J. "From Having a Mystical Experience to Becoming a Mystic." *ReVision*. 1989; 12(1): 41–44. Abstract available at http://www.questia.com/googleScholar.qst;jsessionid=JygdRsmcZxY7dVttfQJsBpjDcTMDknxbpDpjdpLQqv2Bg1mDQ7bN!615987071?docId=95142179. Accessed November 22, 2008.

Larson, E. "Did Psychic Powers Give Firm a Killing in the Silver Market?" *Wall Street Journal*. October 22, 1984.

Lavender, D. *Bent's Fort*. Lincoln: University of Nebraska Press; 1954: 125.

Lawrence, T. Gathering in the Sheep and Goats. A Meta-Analysis of Forced-Choice Sheep-Goat ESP Studies, 1947–1993. Proceedings of Presented Papers: The Parapsychological Association 36th Annual Convention, Toronto, Canada, 1993: 75–86.

Leibovici, L. "Effects of Remote, Retroactive Intercessory Prayer on Outcomes in Patients with Bloodstream Infection: A Randomized Controlled Trial." *British Medical Journal*. 2001(323): 1450–51.

LeShan, L. *How to Meditate: A Guide to Self-Discovery*. Boston: Little, Brown; 1974.

Lorimer, D. *Whole in One*. London: Arkana/Penguin; 1990.

Macnish, R. *The Philosophy of Sleep*. 3rd ed. Glasgow: MM'Phun, 1836: 96. Reprint edition by Kitla, MT: Kessinger Publishing; 2006: 87.

Madgewick, G. *Aberfan: Struggling Out of the Darkness*. Blaengarw, UK: Valley & Vale; 1996: 23.

Maguire, E. A., et al. Navigation-Related Structural Change in the Hippocampi of Taxi Drivers. *Proceedings of the National Academy of Sciences USA* 2000; 97(8): 4398–403.

Maguire, E. A., et al. Navigation Expertise and the Human Hippocampus: A Structural Brain Imaging Analysis. *Hippocampus*. 2003; 12(2): 250–59.

Marcikic, I., et al. "Distribution of Time-Bin Entangled Qubits over 30km of Optical Fiber." *Physical Review* Letters. 2004; 93.

Margenau, H. Quoted in LeShan, Lawrence, *The Science of the Paranormal*. Northamptonshire, UK: Aquarian Press; 1987: 118.

Martin, J., Birnes, W. J. *The Haunting of the Presidents*. New York: Signet/New American Library; 2003: 261.

May, E. C. "The American Institutes for Research Review of the Department of Defense's STAR GATE Program: A Commentary." *Journal of Scientific Exploration*. 1996; 10(1): 89–107.

May, E. C., et al. "Advances in Remote-Viewing Analysis." *Journal of Parapsychology*. 1990; 54, 193–228.

May, E. C., Vilenskaya, L. "Overview of Current Parapsychology Research in the Former Soviet Union." *Subtle Energies*. 1992; 3 (3), 45–67.

May, E. C., Spottiswoode, S. J. P., James, C. L. "Managing the Target-Pool Bandwidth: Possible Noise Reduction for Anomalous Cognition Experiments." *Journal of Parapsychology*. 1994; 58, 303–13.

———. "Shannon Entropy: A Possible Intrinsic Target Property." *Journal of Parapsychology*. 1994; 58, 384–401.

Mayer, E. L. *Extraordinary Knowing: Science, Skepticism, and the Inexplicable Powers of the Human Mind*. New York: Bantam/Random House; 2007: 119.

McCraty, R., Atkinson, M., Bradley, R. T. "Electrophysiological Evidence of Intuition: Part 1. The Surprising Role of the Heart." *Journal of Alternative and Complementary Medicine*. 2004; 10(1): 133–43.

———. "Electrophysiological Evidence of Intuition: Part 2. A System-Wide Process?" *Journal of Alternative and Complementary Medicine*. 2004; 10: 325–36.

McGinn, C. "Can We Ever Understand Consciousness?" *The New York Review*. June 10, 1999; 46(10). http://www.nybooks.com/articles/article-preview?article_id=458. Accessed October 4, 2008.

McLean, I. "On Moles and the Habits of Birds: The Unpolitics of Aberfan." *Twentieth Century British History*, Vol. 8. December 1997.

————. Corporatism and Regulatory Failure: Government Response to the Aberfan Disaster. http://www.nuffield.ox.ac.uk/politics/aberfan.esrc.html. Accessed January 2, 2008.

McLean, I., Johnes, M. *Aberfan: Disasters and Government*. Cardiff: Welsh Academic Press; 2000.

————. Remembering Aberfan. http://www.nuffield.ox.ac.uk/politics/aberfan/remem.htm. Accessed January 2, 2008.

Milton, J. "Effects of 'Paranormal' Experiences on People's Lives. An Unusual Survey of Spontaneous Cases." *Journal of the Society for Psychical Research*. 1992; 58: 314–23.

Mitchell, E. "The Physiological Diagnostic Dream." *New York Medical Journal*. 1923; 188: 416.

Mooney, G. The History of the Gravity poster. http://www.mooneyart.com/gravity/historyof_01.html. Accessed September 16, 2008.

Moore, D. W. "Three in Four Americans Believe in Paranormal." The Gallup Organization, Princeton, NJ. June 16, 2005. Available at http://home.sandiego.edu/%7Ebaber/logic/gallup.html. Accessed October 13, 2008.

Moore, V. "Grim Rea-Purr: The Cat That Can Predict Death." *Daily Mail* online. http://www.dailymail.co.uk/pages/live/articles/news/news.html?in_article_id=470906&in_page_id=1770. Accessed October 2, 2008.

Moss, R. *Dreaming True*. New York: Pocket Books; 2000.

Mott, M. "Did Animals Sense Tsunami Was Coming?" *National Geographic News* online. January 4, 2007. http://news.nationalgeographic.com/news/2005/01/0104_050104_tsunami_animals.html. Accessed October 5, 2008.

Myers, I. B., with Peter B. Myers. *Gifts Differing: Understanding Personality Type*. Mountain View, CA: Davies-Black; 1995.

Nadeau, R., Kafatos, M. *The Non-Local Universe: The New Physics and Matters of the Mind*. New York: Oxford University Press; 1999.

Nasht, S. *The Last Explorer*. New York: Arcade Publishing, 2006: 71–72.

Nelson, R. D., Dunne, B. J., Jahn, R. G. *An REG Experiment with Large Database Capability: HP Operator Related Anomalies: Technical Note PEAR 84003* (September). Princeton, NJ: Princeton Engineering Anomalies Research Laboratory Princeton University School of Engineering/Applied Science; 1984.

Nelson, R. D., et al. *Analysis of Variance of REG Experiments: Operator Intention, Secondary Parameters, Database Structure: Technical Note PEAR 91004*. Princeton, NJ: Princeton Engineering Anomalies Research Laboratory, Princeton University School of Engineering/Applied Science; 1991.

————. "Precognitive Remote Perception: Replication of Remote Viewing." *Journal of Scientific Exploration.* 1996; 10(1): 109–10.

Neppe, V. M. "Temporal Lobe Symptomatology in Subjective Paranormal Experients." *Journal of the American Society for Psychical Research.* 1983; 77(1): 1–29.

————. "Clinical Psychiatry, Psychopharmacology, and Anomalous Experience." In *Psi and Clinical Practice.* Lisette Coly and Joanne McMahon, eds. New York: Parapsychology Foundation; 1993. Available at http://www.pni.org/research/anomalous/classif_art/clinical_psychiatry.html. Accessed September 26, 2008.

Nickerson, C. "Feline Intuition." *Boston Globe* online. http://www.boston.com/yourlife/health/aging/articles/2007/07/25/feline_intuition/. Accessed October 2, 2008.

Oldenburg, D. "A Sense of Doom: Animal Instinct for Disaster. Scientists Investigate Wildlife's Possible Warning Systems." *Washington Post.* January 8, 2005: C1. Available at http://www.dawn.com/2005/01/10/int8.htm. January 10, 2008. Accessed October 5, 2007.

Olshansky, B., Dossey, L. "Retroactive Prayer: A Preposterous Hypothesis?" *British Medical Journal.* December 20, 2003; 327: 1465–68.

Oppenheim, A. L. *The Interpretation of Dreams in the Ancient Near East.* Philadelphia: American Philosophical Society; 1956: 302–303.

Ornstein, C. "State Cites Safety Drug Lapses at Cedars-Sinai." *Los Angeles Times.* January 10, 2008. Available at Portland Tribune online. http://portlandscw.trb.com/news/la-me-cedars10jan10,0,4490595.story?coll=kwbp-news-1. Accessed March 26, 2008.

————. "Quaids Recall Twins' Drug Overdosage." *Los Angeles Times.* January 15, 2008. Available at http://www.zap2it.com/movies/news/zap-story-quaidsrecalltwinsdrugoverdose,0,2286448.story. Accessed March 26, 2008.

Ostrander, S., Schroeder, L. *Psychic Discoveries Behind the Iron Curtain.* New York: Marlowe and Company; 1970: 38–52.

Otto, R . *The Idea of the Holy.* 2nd ed. John W. Harvey, trans. New York: Oxford University Press; 1958: 5–14.

Palmer, J., Neppe, V. M. "Exploratory Analyses of Refined Predictors of Subjective ESP Experiences and Temporal Lob Dysfunction in a Neuropsychiatric Population." *European Journal of Parapsychology.* 2004; 19: 33–65.

Pearce, F. "Ozone hole? What Ozone Hole?" *New Scientist.* September 20, 2008; 199 (2674): 46–47. Available at http://www.tmcnet.com/usubmit/-joe-farmans-old-techtriumph-/2008/09/19/3660472.htm. Accessed October 1, 2008.

Peck, P. Diet, Activity May Help Prevent Alzheimer's. WebMD. http://www.webmd.com/alzheimers/news/20040719/diet-activity-may-help-prevent-alzheimers. July 19, 2004. Accessed May 7, 2008.

Petersen, J. Arlington Institute. TAI Alert 15—Impending Event Alert, at http://www.arlingtoninstitute.org/tai-alert-15-impending-event-alert. Accessed September 15, 2008.

Piersall, P. "The Heart Remembers." *Natural Health.* March–April 1998. Available at http://findarticles.com/p/articles/mi_m0NAH/is_n2_v27/ai_20353562/pg_4. Accessed January 29, 2008.

Pilkington, R. *Men and Women of Parapsycholoogy: Personal Reflections.* Jefferson, NC: McFarland; 1987: 40.

Polanyi, M. "The Stability of Scientific Theories Against Experience." In *Witchcraft and Sorcery.* Max Marwick, ed. New York: Penguin; 1982: 452–59.

Puthoff, H. E., Targ, R. A Perceptual Channel for Information Transfer over Kilometer Distances: Historical Perspective and Recent Research. *Proceedings of the IEEE.* 1976; 64: 329–54.

Puthoff, H. Associative Remote Viewing Experiment. Proceedings of the 1984 Parapsychological Association Conference, Dallas, Texas.

Puthoff, H. E. "CIA-initiated Remote Viewing Program at Stanford Research Institute." *Journal of Scientific Exploration.* 1996; 110(1):75. Available at http://www.biomindsuperpowers.com/Pages/CIA-InitiatedRV.html. Accessed February 6, 2008.

Radin, D. I. "Unconscious Perception of Future Emotions." *Journal of Consciousness Studies Abstracts.* Tucson II conference, University of Arizona, Tucson, April 8–13, 1996; Abstract No. 430: 163.

———. "Unconscious Perception of Future Emotions: An Experiment in Presentiment." *Journal of Scientific Exploration.* 1997; 11(2): 163–80.

———. *The Conscious Universe.* San Francisco, CA: HarperSanFrancisco; 1997: 103–105.

———. Electrodermal presentiments of future emotions. *Journal of Scientific Exploration.* 2004; 18 (2): 253–74.

———. *Entangled Minds.* New York: Paraview/Simon & Schuster; 2006: 168.

———. Preliminary Analysis of a suite of informal web-based psi experiments. http://www.boundary.org/articles/GotPsi-public.pdf. Accessed June 5, 2007.

———. Dean Radin's Blog. http://deanradin.blogspot.com/2007/06/presentiment-in-brain.html. Accessed November 23, 2008.

———. Gazing at the mind's eye and other experiments exploring the capacities of consciousness. Presentation at Mind Before Matter Conference, San Francisco, California, February 23, 2008.

———. Got Psi? http://www.GotPsi.org. Accessed September 19, 2008.

Radin, D. I., Machado, E.R., Zangari, W. Effects of Distant Healing Intention Through Time and Space: Two Exploratory Studies. Proceedings of Presented Papers: The 41st Annual Convention of the Parapsychological Association. Halifax, Nova Scotia, Canada: Parapsychological Association; 1998: 143–61.

Ramsland, K. Death mansion. TrueTV Crime Library. http://www.crimelibrary.com/notorious_murders/mass/heavens_gate/5.html. Accessed March 1, 2008.

Rapoport, C. Aberfan—The Days After. Cardigan: Wales; 2005. http://www.rapo.com/lcgallery/Aberfan.htm. Accessed January 2, 2008.

Rattray, R. S. *Religion and Art in Ashanti.* Oxford: Clarendon Press; 1927: 192–96.

Resnik, S. "The Theatre of the Dream." Alan Sheridan, trans. *New Library of Psycho-analysis*. Vol. 6. David Tuckett, ed. New York: Routledge; 1987: 119–20.

Rhine, J. B. *The Reach of the Mind*. New York: William Sloane; 1947: 66.

Rhine, J. B., Feather, S. R. "The Study of Cases of 'Psi-Trailing' in Animals." *The Journal of Parapsychology*. 1962; 26(1): 1–21.

Rhine, L. E. "Precognition and Intervention." *Journal of Parapsychology*. 1955; 19: 1–34.

Rhine, L. E. "Psychological Processes in ESP Experiences. Part I. Waking experiences." *Journal of Parapsychology*. 1962; 29: 88–111.

Ring, K., Valarino, E. E. *Lessons from the Light: What We Can Learn from the Near-Death Experience*. New York: Insight/Plenum Press; 1998: 93.

Romme, M., Escher, S. *Making Sense of Voices*. London: Mind Publications; 2000.

Ross, R. Heaven's Gate Suicides. Cult Education and Recovery. October 1999. http://www.culteducation.com/hgate.html. Accessed March 1, 2008.

Rubin, C. B., Renda-Tanali, I. Effects of the Terrorist Attacks of September 11, 2001, on Federal Emergency Management in the United States. Institute for Crisis, Disaster and Risk Management, The George Washington University, Washington, DC. http://www.gwu.edu/~icdrm/publications/sept11book_ch22_rubin.pdf. Accessed August 18, 2008.

Rush, J. H. *New Directions in Parapsychological Research. Parapsychological Monographs No. 4*. New York: Parapsychological Foundation; 1964: 18–19.

Russell, S. "Second Sight." *St. Louis Magazine*. July 2007. http://www.stlmag.com/media/St-Louis-Magazine/July-2007/Second-Sight/. Accessed July 26, 2008.

Sagan, C. *The Dragons of Eden*. New York: Random House; 1977: 7.

Saunders, T. Paul Newman—A Life Spent Giving. Look to the Stars: The World of Celebrity Giving. September 29, 2008. http://www.looktothestars.org/news/1287-paul-newman-a<->life-spent-giving. Accessed October 3, 2008.

Schavelzon, J. *Freud, un Paciente con Cancer*. Buenos Aires, Argentina: Editorial Paidos; 1983.

Scheib, R. "Timeline." *Utne Reader*. January–February 1996: 52–61.

Scherk, M. Quoted in Doheny, K. "Cat's 'Sixth Sense' Predicting Death?" CBSNews.com. http://www.cbsnews.com/stories/2007/07/25/health/webmd/main3097899.shtml. July 25, 2007. Accessed October 3, 2008.

Schlitz, M. J., Honorton, C. "Ganzfeld Psi Performance Within an Artistically Gifted Population." *Journal of the American Society for Psychical Research*. 1992; 86: 83–98.

Schmeidler, G. R. *Parapsycholoogy and Psychology: Matches and Mismatches*. Jefferson, NC: McFarland; 1988.

Schmeidler, G. R., McConnell, R. A. *ESP and Personality Patterns*. Westport, CT: Greenwood Press; 1958.

Schmidt, H., Morris, R., Rudolph, L. "Channeling Evidence for a Psychokinetic effect to Independent Observers." *Journal of Parapsychology*. 1986; 50: 1–15.

Schmidt, H., Schlitz, M. *A Large Scale Pilot PK Experiment with Prerecorded Random*

Events: Mind Science Foundation Research Report. San Antonio, TX: Mind Science Foundation; 1988.

Schmidt, H., Morris, R. L., Hardin, C. L. *Channeling Evidence for a Psychokinetic Effect to Independent Observers: An Attempted Replication: Mind Science Foundation Research Report.* San Antonio, TX: Mind Science Foundation; 1990.

Schmidt, H., Braud, W. "New PK Tests with an Independent Observer." *Journal of Parapsychology.* 1993; 57: 227–40.

Schmidt, I., Stapp, H. "PK with Prerecorded Random Events and the Effects of Preobservation." *Journal of Parapsychology.* 1993; 57: 331–49.

Schneider, D. *Revolution in the Body-Mind. I. Forewarning Cancer Dreams and the Bioplasma Concept.* Easthampton, NY: Alexa Press; 1976: 7.

Schrödinger, E. *What Is Life? and Mind and Matter.* London: Cambridge University Press; 1969: 145.

Schwartz, S. A. *Opening to the Infinite.* Buda, TX: Nemoseen; 2007: 111–12.

———. "An Arrow Through Time." *Explore* (NY): *The Journal of Science and Healing.* 2008; 4(2): 95–100.

Schwarz, B. E. "Possible Telesomatic Reactions." *Journal of the Medical Society of New Jersey.* 1967; 64(11): 600–603.

Sheldrake, R. *Dogs That Know When Their Owners Are Coming Home.* New York: Crown; 1999.

———. *The Sense of Being Stared At, and Other Aspects of the Extended Mind.* London: Arrow/Random House; 2003: 242.

Shoup, R. Physics Without Causality—Theory and Evidence. Paper presented to the Society for Scientific Exploration, 26th Annual Meeting, East Lansing, Michigan, May 30–June 2, 2007: 16–17.

SIDS: Reducing the Risk. California SIDS Program. http://www.californiasids.com. Accessed January 8, 2008. The changing concept of sudden infant death syndrome: Diagnostic coding shifts, controversies regarding the sleeping environment, and new variables in consider in reducing risk. American Academy of Pediatrics Task Force on Sudden Infant Death Syndrome. *Pediatrics.* 2005; 116(5): 1245–55. Abstract available at http://www.ncbi.nlm.nih.gov/entrez/query.fcgi?db=pubmed&cmd=Retrieve&dopt=AbstractPlus&list_uids=16216901&query_hl=3&itool=pubmed_docsum. Accessed January 8, 2008.

Sinclair, U. *Mental Radio.* Republication of the 1930 edition by Charlottesville, VA: Hampton Roads; 2001: 124.

Spottiswoode, S. J. P., May, E. C. "Skin Conductance Prestimulus Response: Analyses, Artifacts and a Pilot Study." *Journal of Scientific Exploration.* 2003; 17(4): 617–41.

Sprengnether, M. *Mouth to Mouth: Freud, Irma, and the Dream of Psychoanalysis.* American Imago. 2003; 60(3): 259–84. Abstract available at http://muse.jhu.edu/login?uri=/journals/american_imago/v060/60.3sprengnether.html. Accessed September 21, 2008.

St. Augustine. Chapter XIV. *The Confessions of St. Augustine, Bishop of Hippo.* CyberLibrary. http://www.leaderu.com/cyber/books/augconfessions/bk11.html.

Steering Committee of Physicians' Health Study Research Group. Preliminary Report: Findings from the Aspirin Component of the Ongoing Physicians' Health Study. *New England Journal of Medicine.* 1988; 318: 262–64.

Stevenson, I. *Telepathic Impressions: A Review of 35 New Cases.* Charlottesville, VA: University Press of Virginia; 1970.

Storm, L., Thalbourne, M. A. "The Effect of a Change in Pro Attitude on Paranormal Performance: A Pilot Study Using Naïve and Sophisticated Skeptics." *Journal of Scientific Exploration.* 2005; 19: 11–29.

Surowiecki, J. *The Wisdom of Crowds.* New York: Anchor/Random House; 2005.

Sutherland, P. "End of the World Due in Nine Days." *The Sun* online. September 1, 2008. http://www.thesun.co.uk/sol/homepage/features/article1630897.ece. Accessed October 31, 2008.

Szpakowska, K. M. The Perception of Dreams and Nightmare in Ancient Egypt: Old Kingdom to Third Intermediate Period. Ph.D. dissertation; University of California, Los Angeles; 2000: 273.

Szpunar, K. K., Watson, J. M., McDermott, K. B. *Neural Substrates of Envisioning the Future. Proceedings of the National Academy of Sciences USA* 2007; 104(2): 642–47.

Targ, E., Schlitz, M., Irwin, H. J. "Psi-Related Experiences." In *Varieties of Anomalous Experience: Examining the Scientific Evidence.* Cardeña, E., Lynn, S. J., Krippner, S. (eds.) Washington, DC: American Psychological Association; 2000: 219–52.

Targ, R. "Remote Viewing at Stanford Research Institute in the 1970s: A Memoir." *Journal of Scientific Exploration.* 1996; 10(1): 77–88.

———. Preface to Dunne, J. W. *An Experiment with Time.* Charlottesville, VA: Hampton Roads; 2001: viii–ix.

———. *Limitless Mind.* Novato, CA: New World Library; 2004.

Targ, R., Katra, J., Brown, D., Wiegand, W. "Viewing the Future: A Pilot Study with an Error-Detecting Protocol." *Journal of Scientific Exploration.* 1995; 9(3): 367–80.

Targ, R., Puthoff, H. E. "Information Transmission Under Conditions of Sensory Shielding." *Nature.* 1974; 251: 602–607.

Thaheld, F. H. "An Interdisciplinary Approach to Certain Fundamental Issues in the Fields of Physics and Biology: Toward a Unified Theory. *BioSystems,* 2005; 80: 41–56.

Thwaites, R. G., ed. *Jesuit Relations and Allied Documents: Travels and Explorations of the Jesuit Missionairies in New France, 1610–1791.* Cleveland, OH: Burrows Brothers; 1896–1901; 12: 121–23.

Tierney, J. "Living in Fear and Paying a High Cost in Heart Risk." *New York Times* Online. January 15, 2008. http://www.nytimes.com/2008/01/15/science/15tier .html. Accessed January 25, 2007.

————. "The Endless Fear of Terrorism." *New York Times* Online. January 16, 2008. http://tierneylab.blogs.nytimes.com/2008/01/16/the-endless-fear-of-terrorism/. Accessed January 25, 2008.

Tittell, W., et al. "Experimental Demonstration of Quantum Correlations over More Than 10 km." *Physical Review*; 1998; 57: 3229–32.

Torres, K. Legislators Seek Investigation in Utah Mine Disaster. Occupational Hazards.com. http://www.occupationalhazards.com/News/Article/70536/Legislators_Seek_Investigation_into_Utah_Mine_Disaster.aspx. August 28, 2007. Accessed October 15, 2007.

Utts, J. "An Assessment of the Evidence for Psychic Functioning." *Journal of Scientific Exploration*. 1996; 10(1): 3–30. Available at http://anson.ucdavis.edu/~utts/air2.html. Accessed February 6, 2008.

Van de Castle, R. *Our Dreaming Mind*. New York: Ballantine; 1994.

Van Dyke, H. Time Is. ThinkExist.com http://thinkexist.com/quotation/time_is_too_slow_for_those_who_wait-too_swift_for/8953.html. Accessed September 28, 2008.

Vassy, Z. "Method for Measuring the Probability of One-Bit Extrasensory Information Transfer Between Living Organisms." *Journal of Parapsychology*. 1978; 42: 158–60.

————. "A Study of Telepathy by Classical Conditioning." *Journal of Parapsychology*. Fall 2004. Available at http://findarticles.com/p/articles/mi_m2320/is_2_68/ai_n16107401/pg_1. Accessed February 8, 2008.

Veacock, C. *Titanic: Anatomy of a Disaster Shrouded in Mystery*. Merseyside Anomalies Research Association. http://www.mara.org.uk/titanic.htm. Accessed July 23, 2008.

Von Lucadou, W. Quoted in Broderick, D. *Outside the Gates of Science: Why It's Time for the Paranormal to Come in from the Cold*. New York: Thunder's Mouth Press/ Avalon; 2007: 270.

Watson, L. "The Importance of Pattern." In *The Dreams of Dragons*. Rochester, VT: Destiny Books; 1992: 28–29.

————. *Dreams of Dragons*. Rochester, VT: Destiny Books; 1992: 26.

Weaver, W. *Lady Luck: The Theory of Probability*. New York: Dover; 1982.

Wilkins, Sir H., Sherman, H. M. *Thoughts Through Space: A Remarkable Adventure in the Realm of the Mind*. 2nd ed. New York: C & R Anthony; 1951: 34. Cited also in: Simon Nasht. *The Last Explorer*. New York: Arcade Publishing; 2006: 267.

Zangari, W., Machado, F. R. Incidence and Social Relevance of Brazilian University Students' Psychic Experiences. Paper presented at the 37th Annual Convention of the Parapsychological Association, Amsterdam, August 1994.

Zimmer, C. "Lots of Animals Learn, but Smarter Isn't Better." *New York Times* Online. May 6, 2008. Accessed May 21, 2008.

ACKNOWLEDGMENTS

I t has been my privilege to be closely acquainted for nearly three decades with some of the key individuals involved in consciousness research. Many of them have become close friends. Their insights, counsel, and shared knowledge have sustained and inspired me over the years.

These individuals recur frequently throughout this book. They come from diverse fields—medicine, nursing, psychology, archaeology, biology, epidemiology, physics, engineering, materials science, statistics, and philosophy. Rather than mention them all here, which would be a perilous task, as I no doubt would unintentionally omit some of them, I have let them speak for themselves in the preceding pages.

The most important acknowledgment of these individuals comes not from me, of course, but will be provided by history. When an account of consciousness research is written at some future time, many of the researchers who appear in this book will occupy a very high place.

When I first began practicing internal medicine, many of my patients shared with me their premonitions of health and illness. This is not easy for patients to do, for fear of being misunderstood and rejected by their doctor. Their stories opened a dimension I'd not taken seriously. To them, much gratitude.

Four centuries ago Sir Francis Bacon said, "Send out your little book upon the waters and hope." My literary agent, James Levine of the Levine/Greenberg Literary Agency; my lecture representative, Kitty Farmer; and my publicist, Anita Halton have helped me launch this little book. I'm grateful for their support and unstinting generosity. They've done more than provide professional help; they've been there with friendship and understanding every step of the way.

It has been an uncommon pleasure to work with Amy Hertz, my editor, and Melissa Miller, her assistant. Amy is one of the most skillful editors I've ever encountered. She has been the perfect corrective to my incurable blovi-ation. Amy wields a scalpel that is so sharp and precise, yet caring, that her surgery on my manuscript was almost painless. Every author prays for an editor who has an intuitive understanding of his or her topic. With Amy, I got my wish—as I also did with Brian Tart and Susan Petersen Kennedy at Dutton/Penguin, who trusted what my manuscript might become.

Thanks, too, to science journalist, novelist, and poet Jill Neimark for reading the manuscript and offering suggestions that helped shape this book. I've admired her science writing for years, and we've often bounced ideas back and forth. I had a premonition—well, maybe an inference—that Jill's input would be invaluable, and I was right on target.

Some research assistance deserves special mention. Thanks to Stephan A. Schwartz, my nominee for the first Indiana Jones Award if it ever becomes available. Stephan is one of the original architects of the field of remote viewing. Because of the similarity of remote viewing to precognition, his research has been invaluable to me. For years he has gracefully tolerated my badgering for information and advice, as only a true friend would do.

Perhaps no one has done more in the past two decades to advance our understanding of future knowing than researcher Dean Radin, whom I con-sider the Einstein of research in this field. Dean has transformed our under-standing of premonitions with his presentiment experiments. Our paths have often crossed during the writing of this book, and I've benefited enor-mously from our association.

I extend special gratitude to Rupert Sheldrake, the courageous British biologist, researcher, and proponent of extended mind, who read the manu-script. Rupert is a Jedi master of the premonitions universe, and his advice and feedback have been inspiring.

I am grateful also to my colleagues at the peer-reviewed journal *Explore: The Journal of Science and Healing*, on which I serve as executive editor. They continually encourage and support my essays on consciousness-related subjects and their relevance to healing. Should readers care to follow my thoughts on this subject, they may do so through www.explorejournal.com.

An ultimate value of premonitions is the unity and oneness they reveal between humans and all else. My touchstone for this understanding now and for most of my life has been Barbara, my wife, my love. To any writer contemplating a book on premonitions or any other manifestation of nonlocal mind, I say: First, fall in love, for without love you'll miss the plot. Your book will be a lifeless exercise in dull fact. We do not need more dry chronicles of facts; we need messages that are so full-throated and bone-deep that they are adequate to the urgency of our time—and what can exceed the power of love to see us through? This view is hardly original. Nearly two thousand years ago, St. Paul elevated love above future knowing in importance: "If I have the gift of prophecy . . . but have not love, I am nothing." (1 Corinthians 13:2, New International Version)

To my twin brother, Garry, and my sister, Bet: by showing me that nonlocal connections happen in real life, you've helped make this work possible.

Has an author yet thanked his laptop in print? I do so now. My MacBook Pro has been a faithful friend at home and in airports and hotels across the land. It never complains, no matter what idiotic thoughts I tap into its innards.

Thanks, too, to my avian companions—the nuthatches, chickadees, juncos, titmice, and piñon jays—at the feeder outside my study, and the occasional deer and coyote, who are a reminder that nonlocal mind is not restricted to the two-leggeds.

During the writing of this book, I, like most authors, was often asked by friends, relatives, and colleagues, "What are you working on now?" I'd answer, "A book about premonitions." They would invariably light up and respond, "Premonitions? Really? Let me tell you about mine!" And they would. This conversation occurred so often, so predictably, that it became an amusement and assured me that I was pursuing something that was personally important to a great many people. To all who shared their stories, thank you. Your encouragement was more important than you know.

INDEX

ABOUT THE AUTHOR

Larry Dossey, M.D., has been a leader in bringing scientific understanding to spirituality, and rigorous proof to integrative medicine. He is the author of *The New York Times* bestseller *Healing Words*, the first serious look at how prayer affects healing. He is an international advocate for the role of the mind and spirituality in health. He lives in Santa Fe, New Mexico, with his wife, Barbara Dossey.

We hope you enjoyed this Hay House book.
If you would like to receive a free catalogue featuring additional
Hay House books and products, or if you would like information
about the Hay Foundation, please contact:

Hay House UK Ltd
292B Kensal Road • London W10 5BE
Tel: (44) 20 8962 1230; Fax: (44) 20 8962 1239
www.hayhouse.co.uk

***

Published and distributed in the United States of America by:
Hay House, Inc. • PO Box 5100 • Carlsbad, CA 92018-5100
Tel: (1) 760 431 7695 or (1) 800 654 5126;
Fax: (1) 760 431 6948 or (1) 800 650 5115
www.hayhouse.com

***

Published and distributed in Australia by:
Hay House Australia Ltd • 18/36 Ralph Street • Alexandria, NSW 2015
Tel: (61) 2 9669 4299, Fax: (61) 2 9669 4144
www.hayhouse.com.au

***

Published and distributed in the Republic of South Africa by:
Hay House SA (Pty) Ltd • PO Box 990 • Witkoppen 2068
Tel/Fax: (27) 11 467 8904
www.hayhouse.co.za

***

Published and distributed in India by:
Hay House Publishers India • Muskaan Complex • Plot No.3
B-2 • Vasant Kunj • New Delhi - 110 070
Tel: (91) 11 41761620; Fax: (91) 11 41761630
www.hayhouse.co.in

***

Distributed in Canada by:
Raincoast • 9050 Shaughnessy St • Vancouver, BC V6P 6E5
Tel: (1) 604 323 7100
Fax: (1) 604 323 2600

***

Sign up via the Hay House UK website to receive the Hay House
online newsletter and stay informed about what's going on with your
favourite authors. You'll receive bimonthly announcements
about discounts and offers, special events, product highlights,
free excerpts, giveaways, and more!
www.hayhouse.co.uk